California Tenants' Handbook

Tenants' Rights

by California attorneys
Myron Moskovitz
&
Ralph Warner

Note: We gratefully acknowledge the contributions of
Charles E. Sherman, who co-authored the original edition of this book.

edited by Toni Lynne Ihara
&
Stephen Elias

Illustrations by
Linda Allison

Important: The information in this book changes rapidly and is subject to differing interpretations. It is up to you to check it thoroughly before relying on it. Neither the author nor publisher of this book makes any guarantees regarding the outcome of the uses to which this material is put.

NOLO PRESS 950 Parker Street, Berkeley, CA 94710

Important

Nolo Press is committed to keeping its books up-to-date. Each new printing, whether or not it is called a new edition, has been revised to reflect the latest law changes. This book was printed and updated on the last date indicated below. Before you rely on information in it, you might wish to call Nolo Press (415) 549-1976 to check whether a later printing or edition has been issued.

Printing History

Difference between new "Editions" and "Printings":

New "**Printing**" means there have been some minor changes, but usually not enough so that people will need to trade in or discard an earlier printing of the same edition. Obviously, this is a judgment call and any change, no matter how minor, might affect you.

New "**Edition**" means one or more major, or a number of minor, law changes since the previous edition.

First Edition	August 1972
Second Printing	January 1973
Second Edition	May 1974
Second Printing	February 1975
Third Edition	November 1975
Second Printing	April 1976
Fourth Edition	January 1977
Second Printing	December 1977
Third Printing	August 1978
Fourth Printing	July 1979
Fifth Edition	January 1980
Sixth Edition	March 1981
Seventh Edition	August 1982
Second Printing	February 1983
Eighth Edition	February 1984
Second Printing	July 1984
Third Printing	January 1985
Fourth Printing	July 1985
Ninth Edition	May 1986
Second Printing	November 1986
Third Printing	September 1987
Tenth Edition	January 1989
Second Printing	January 1990

We wish to thank the following people associated with the first Moskovitz manuscript: Pedro Echeverria and Ronald Vera for their research assistance, Mary Durant and Madeline Finlay for their secretarial assistance, Allan David Heskin for his editorial assistance and Ann Curtis for her artwork.

We also wish to express our gratitude to some friends who helped to make this a better book. Thanks to Lucretia Edwards, Jeffrey Carter, David Brown, Mary Randolph, Barbara Kaufman, Steve Elias and J. Wallace Oman. We would also like to acknowledge the many excellent contributions of our original co-author Charles Sherman, many of whose original words still appear fifteen years (and nine editions) after his valuable contributions to the first edition.

RECYCLE YOUR OUT-OF-DATE BOOKS &
GET 25% OFF YOUR NEXT PURCHASE!

Using an old edition can be dangerous if information in it is wrong. Unfortunately, laws and legal procedures change often. To help you keep up to date we extend this offer. If you cut out and deliver to us the title portion of the cover of any old Nolo book we'll give you a 25% discount off the retail price of any new Nolo book. For example, if you have a copy of TENANT'S RIGHTS, 4th edition and want to trade it for the latest CALIFORNIA MARRIAGE AND DIVORCE LAW, send us the TENANT'S RIGHTS cover and a check for the current price of MARRIAGE & DIVORCE, less a 25% discount. Information on current prices and editions is listed in the NOLO NEWS. Generally speaking, any book more than two years old is of questionable value. Books more than four or five years old are a menace. This offer is to individuals only.

OUT OF DATE = DANGEROUS

CTEN 10/89

Table of Contents

Introduction

Here is a detailed legal guide designed for use by California residential tenants. Our purpose in writing it is twofold. First, we explain California landlord-tenant law in as straightforward a manner as possible. Second, we focus on how you can use this knowledge to anticipate and, where possible, avoid legal problems. In this latter regard, particularly, ours is a result-oriented approach. We have specifically designed this book so that a tenant who believes that his or her rights have been violated can quickly understand the relevant law that covers the area, as well as the remedies available to deal with the problem.

This is the 10th edition of the *California Tenants' Handbook—Tenants' Rights.* Over the years, landlord-tenant law has experienced so many changes that little of the original book remains. Of far more importance to you, however, is the fact that today the legal and practical strategies necessary to be a successful tenant are far different than they were just a few years ago.

The reasons for this have to do with two major changes in the California landlord-tenant scene. To successfully protect your rights as a tenant, you must understand both. The first big change is that in the last decade, the legal rights available to tenants to protect themselves from outrageous landlord conduct have greatly improved. For example, today a tenant has a number of fairly powerful weapons when it comes to dealing with a landlord who does any one of a number of obnoxious things, including discriminating against her for almost any reason not directly related to her being a bad tenant, invading her privacy, refusing to fix dangerous conditions on the rental premises, or failing to return a security deposit when a unit has been left clean and undamaged.

So far, so good, but unfortunately, the other major change in the landlord-tenant relationship is not beneficial to tenants. This is simply that, in the great majority of California cities and counties, there is not enough rental housing to go around. The fact that there are too many tenants chasing not enough rental units is, of course, not lost on landlords, many of whom have taken advantage of it to raise rents, reduce services and adopt all sorts of other strategies to maximize their economic return.[1] And sadly, it has also made a deep impact on many tenants who have become so worried about not having a place to live that they are reluctant to assert their obvious legal rights, for fear the landlord will ask them to leave.

Our job is to explain your rights as a tenant and the remedies available to you should any of these rights be violated. But we do so with emphasis on how you can both take advantage of your legal rights and feel as secure as possible in doing so. In other words, we want you to know how to improve the condition of your tenancy, while at the same time you don't risk losing it.

Here at the beginning, let us confess an important bias. We believe that in the long run a tenant is best served if he establishes a positive relationship with his landlord (or property man-ager, if the landlord is not on the scene). Why? First, because it's our view that adherence to the law and principles of fairness is a good way to live. Second, because your landlord is intimately involved with providing you one of your most important services, the roof over your head, ideally, you want your relationship with this person or corporation to be free of paranoia and hostility. For these reasons, we present your legal rights and remedies in the context of using them to arrive at solutions both you and your landlord can feel good about.

Occasionally, however, tenants must deal with a landlord so neglectful, hostile, or just plain difficult that a positive approach is just plain impossible, and perhaps even counter-productive. If you find yourself in this unpleasant situation, there is little that you can do except assert your legal rights early and often. We are mindful of this possibility and provide detailed information as to how to cope with the obnoxious landlord.

Now, here are a few tips about using this book. Landlord-tenant law is a complicated and intertwined subject. Necessarily, when laying it out in a linear fashion on the pages of this book, we have had to make dozens of organizational decisions. Thus, because getting deposits returned is principally of interest when you move out, we deal with the law on this subject in Chapter 10, in the context of ending a tenancy. However, we discuss the process of renting a place in Chapter 2, another time when understanding the law as it applies to deposits is important. The point is that unless you are very knowledgeable about California landlord-tenant law to begin with, your best bet is to read this entire book at least once. You will then have the perspective and background necessary to be able to focus on those specific legal areas which concern you.

A special word is appropriate for those of you who live in areas covered by rent control ordi-nances. These laws generally establish how much your rent can be increased for most residential living spaces. It is also of great importance, however, that they can, and often do, override general California law in a number of other ways. For example, in many cities (including San Francisco and Los Angeles) rent-control ordinances restrict a landlord's ability to terminate month-to-month tenancies: these laws require "just cause" to evict. We handle rent control in two ways. First, throughout this book, as part of explaining tenants' rights and responsibilities under general state law, we indicate those areas in which rent control laws are likely to modify or change these rules. Second, we provide a detailed discussion of rent control in Chapters 4 and 11. These chapters are designed to be used along with a careful reading of a current copy of your local rent control ordinance.

---

[1] As we discuss in detail in Chapter 4, the adoption of rent control ordinances in several communities has helped counter this trend in those geographical areas, but has done nothing to protect tenants in most areas of the state where rent control has not been enacted.

We come now to the pesky personal pronoun. Our solution to the problem of how to handle gender is by using "he" and "she" more or less alternatively throughout the book. While this isn't perfect, it makes more sense than "she/he" or other cumbersome devices, such as writing "he and she" every time an abstract person must be identified.

Finally, may we wish you nothing but good landlords, understanding managers, and, above all else, good luck.

Chapter 1:

Some General Things You Should Know

A. Who Is Your Landlord?

1. Know Your Landlord

Your landlord may be a little old man with a Siamese cat and a bad head for arithmetic or you may rent from a large corporation. There is no typical landlord. In this book we give you a lot of information about your legal rights, but we can't tell you what kind of a landlord you have. It is extremely important that you find out what kind of person your landlord is, because having complete knowledge of your legal rights will help you very little if you lack a good human understanding of the person with whom you are dealing. Coupled with such an understanding this book can be of great value.

Along with understanding the personality of your landlord, it is important to know his problems, circumstances and style of operating. Dealing with a retired schoolteacher managing her late uncle's duplex will obviously be a lot different from dealing with an institution with 500 units, managers, rules and red tape.

2. Know Your Manager

Many medium to large apartment complexes have managers. The owner wants to make money, but he wants somebody else to do the work of actually managing the rental property. More and more owners are hiring management corporations who specialize in managing lots of rental units and who get paid a percentage (usually between 5% and 10%) of the rental income. Such companies tend to be sticklers for rules and procedures, but are usually less emotionally involved than owners, and are often more rational at arriving at business-like compromises.[1] Often, however, the owner will simply give a student or older person free or reduced rent to look after his property on a part-time basis. This can be either good or bad as far as you are concerned, depending on the personality of the manager and whether he has any real authority to take care of problems. Just as there are all sorts of landlords, there is an equal variety of managers.

In dealing with a manager on a day-to-day basis, it is important not only to notice who he is and how best to deal with him; it is also important to notice his relationship to the owner. Remember, the owner and the manager may have very different interests. Some owners, for example, may want the property to yield a maximum amount of profit with a minimal amount of trouble, while others may be investing for long-term real property appreciation and be willing to be reasonably generous to tenants in the meantime. Similarly, some manager's major concern is probably doing as little work as possible for his free rent, while others, especially those who are in the business, may want to do a bang up job in hopes that word will spread and they will get other jobs.

Should you be in a situation in which the premises are not being kept clean or in good repair or if the manager is impolite, you will probably want to deal directly with the owner if possible. In any case, where communications are sticky or broken down, you should consider sending duplicate copies of letters and other communications to the owner as well as to the manager.

3. Finding Out the Name of the Owner

In the past, some owners have instructed their managers not to tell the tenants who they were or where they could be located, so the tenant could not "bother" them. California Civil Code Section 1962 tries to solve this problem. It provides that:

a. The rental agreement must state the name and address of both the manager and the owner (or person authorized by him to receive notices, demands and lawsuits against the owner). This information must be kept current with the tenant being informed of all changes,

or,

b. Instead of putting this information in each rental agreement, the owner may choose to post notices containing the same information in the building. A notice must be posted in at least two easy-to-see places (including all elevators).

---

[1] Usually a rental management corporation manages a lot of units in a relatively small geographic area. This makes checking their reputation fairly easy. It is wise to do so. If the building or development has 16 or more apartments, there must be a resident manager living there. 25 California Administrative Code § 42.

If the owner fails to follow this law, then the person who rented the dwelling for the owner automatically becomes his agent for receiving notices, demands and lawsuits.

B. The Landlord Business

You may choose not to read this section and still learn all you need to know about what you face as a tenant. For those who are interested, however, we thought it would be helpful to understand how the landlord business works. We believe that a tenant or group of tenants will be in a better position to make wise decisions if they have an idea of what it's like to walk a mile in their landlord's boots.

Making money as a landlord depends a great deal on making wise initial investment decisions and on having an ability to manage property. This is true whether the landlord owns one unit or a thousand units. Given average ability in these directions, however, it is pretty difficult to lose money in the landlord business. Indeed, many landlords achieve spectacular returns. This is possible because the landlord is able to take advantage of a number of favorable tax laws and is able to use **your money** to do it.

The landlord business works something like this. To buy a building or building complex the landlord must usually put down between 10% and 25% of the purchase price. A bank or insurance company puts up the rest. If he buys a decent building he is then able to set the rents at a level that will allow him to cover all of his mortgage, tax and upkeep payments and pocket a little money besides. If you ask a landlord about his yearly profit, he will doubtless tell you that it is small, or perhaps even nonexistent, but will not tell you that each year he owns more of the building and in addition is receiving tax deductions on his personal tax returns. He will also not point out that in most areas the market value of the building is constantly going up.

You have probably heard about "tax shelters" and "tax loopholes." There are still many of these available to landlords although they were severely curtailed by the Tax Reform Act of 1986. Here is how tax laws work to benefit landlords:

• All the money a landlord pays for building maintenance, upkeep expense and interest on his mortgage payments is subtracted from the landlord's profit figure before taxes are paid.

• All the money a landlord pays in local property taxes constitutes a tax deduction.

• A percentage of the value of a landlord's building is deductible each year under the heading of "depreciation." The depreciation deduction allows the landlord credit for wear and tear to his building and the fact that the building is supposed to get less valuable as it gets older. If a landlord claims that a particular building has a useful life of 20 years, he is able to deduct 5% of the building's value each year. In some situations, a landlord is able to take advantage of laws that allow him to take extra depreciation in the early years of a mortgage. The depreciation deduction is often a major windfall for a landlord. This is because in most cases a building is more valuable after 20 years than it was when first purchased. Thus, the landlord gets his yearly tax deduction and a more valuable building too! As soon as the depreciation credits are used up, the wisdom of the landlord business dictates that the building be sold to a new landlord, who then declares a new life expectancy for the building and starts the depreciation process all over again!

Usually the landlord will buy the building with a little bit of his own money and a lot of borrowed money. He collects rent from you and other tenants, then uses your rent money to pay off his loan and to pay property taxes and upkeep.

Landlords also get certain built-in advantages in times of inflation. In non-rent control areas, a landlord is able to raise rents while his mortgage and interest payments remain pretty constant. In a similar way, the landlord often gets a break on his real property taxes. Normally, a building is assessed for local property tax purposes on the basis of the original purchase price. In periods of inflation, however, rents often go up faster than do tax assessments.

With so much in the landlord's favor, it is truly amazing that any landlords are in unfavorable financial situations. When such is the case, however, it always goes hard on the tenants. If the landlord is a bad businessperson, he may get over-extended on his loans (that is, he may try to buy too much property without enough money, or may have paid too much for the property in the first place). Then he will have to raise rents or cut back on repairs and services. This can lead to a high turnover of dissatisfied or resentful tenants. Such circumstances can make the landlord harder to deal with, almost desperate.

Note: You may want to ask your landlord about his finances and problems, especially if you are on good terms. He might appreciate your interest (making for an easier relationship), and you may learn some things that will increase your understanding of his problems.

Landlords' profits can be hurt quickly:

1. By periods of deflation and depression (the 1930's was a bad time for landlords), when they can't fill up their buildings with tenants at favorable rents;

2. By any action by tenants to jointly withhold rents; and

3. By extremely tough rent control ordinances.

None of these conditions has been widespread in California in recent years. As a result, most landlords have done very well and in many cases have made enormous profits. To see that these profits keep coming, landlords have organized at the local, state and federal levels. Through real estate associations, apartment house owners associations and similar groups, landlords keep a close watch on government—from your local city council and planning commission to the state and federal legislatures. Lobbyists maintain offices in Sacramento and Washington with the specific purpose of furthering the landlord business and seeing to it that no law harmful to landlords is passed by any legislature anywhere. Landlord lobbyists are often very successful at getting legislation introduced and enacted that is favorable to landlords.

C. Renters' Tax Credit—California Income Tax

California allows a tax credit of $60 for single people and $137 for married couples and heads of household to people who rent their principal dwelling place and who are not claimed as a dependent by another taxpayer.[2] If you pay taxes, you subtract the credit from the amount owed. If you don't pay taxes, you can still get the credit. This means you file a return and the state pays

---

[2]Revenue and Taxation Code § 17053.5.

you. Married couples can only get one credit, but people living together can each claim one. In addition, tenants 62 years of age or older and tenants who are blind or disabled and whose annual income is $12,000 or less are eligible for tax benefits due to the fact that part of their rent is used to pay property taxes.[3] For technical details on these benefits, see the Individual Income Tax guide put out by the California Franchise Tax Board.

D. Lawyers

This book is not designed to replace an attorney. It is meant to give you a clear understanding of your rights and obligations and help you decide whether or not you **need** one. The law says that you have a right to have an attorney represent you if you want one; no law says that you must have one.

Lawyers, like most of the rest of us, are in business to make money. They have to pay a lot of office overhead as well as support themselves and their families in a style to which they are, or would like to be, accustomed. Thus, most charge fairly high fees, normally in a range of $80 to $150 an hour. Clearly, when you have a dispute with your landlord which involves a few hundred dollars, it does not make good sense to pay someone as much (or more) than that to try to vindicate your position. In addition, there is always the danger that you will lose and end up paying both your landlord and your attorney, too.

Legal Research Note: Many people wish to do some of their own legal research before visiting a lawyer. County law libraries (which are located in many county courthouses) are free and open to the public. We review the basics of legal research in Section F of this chapter.

1. When Do You Need A Lawyer?

There is no simple answer to the question of when you need a lawyer. This is because there are many possible areas of dispute between landlord and tenant, and many levels of tenant ability to

---

[3]Revenue and Taxation Code § 19523.5.

deal with problems. Throughout this book, we suggest times when the advice or other services of an attorney would be useful, but here are a few general pointers:

a. If a lease or written rental agreement allows attorney fees for your landlord, then California law says that the tenant is also entitled to recover attorney fees, if he wins a lawsuit based on the terms of that agreement.

b. If your landlord sues you for a lot of money, or if you suffer a physical or emotional injury because of action or inaction by the landlord or manager, see an attorney.

c. If you have any problem that you can't understand or solve by reading this book, you should do some legal research yourself or get some professional advice.

2. What Lawyers Can Do For You

There are three basic ways a lawyer can help with the kinds of problems that face a tenant:

a. Consultation and Advice

The lawyer can listen to the details of your situation, analyze it for you, and advise you on your position and best plan of action. Ideally he will give you more than just conclusions—he can educate you about your whole situation and tell you all the various alternatives available. Then you can make your own choices. Or, you may just want a lawyer to look over the papers you have prepared, to be sure they are correct. This kind of service is the least expensive, as it only involves an office call and a little time. Find out the fee before you go in.

b. Negotiation

The lawyer can use his special talents, knowledge and experience to help you negotiate with the landlord to your best advantage. In case of serious problems, he can probably do this more successfully than you, especially if you are at odds with the landlord, or if your landlord has an attorney. Without spending much of his own time, he can often accomplish a lot through a letter or phone call. Receiving a message on an attorney's letterhead is, in itself, often very sobering to a landlord. A lawyer can sometimes possess considerable skill as a negotiator. Also, if bad turns to worse, a lawyer can convincingly threaten legal action. You can then decide at a later time whether actually to pursue it.

c. Lawsuits

In some instances your case may merit going into court with a lawsuit. Having your lawyer go into court can be expensive, and only rarely warranted. If the landlord sues you first, it is more likely that you will end up in court, and very likely that you will need a lawyer's help.

Whenever you think of using a lawyer, keep in mind this view of clients that is held by a lawyer-friend of ours: he imagines a man who has built a shack on some old railroad tracks in a high mountain valley. One day, when he puts his ear to the track, the man hears a distant vibration. A few days later he can hear the sound of a train rumbling on the warm breeze that blows up to the canyon, and soon the sound is distinctly audible. At this point he can begin to see the smoke of the engine, and not much later the train is running down on him, spitting fire and belching smoke. When the thing is fifty yards away, he picks up his phone, calls his lawyer and asks him to get an injunction against the railroad company! What we mean to say is...if you decide to use a lawyer, don't wait until it's too late.

3. Finding A Lawyer

Finding a lawyer who charges reasonable prices and whom you feel can be trusted is not always an easy task. There is always the danger that by just picking a name out of the telephone book you may get someone unsympathetic (perhaps an attorney who specializes in representing landlords) or an attorney who will charge too much. Here are some suggestions:

a. Legal Aid

If you are **very** poor, you may qualify for free help from your Legal Aid (often called Legal Services) office. Check your phone directory for their location, or ask your County Clerk.

b. Tenants' Rights Organizations

In a number of California communities, tenants have gotten together and established tenants advocacy organizations. Many of these groups provide free or low cost tenant counselling. Often counselling is provided by paralegals and (sometimes) by volunteer lawyers. It often involves helping tenants understand their rights and sometimes extends to helping them prepare paperwork necessary to file or defend a lawsuit. Local bar associations also sometimes provide clinics for low-income tenants.

c. Personal Referrals

If you're looking for a lawyer on your own, this is the best approach. If you know someone who has consulted a lawyer on a landlord-tenant matter and was pleased with the lawyer, call that lawyer first.

d. Pre-Paid Legal Plans

Many unions, employers and consumer groups now offer membership in pre-paid legal plans. You can also sign up as an individual with plans offered by private companies such as Bank of America or Montgomery Ward.

The services provided by the plans vary widely. Some give legal services at reduced fees; some offer free advice. If a plan offers extensive free advice, your initial membership fee may be worth the consultation you receive, even if you use it only once. Most plans have renewal fees; it's common to join a plan for a specific service and then not renew.

There's no guarantee that the lawyers available through these plans are any good. Check out the plan, and if possible, its lawyers, in advance. And when using any of these prepaid plans, remember this: the lawyer is typically getting only $2-$3 per month from the pre-paid plan for dealing with you; some lawyers sign up in the hope they can talk you into buying extra services not covered by your monthly premium.

e. Private Law "Clinics"

To market their services, law firms such as Hyatt Legal Services and Jacoby & Meyers advertise on T.V. and radio, offering low initial consultation fees. This generally means that a basic consultation is cheap (often about $20), but anything after that isn't. If you consult a law clinic, the trick is to quickly extract what information you need and to resist any attempt to make you think you need further services.

f. Lawyer Referral Panels

Most county bar associations maintain lawyer referral services. Usually, you can get a referral to an attorney who specializes in landlord-tenant law, and an initial consultation for free or for a low fee. But the panels don't really screen the listed attorneys, and the attorneys participating may not have much experience or ability. If you contact an attorney this way, be sure to ask about experience with tenant problems, and make sure she's sympathetic to tenants' rights.

g. Yellow Pages

If all else fails, every Yellow Pages has an extensive list of lawyers (under Attorneys) both by specialty and by alphabetical order. Many of the ads quote initial consultation rates.

Shop around by calling different law offices and stating your problem. Ask to talk to a lawyer personally; if you can't, this should give you an idea of how accessible the lawyer is. Ask some specific questions. Do you get clear, concise answers? If not, try someone else. If the lawyer says little except to suggest that he handle the problem (with a substantial fee, of course), watch out. You are talking with either someone who doesn't know the answer and won't admit it (common), or someone who pulls rank on the basis of professional standing. Don't be a passive client or deal with a lawyer who wants you to be one.

Keep in mind that lawyers learn mostly from experience and special training, not from law school. Because you're already well informed (you've read this book), you should be in a good position to evaluate a lawyer's credentials.

Remember, lawyers whose offices and life styles are reasonably simple are more likely to help you for less money than lawyers who feel naked unless wearing a $1,000 suit. You should be able to find an attorney willing to represent you for either a flat rate or an hourly rate of between $75-$150, depending on where the lawyer's office is located (big city lawyers tend to be pricier) and how complex your case is.

E. Typing Services

What if you don't want to hire a lawyer but don't want to do all your legal paperwork yourself? Now, there's a middle ground. A number of businesses, known as "typing services" or "independent paralegals," now assist people doing their own legal work in filling out the forms. Most typing services concentrate on family law or bankruptcy, but some handle landlord-tenant matters, too.

Typing services aren't lawyers. They can't give legal advice and can't represent you in court (only lawyers can). You must decide what steps to take in your case, and the information to put in any needed forms. Typing services can, however:

- provide written instructions and legal information needed to handle your own case;

- provide the appropriate forms; and

- type your papers so they'll be accepted by the court.

Typing services commonly charge far less than attorneys, because typing service customers do much of the work and make the basic decisions. Also, most typing services handle only routine cases.

If you're looking for a typing service, check classified sections of newspapers under Referral Services, usually immediately following attorneys. Also check the yellow pages under "divorce assistance" or "legal clinics." A local legal aid office may provide a reference, as will the occasional court clerk. Finally, many offices have display ads in local throwaway papers like the Classified Flea Market.

Occasionally, a typing service has taken money from a customer and then failed to deliver the services as promised. As with any other business ripoff, you, as a consumer, can sue in small claims or regular court, and report the matter to your local district attorney's consumer fraud division. But legal remedies are often ineffective. The best precaution is to select a reliable typing service at the beginning. As with finding a lawyer, a recommendation from a satisfied customer is best. Also, as a general matter, the longer a typing service has been in business, the better. A list of reputable California typing services is maintained by the National Assocation For Independent Paralegals (800)542-0034.

F. Legal Research Notes

We don't have space here to show you how to do your own legal research in anything approaching a comprehensive fashion. *Legal Research: How to Find and Understand the Law* (Nolo Press), by Steve Elias is an excellent resource if you wish to learn basic legal research skills, something we highly recommend. Our goal here is only to tell you how to find the basic laws that control your residential tenancy. In addition, we show you how to locate the important judicial decisions (most of which are mentioned in this book) which interpret these laws.

Before you can find the laws, though, you've got to find the law library. Every California county maintains a law library which is open to the public. All have the California statutes, written court opinions, and expert commentary. You can find and read any statute or case we've referred to at the law library by looking it up according to its citation.

Or you may want to start your research with a good background resource. We mention several of these (*The California Eviction Defense Manual*, for example) throughout the book.

Landlord-tenant laws and legal procedure are principally contained in two codifications (Codes) of California law—the Civil Code (C.C.) and the Code of Civil Procedure (C.C.P.), both of which are available at all law libraries and most public libraries. The Civil Code is divided into numerous sections, dealing generally with people's legal rights and responsibilities to each other.

Most of California's substantive landlord-tenant law is contained in Sections 1940 through 1991 of this code. The Code of Civil Procedure is a set of laws which tells how people enforce legal rights in civil lawsuits. Eviction lawsuit procedures are contained in Sections 1161 through 1179 of the Code of Civil Procedure. Also of interest are the small claims court procedures mentioned in Sections 116 through 117.22.[4]

Although these codes contain the text of applicable laws passed each year by the legislature, they don't contain the text of any of the appellate court decisions which determine what those laws mean. Sometimes these cases are extremely important. For example, the case of *Green v. Superior Court* adopted a "common law" rule allowing tenants in substandard housing to withhold rent—without paying to make repairs themselves (see Chapter 7A5). To gain access to the printed reports of important court decisions, you have to go to a law library.

The best way to learn of the existence of written court decisions which interpret a particular law is to first look in an "annotated code." An annotated code is a set of volumes of a particular code, such as the Civil Code or Code of Civil Procedure mentioned above, that contains not only all the laws (as do the regular codes), but also a brief summary of many of the court decisions interpreting each one. These annotated codes—published by West Publishing Company (*West's Annotated California Codes*—blue volumes) and by Bancroft-Whitney (*Deering's California Codes*—brown volumes)—can be found in some public libraries and any county law library or law school library in the state. They have comprehensive indexes by topic, and are kept up to date each year with paperback supplements ("pocket parts") located in a pocket in the back cover of each volume. Don't forget to look through these pocket parts for the latest law changes or case decisions since the hardcover volume was printed.

Each brief summary of a court decision is followed by the title of the case, the year of the decision, and the "citation." The "citation" is a sort of shorthand identification for the set of books, volume, and page where the case can be found. The "official" volumes of cases are published by the California Supreme Court as the *Official Reports of the California Supreme Court* (abbreviated "Cal.," "Cal. 2d," or "Cal. 3d," respectively, representing the first, second and third "series" of volumes, the third containing all cases decided since 1969) and by the California Courts of Appeal[5] as *Official Reports of the California Courts of Appeal* (similarly abbreviated "Cal. App.," "Cal. App. 2d," and "Cal. App. 3d"). The same cases are also published in "unofficial volumes" by the West Publishing Company. These are *California Reporter* (abbreviated "Cal. Rptr.") and *Pacific Reporter* (abbreviated "P." or "P.2d," respectively, for the first and second series). The case is the same whether you read it in the "official" or "unofficial" reporter.

Here are some examples of case citations:

---

[4]You can buy the Civil Code and the Code of Civil Procedure in law book stores. If you are involved with questions of landlord-tenant law on a daily basis, it is almost essential that you own both.

[5]The Courts of Appeal are California's "intermediate" level appeals courts, on a lower legal level than the California Supreme Court, but "higher" than the superior, municipal and justice courts of the counties. There are six appellate districts in the state, with courts in San Francisco, Los Angeles, Sacramento, San Diego, Fresno, and San Jose. (The California Supreme Court is headquartered in San Francisco.)

case name

year of decision

volume number

3rd series
*Official Reports of
California Supreme Court*

page no.

volume no.

case is also listed in
Calif. Reporter,
the "unofficial" reports

page no.

volume no.

case is also listed
in 2nd series of
Pacific Reporter

page no.

Green v. Superior Court   (1974) 10 Cal.3d 616, 11 Cal.Rptr. 704, 517 P.2d 1168.

case name

year of decision

3rd series of
*Official Reports of California
Courts of Appeal,*
volume 137, page 770.

case is also listed in
Calif. Reporter,
the "unofficial" reports,
volume 187, page 242.

Glaser v. Myers   (1982) 137 Cal.App.3d 770, 187 Cal.Rptr. 242.

case name

year of decision

3rd series of
*Official Reports of the
California Court's of Appeal*
Volume 98, page 24 of the supplement
in the back of the volume

The case also appears in
volume 160, page 79 of the
Calif. Reporter.

Lee v. Vignoli   (1979) 98 Cal.App.3d Supp. 24, 160 Cal.Rptr. 79.

volume 405, page 56 of
*Official Reports of the
United States Supreme Court*

also published in volume 92, page 862 of the
Supreme Court Reporter—
an "unofficial" source

also published in the 2nd series
of "Lawyers' Edition" of the
U.S. Supreme Court Reports,
volume 31, page 36

Lindsey v. Normet   (1972) 405 U.S. 56, 92 S.Ct. 862, 31 L.Ed.2nd 36.

The above examples should take some of the mystery out of legal research. If, in the course of your research, you still have questions, again we recommend Elias, *Legal Research: How to Find and Understand the Law* (Nolo Press).

G. Mediation

Mediation involves bringing in a neutral third party to help disputants settle differences. The mediator normally has no power to impose a solution if the parties can't agree. Generally, it works well in situations where the parties want to settle their disputes in order to work together in the future. In a landlord-tenant context, mediation can be extremely helpful in a number of areas, such as disputes about noise, the necessity for repairs, a tenant's decision to withhold rent because defects have not been repaired, rent increases, privacy and many more. Many tenants and especially groups of tenants with a list of grievances, find that mediating disputes with a landlord is a better approach to problem solving than is withholding rent, filing a lawsuit, etc.

A mediator does not impose a decision on the parties, but uses her skills to facilitate a compromise. Mediation is most effective when procedures are established in advance. Typically, the tenant or landlord with a problem contacts some respected neutral organization, such as a city or county landlord-tenant mediation project (not every area has one, but many do), the American Arbitration Association, or a neighborhood dispute resolution center, such as San Francisco's Community Board Program, and arranges for this group to mediate legitimate landlord-tenant disputes, should the need arise. There are a great number of mediation programs in California, and if you ask around in your area, you should find one.

At the mediation session, each side gets to state their position. Just doing this often cools people off considerably and frequently results in a compromise. If the dispute is not taken care of easily, however, the mediator may suggest several ways to resolve the problem, or may even keep everyone talking long enough to realize that the problem goes deeper than the one being mediated. For example, a landlord who thinks he runs a tight ship may learn that the real problem from the tenant's point of view is that her manager is lazy and slow to make repairs. This, of course, may lead to the further discovery that the manager is angry at several tenants for letting their kids pull up his tulips and call him a "big dummy."

The point is that because mediation lets both sides air their grievances it often works well to improve the climate of stormy landlord-tenant relationships. And if it doesn't, you haven't lost much, especially if you make sure mediation occurs promptly and you use it only in situations where your landlord has some arguably legitimate position. If mediation fails, you can still fight it out in court.

Chapter 2:

Looking for a Place and Renting It

A. Get Organized

Looking for a house or apartment to rent is often a frustrating and time-consuming task. Since it is human nature to become harried and frazzled under pressure, many mistakes are made at this stage which later turn out to be costly, both in time and money. Try to stay cool.

Before you start looking for a place, decide:

- How much you want to pay,
- How long you plan on staying, and
- What sort of area you want to live in.

Be realistic both as to your budget and as to what is available, and set definite guidelines in advance. If you can't find a place that meets your guidelines, don't change them without taking time to think the matter over carefully. Some of the worst and most costly mistakes are made by people who sign a lease or put down a deposit at the end of a long, frustrating day only to realize later that the place is completely unsuitable.

It is extremely important that you keep all records. As part of your getting organized, get a large manila envelope or file folder in which to keep all papers having to do with your rental transaction. Misplacing and losing papers (deposit agreements, leases, rent receipts, etc.) is a com - mon mistake that should be avoided. Your landlord is in business and has probably learned how not to make such basic mistakes, so you should do the same. Set up a safe place in which to save your papers, receipts, cancelled checks, and anything else that you think might possibly be important at a later time.

Be wary of companies that claim to be "homefinding services." Some do a good job of trying to help people find a place to rent, but some are sloppy, and a few are actually crooked. For example, several homefinding services have been caught running ads about imaginary apartments in good locations at low rents, only to tell people who show up, "We just rented that one, but here's another one"—at a higher rent—"you will really like." Another problem has been companies that sell lists of addresses of apartments for rent which are so outdated that most or all of the apartments have been rented. In other words, do a little investigating (e.g., talk to some other home-seekers or check with the Better Business Bureau) before you pay anyone to help you find a home. If you feel an apartment locator service has seriously misrepresented its service, ask for your money back and file a complaint with the Consumer Fraud Division of your local district attorney's office.

B. Learn About Rental Agreements

Before you start looking for a place, you should know a little about rental agreements. First—the most important rule—*don't sign any papers until you understand what's in them, or you may regret it later!*

Fortunately, there are only three different kinds of rental agreements, and all you really need to know is what they are like and the consequences to you of each. If you know these things, you may be able to bargain for better terms, and you'll certainly know when to turn down an agreement altogether. If you read this chapter and still don't understand what's in your agreement, you should probably get some advice (see Chapter 1, Part C) before you make the deal.

The Three Kinds of Rental Agreements

The three basic ways that residential rentals are commonly made are:

• The Lease,

• The Written Rental Agreement, and

• The Oral Rental Agreement.

An oral agreement is made without anything being written down—you just talk over what the deal is and agree to it. The other two, the Lease and the Written Rental Agreement, have all the terms you agree to written down on a paper which you and the landlord sign. Let's look at each in some detail.

1. Oral Agreements

It is perfectly legal to make a deal orally—that is, without writing anything down, and no sig - natures. The landlord agrees to let you move in and you agree to pay a certain amount of rent on some schedule, like weekly, every other week or every month. The period between rent payments is what determines how much notice you are entitled to for rent raises or orders to get out. If you pay (a) weekly or (b) monthly, then you are entitled to (a) a week's or (b) 30 days' notice.

The Oral Agreement has some advantages: it is relatively informal, you can move out on short notice, and you aren't subjected to the long list of terms and rules contained in most Leases and Written Rental Contracts. However, if you want the clarity of having everything written down, you will probably want your deal in writing. If you want long-term security from rent raises and orders to move out (unless you live in one of the rent control cities that provide these advantages to everyone—see Chapter 4), you will want a lease.

Oral agreements are legal and enforceable. But as time goes by and circumstances change, peo - ple's memories can have a funny habit of changing, too. Then, if something goes wrong, both sides end up in front of a judge who has to decide whose recollection of the agreement to believe. For this reason, even if you make an oral agreement, it is wise to get some of the landlord's pro - mises in writing. For example, if your landlord promises to make repairs, allow you to have a pet, or do anything else which you want to make sure he remembers, ask him to write it down, date and sign it, as illustrated in Section F below.

2. Leases and Written Rental Agreements

The Lease and the Written Rental Agreement are basically the same except for one terribly important difference. The lease fixes all the terms of the agreement so that no changes can be made for a given period of *time*—most commonly, one year. If you rent under a Lease, your rent cannot be raised until the Lease runs out, nor can you be told to move unless you break the terms of the Lease. On the other hand, you are expected to perform your obligations under the Lease (including rent payments) until it runs out, or a qualified substitute tenant is found to replace you.

The written rental agreement—often called a "month-to-month" agreement—has everything written down, just like the Lease, but the time period of your tenancy is indefinite. This means that you can move out or your landlord can raise your rent or order you to move out on only 30 days' notice (sometimes less)[1]—except in certain communities which have rent control laws including requirements that landlords show "just cause" to evict. See Chapter 4 for a list.

---

[1]Civil Code Section 1946 allows the notice of tenancy termination period to be shortened to any amount of time not less than seven days before the end of the month, by an agreement made at the time the tenancy is created. This is very rarely done.

Except for these very important differences, Leases and Written Rental Agreements are so much alike that they are sometimes hard to tell apart. Both of them cover the basic terms of rental (names, addresses, amount of rent and date due, deposits, etc.) and both of them tend to have a lot of other fine print provisions to protect the landlord.

Be Careful! Since they look so much alike, some forms can look like a lease, and sound like a lease, and even cover a year's period, but if they contain a provision that rent can be raised or that the agreement can be terminated on 30 days' notice, then they are really only written rental agreements.

Read It Carefully! It is crucial that you read the entire lease or rental agreement and understand it before you sign it. If the main document refers to another document such as "house rules," make sure you read a copy of these too. If there is any part of the written document that you don't understand, get advice (but not from the people who want you to sign it). If you want your rights protected, you will have to see to it yourself.

Legally, a written agreement can be typed or written down in longhand on any kind of paper, in any words, so long as the terms are understandable. However, as a practical matter, nearly all landlords use standard printed forms which they buy in stationery stores or get from landlord associations. These forms have been prepared by lawyers or real estate associations, and they are usually as favorable as possible to the landlord. These forms need not look like death certificates, nor read like acts of Congress, but such is often the case. Some of the worst ones include clauses requiring you to waive your privacy, accept shorter than normal notice periods for rent increases and termination, accept responsibility for fixing things that should be handled by your landlord, and generally leave the tenant in a very vulnerable position. We discuss the common provisions and tell you some things to watch out for below. At the back of this book you will find a lease and rental agreement form which is fair to *both* landlord and tenant.

Spanish Language Note: If a lease or month-to-month rental agreement is negotiated primarily in Spanish, then the landlord must give the tenant a Spanish translation of the lease or rental agreement before it is signed. Civil Code § 1632.

If the lease offered to you by the prospective landlord is not satisfactory, it is legal and simple to change it if both parties can agree on the changes. All you do is cross out unwanted portions, write in desired changes, and have all parties who are going to sign the document initial the changes. Make sure that you sign the lease at the same time as the landlord and that you get a copy then and there. This assures both sides that no changes can be made after only one party has signed.

Whenever there is a written agreement, the law presumes that the parties wrote down all of the parts to it before they signed it. If the landlord makes promises which aren't written, it is assumed they weren't made. So again, get everything you want included in writing before you sign.

3. Printed Forms: What to Watch Out For

This section is about the fine print on the form agreements. There are probably hundreds of different printed forms and the provisions in them are all worded a little differently. It is often not at all obvious what some provisions mean. (Contrary to what some form writers seem to think, it is not illegal to use plain English and be clear.) We try to simplify the whole problem for you by setting out, in the list below, the most common kinds of printed form provisions, together with what they usually mean, and what to watch out for.

As will be seen, some of the provisions are illegal and therefore unenforceable. When it comes to these provisions, you should probably *not* waste your bargaining power by trying to get the landlord to scratch them out. It may sometimes help, however, to mention to him that these pro-visions are illegal, in order to show him how one-sided the agreement is, and then ask him to eliminate or change other (enforceable) provisions.

Whether you want to use your bargaining power on lease changes, however, rather than on trying to get repairs or a lower rent or lower security deposit, is a judgment you will have to make.

a. Provision Against Assignment or Sub-Lease Without Landlord's Consent

This provision might restrict your ability to get out of your lease by finding another tenant to take your place. It might also restrict your ability to bring in a new roommate to help you pay the rent. It is probably better for you if this provision is not included. Without this provision, you have the right to assign or sublease without your landlord's consent. Keep in mind, however, that even if this provision is included, the landlord might not be able to arbitrarily withhold her consent to your transferring your lease to someone else.[2]

For example, she cannot withhold consent simply because she thinks the rent set by the lease is too low and will not consent unless the rent is increased. It is not arbitrary, however, to with-hold consent because the new tenant has a poor credit rating or poor housekeeping habits.

b. Provision that the Landlord Is Not Responsible for Damage

This provision says that if the landlord is negligent in maintaining the place and you, your family, or your property is injured (for example, by falling down broken stairs), the landlord is not responsible for paying for your losses. This is called an "exculpatory" provision. Under Civil Code Section 1953, such a provision is invalid.

c. Provision Making Tenant Responsible for Repairs

This provision requires the tenant to waive his rights under Civil Code Sections 1941 and 1942 to make repairs himself and deduct the cost from his rent. This waiver is not valid, so don't use up your bargaining power by making an issue of it.

The agreement might instead contain a provision requiring you to repair or maintain the pre-mises. This provision does not relieve the landlord of his legal obligation to see that the place complies with the housing codes. It might, however, stop you from exercising any rights you have to "repair and deduct," if he fails to make repairs (see Chapter 7A4).

---

[2]*Kendall v. Pestana* (1986) 40 Cal. 3d 488.

d. Waiver of Right to Legal Notice

This provision says the landlord can sue to evict you or can raise the rent or change the terms of the lease without giving notice (such as a three day notice to pay your rent or vacate) required by law. It is not valid. Civil Code § 1953.

e. Provision Setting Notice Period

This provision sets the amount of time the landlord must give you before his notice of termi - nation or rent raise or change in terms becomes operative. If there is no such provision, and you are a month-to-month tenant, the law requires that he give you at least 30 days' notice. Section 1946 of the Civil Code permits, however, such a provision to cut the notice period down to as low as seven days before the end of the term (e.g., the landlord may serve a rent increase notice on June 24, to raise the rent due on July 1). This is very bad for you. If there is such a provision in the agreement, try to get it scratched out. Tell the landlord that you will need at least 30 days to find another place if he decides to terminate your tenancy or raise your rent.

f. Right to Inspect

Many forms have a provision which gives the landlord the right to come into your place to inspect it, or for other purposes. Under Civil Code Section 1954, the landlord's right to enter the dwelling is limited to certain reasons, and any attempt to add to these reasons in the lease or rental agreement is void. We discuss your rights to privacy in detail in Chapter 6.

g. "Right of Re-entry" Provision

This provision permits the landlord to come in and throw you out if you don't pay the rent, without giving you legal notice or going to court. It is not valid. Civil Code § 1953.

h. Waiver of Jury Trial

This provision says that you waive your right to a trial by jury in any eviction lawsuit brought by the landlord. It is not valid. Civil Code § 1953.

i. Waiver of Right to Appeal

This provision prevents you from appealing a court decision in any eviction lawsuit. It is not valid. Civil Code § 1953.

j. Treble Damages

This provision says that if the landlord sues to evict you and wins, he may get not just the actual damages he has suffered (usually unpaid rent), but three times as much. The law provides for this possibility anyway, so you might as well leave this provision alone.

k. Landlord's Attorney's Fees

This provision says that if the landlord has to sue to evict you or collect rent, you will pay his attorney's fees. This can amount to $200 to $400 or more. This provision is valid, and the land-lord cannot get attorney's fees unless he has such a provision. Therefore, you may want to ask that it be scratched out. If it stays and you lose your job or your income is otherwise cut off and you can't pay the rent, you risk getting a judgment against you for attorney's fees in addition to back rent.

However, you should understand that whenever there is an attorney's fee provision in a lease or written rental agreement, the law (Civil Code § 1717) says that the attorney's fee provision entitles you to collect your attorney's fees from the landlord if you win the eviction lawsuit, even if the provision does not say this. For this reason some tenants actually prefer to have an attorney's fees clause—even a seemingly one-sided one—in their written agreement, feeling that if their landlord seriously violates a provision of the agreement and they have to sue her, they want to be able to collect their attorney's fees.

l. Late Charges

This provision requires the tenant to pay a "late charge" if the rent is paid late. The charge may be set as a percentage of the rent (such as 4%), a flat charge (such as $10.00), or a flat charge per day (such as $2.00 each day the rent is late). This provision is probably valid, if the late charge set is a reasonable estimate of the amount the lateness of your payment will cost the landlord, i.e., her administrative cost of processing the late payment and her loss of interest on your rent. However, if the charge is set higher than this, in an effort to "terrorize" you into paying your rent on time, the charge is probably a "penalty" provision, which is invalid. If the late charge seems suspiciously high to you (e.g., a $30 charge on a $300 rent payment late by a few days), ask the landlord to justify it or lower it.

m. Restrictions on Occupants and Guests

Restrictions on the number of occupants and the length of time guests may stay are common in leases and rental agreements. These are valid so long as they are not arbitrary. The landlord has legitimate interests in seeing that the number of occupants does not get so high that there would be excessive wear on the apartment, common area and facilities. The landlord also has a legitimate interest in ensuring that new occupants and guests will not be obnoxious people who might dis - turb other tenants or wreck the place.

These restrictions may not, however, be based on the age or sex of the occupant or guest. A provision forbidding any overnight guests of the opposite sex of the tenant, for example, would be illegal. Civil Code § 51. See also *Atkisson v. Kern County Housing Authority* (1976) 59 Cal. App. 3d 89. So would a provision saying, "No overnight guests under 12 years of age." Civil Code § 51. See also *Marina Point, Ltd. v. Wolfson* (1982) 30 Cal. 3d 721 and Chapter 5B(2).

Restrictions on "guests" are generally not intended to apply to daytime guests, but to overnight guests. While the restriction may not be clear on this distinction—simply limiting "guests"—this word should usually be interpreted to apply only to overnight guests.

Some agreements require the tenant to give the landlord prior notice of overnight guests, or to obtain the landlord's prior consent. These provisions are probably valid, though a provision regard - ing consent would probably be read to mean that the landlord could not arbitrarily withhold his consent. These provisions can be annoying, however, as they allow the landlord to nose into the tenant's private affairs. You might ask the landlord to write in something like, "This restriction shall apply only to overnight guests who stay more than five nights in any 30-day period."

n. Restrictions on Pets

A landlord may completely restrict a tenant's right to keep any pet or restrict the right to keep certain types of pets (e.g., no dogs, or cats, but birds are okay). However, a landlord may not prohibit properly trained dogs needed by a blind, deaf or physically handicapped tenant. Civil Code § 54.1(b)(5).

o. Entire Agreement

Somewhere in the fine print, usually at the end, most leases have a provision which says that the agreement is the entire agreement of the parties. That means that if the landlord made any promises which weren't written down, then they don't count and can't be enforced. It pays, under all circumstances, to get all promises from the landlord in writing. Do this either on the lease or rental agreement itself, or you do it on a separate piece of paper (but make sure it states that the additional material is made a part of the lease or rental agreement).

p. Provision Restricting Water-filled Furniture

It is no longer legal for a landlord to ban water-filled furniture. A landlord may, however, require you to have $100,000 of liability insurance to cover potential damage. A policy should be available for $25 to $50 a year (see Chapter 13).

q. Provision Against Violating Law, Causing Disturbances, Etc.

This type of provision—which allows a landlord to evict if you violate the law in the use of the premises or seriously damage the property—is legal and many landlords insist on it. However, a court is unlikely to enforce this provision for trivial violations.

r. Liquidated Damages Provision

Occasionally, a lease includes a "liquidated damages" clause. Such a clause says that if you move out before the lease expires, you are supposed to pay the landlord a certain amount of money (damages) for the losses caused by your early departure. Usually, landlords set the amount of liquidated damages at several hundred dollars.

If you think that sounds unfair, you're right. As is discussed in Chapter 9, if you move out before your lease expires, you are legally responsible to pay the landlord only for the actual losses you cause. Further, the landlord is legally obligated to minimize those losses by trying to find a new tenant to replace you as soon as possible. Why should the landlord, who didn't lose any money when you moved out, get a windfall?

Courts don't look kindly on liquidated damages, either. If the amount of liquidated damages far exceeds the landlord's actual damages, a judge will probably rule that you don't have to pay them. Of course, it takes time and trouble to go to court, so it's better to get a clause like this crossed out of the lease before you sign it.

4. Which Is Better, a Lease or a Month-to-Month Rental Agreement?

If you have a lease for a substantial term, like a year or more, you are assured that the landlord cannot evict you or raise the rent so long as you pay your rent on time and meet your other obligations under the lease. This kind of security is extremely valuable where housing is hard to find and rents are rising, which, as you know all too well, describes the rental market in most California communities.

If your unit is covered by a local rent control and eviction control ordinance, your need for the protection which a lease provides is lessened. Nevertheless, such ordinances do allow some rent increases, and they usually allow the landlord to evict in order to move himself or a relative into the place, or to make certain repairs. A lease will normally protect you against these dangers.

Of course, if you expect to be moving in a very short time, you may prefer a month-to-month rental agreement, so that you can leave simply by giving 30 days' notice. But don't be too sure that a month-to-month tenancy is what you want. In today's tight rental market, it is usually not difficult to "break" a lease if you have to. We discuss this possibility in Chapter 9. Basically, the rule is that if you have a lease and move out before the term is up, the landlord can sue you for the rent as it comes due until the lease runs out, only as long as she makes a reasonable effort to find another tenant. But, because finding another tenant at the same rent or more is usually very easy these days with even minimal effort, there is normally little risk of loss to the tenant who leaves before a lease runs out. (But see Chapter 9 for the details.)

All things being equal, a lease is commonly preferable to a rental agreement because it gives you additional security from rent increases and eviction, especially in cities that do not have a provision in their rent control ordinances requiring just cause for eviction. But if it is likely that you will be a very short-term tenant, you will probably wish to rent under a written rental agreement, as getting out of a lease does involve some trouble.

If you prefer a lease, but are worried about some specific event which might force you to leave the area, consider simply providing for that event in the lease. If your boss might transfer you to Phoenix, put a provision in your lease saying, "Tenant may terminate this lease upon 30 days' written notice, provided that, with such notice, Tenant also gives Landlord a copy of a note from Tenant's employer saying that Tenant is being transferred to a location out of the city." Such a provision might be especially important for a tenant who is in the military service.

The written rental agreement is often preferred by landlords. It gives them the right to raise the rent as often as they wish (unless there is a local rent regulation ordinance) and to get rid of tenants that they don't like. In most cases, from a tenant's point of view, the written rental agreement does not have the advantages of either a lease or an oral agreement.

On the other hand, the truth is that you often have to take what you can get.

5. Model Lease and Model Rental Agreement

Landlord's forms are often very unfair. They impose many requirements on the tenant and very few on the landlord. We offer a positive alternative for you to use, if you get the chance. You will find tear-out copies of both a lease and rental agreement which are fair to both parties at the back of this book. They require the tenant to pay his rent and keep up his apartment, while requiring the landlord to make repairs and not hassle the tenant. They leave out the harsh provisions found in most landlord's leases. Try to get your landlord to agree to use one of these forms instead of his. Read the sections above to help you decide whether you want to use the Lease or the Rental Agreement.

C. Fees and Deposits

Almost every landlord requires the tenant to give a substantial security deposit, sometimes including "last month's rent." The laws concerning how much can be charged and when deposits must be returned are discussed in Chapter 10. Here we will discuss some other fees and deposits that are occasionally required.

1. "Holding" Deposit

Sometimes, if you make a deal with a landlord, he will want some type of cash deposit, then and there, to make sure you don't change your mind and back out of the deal. If you give him the cash, sometimes as much as a month's rent, he will "hold" the place for you until you bring him your first month's rent and any deposits or fees you agreed on. This is called a "holding" or "bond" deposit.

If you give a landlord a holding deposit and later decide not to take the place, you probably will be unable to get your deposit back. Therefore, be sure you really want the place before giving this kind of deposit. If you and the landlord agree on anything else, such as your right to get half of the holding deposit back if you decide not to take the place within a certain number of days, be sure you write it down.

Be sure you and the landlord understand what is to happen to the deposit when you take the place. Usually it will be applied to the first month's rent. To make this clear, have the landlord give you a receipt for the deposit and have her write on the receipt what is to happen to the deposit when you come back with the rent.

2. "Finder's Fees"

Some landlords--especially in cities with rent control--try to collect high "finder's fees" and the like just for renting the place to the tenant.

It works like this. When a prospective tenant applies to a landlord or management company, he is told that he must either (1) pay a finder's fee directly to the landlord or management company to qualify to get a particular unit, or (2) go to an apartment locator service and pay a finder's fee. In some situations, the locator service will have been set up primarily to collect the fee and isn't real-ly in the business of locating apartments.

In a rent control city, this sort of fee is probably a sneaky way to get a higher rent--illegally. To get the place, you may want to pay the fee. After you move in, however, try to get it back! You have a right to, as your payment of the fee was not really voluntary, and a tenant generally cannot be required to waive his rights under a rent control law. Contact your local rent control board, city attorney, or district attorney's office (consumer fraud unit)--or sue the landlord in Small Claims Court.

Even in a city without rent control, a "finder's fee" which goes to the landlord (or his agent) rather than to a true finder is probably still illegal. *People v. Sangiacomo* (1982) 129 Cal. App. 3d 364. This issue is covered by Civil Code Section 1950.5, which allows fees and deposits to be used only to remedy tenant defaults in payment of rent, cleaning the premises, and paying for damage to the premises. The landlord who simply pockets the "finder's fee" is probably violating this statute, and you can sue him in Small Claims Court to get it back.

3. Credit Check Fees

Landlords can, and often do, charge a fee to check the credit of prospective tenants. Credit checks normally cost no more than $25, and we believe that charging more is unreasonable. Some landlords have been known to take credit check fees from a number of prospective tenants and pocket some or all of the money. Problems can also develop if the landlord takes a long time to check a tenant's credit and the tenant, not knowing whether or not the rental will be approved, rents another place. To avoid these and other possible areas of dispute, it is wise to sign a brief agreement with a landlord such as the following:

CREDIT INFORMATION

Tenant authorizes Owner to verify all credit information for the purpose of renting the premises at_____. Owner shall not release such information for any other purpose without the express written approval of the Tenant.

If Owner does not agree to sign Lease within _____ days of receiving a deposit from Tenant for the purpose of reserving the premises, the total deposit shall be refunded to Tenant, less the amount actually spent to verify credit information.

Tenant may withdraw from the agreement and receive a refund of the total deposit (less an amount used to verify credit information) up until such time as Owner/Agent signs the lease.

_____   and   _____
Landlord   Tenant

D. Credit Reports

A number of organizations, generally called "consumer credit reporting" or tenant-screening G15 agencies, collect information about tenants, such as whether they pay rent on time or were ever involved in an unlawful detainer action. Larger landlords especially routinely check with these agencies before renting to a prospective tenant. Civil Code Sections 1785.1-1786.4 provide that if a landlord does not rent to a tenant or charges more for a unit because of information in a credit report, the tenant must be notified and told the identity of the credit reporting agency. It also prohibits a credit agency from including any information about unlawful detainer lawsuits where the tenant was adjudged the prevailing party. If the credit report is to discuss the tenant's character, general reputation, personal characteristics or mode of living, the tenant must be notified in writing within three days. If you believe a credit bureau or reporting agency may have given incorrect information about you to any creditor, including a landlord, you have a right to check and see for yourself, and to make such corrections as you desire.

E. How To Check a Place Over

If you see a place that you think you will like, take a walk around the neighborhood. Check out where there are stores, schools and bus stops. Walk around the building you are interested in renting and try to meet some of the neighbors. Ask them how they have gotten along with the landlord. Make sure that you can feel at home in all respects. Take an especially close look at the condition of the unit you may rent. Look for dirt and damage, and carefully check all doors, windows, screens, stoves, furnaces, hot water heaters and any other appliances. Make lists of any defects you find--later you can negotiate with the landlord for improvements and repairs. At the very least, be sure to get her to sign an acknowledgment of the existing conditions, so she can't blame you later for causing them. The best way to do this is by completing the landlord-tenant Checklist discussed in Section H, below.

In the section below we cover the landlord's responsibilities for the condition of the premises he rents. In addition we show you exactly how to carefully check a place out to see if it meets legal standards.

1. Housing Codes and Enforcement

Housing codes are laws which require a landlord to put his apartments and houses in good condition before renting them and to keep them that way while people are living there. The landlord cannot escape this duty by trying to impose it on the tenant in the lease or rental agreement.

California has a State Housing Law.[3] The main part of this law is contained in a little book called the Uniform Housing Code. You can get a copy from the International Conference of Building Officials, 5360 South Workman Mill Road, Whittier, California 90601. Repeated severe violations of the State Housing Law is a crime, punishable by a fine of up to $5,000 or imprisonment for up to one year, or both.[4]

Many cities and counties have also enacted housing codes. Local rules are at least as strict as the State Housing Law and sometimes stricter. Check with your City Clerk and County Clerk to see if you have such laws in your community.

The State Housing Law and local housing codes are enforced by local agencies. These are usually city and county Building Inspection and Housing Departments. Other local agencies which might help you with certain health and housing conditions are the Health Department and Fire Department.

If you call a local agency such as a Building Inspection Department and tell them that your landlord won't make repairs, they will send out a building inspector. He will inspect the place and make a report. If he finds housing code violations, he should send a letter to the landlord ordering her to make repairs. If she does not make them within a reasonable time, the inspector may order the building vacated until repairs are made, order the building demolished, or have the work done and charge the cost to the landlord.

In addition, you may be able to "enforce" the codes by suing the landlord, using rent money to make repairs, or withholding rent. These remedies are discussed in Chapter 7.

2. A Checklist of Things to Inspect

Here is a checklist of things you should look for when inspecting a place. All requirements mentioned are contained in the State Housing Law. While checking some items on this list may seem obvious almost to the point of being simple-minded, the unhappy truth is that many people do not check a rental unit thoroughly before moving in and have all sorts of trouble getting repairs made later. So please slow down and look carefully (and then look again) before you sign on the dotted line.

a. Check the STRUCTURE (floors, walls, ceiling, foundation)

The structure of the place must be weatherproof, waterproof and rodent proof.

---

[3]For a list of those conditions which violate the law, see Health and Safety Code Section 17920.3.
[4]Health & Safety Code§17995.3. First time offenders face a fine of $500 and up to six months in jail or both, Health & Safety Code§17995.

"Weatherproof" means there must be no holes, cracks, or broken plaster. Check to see if all the walls are flush (that they meet directly, with no space in between). See if any floorboards are warped. Does wall plaster fall off when you touch it?

"Waterproof" means no water should leak in. If you see dark round spots on the ceilings or dark streaks on the walls, rain water might have been leaking through.

"Rodent proof" deals with cracks and holes which rats and mice could use.

b. Check the PLUMBING

The landlord does not have to provide you with water, but he must provide a plumbing system connected to your community's water system and also to its sewage system (unless you have a cesspool).

All plumbing must be in good condition, free of rust and leaks. Sometimes the condition of the plumbing is hard to discover, but there are several tests you can run to see if there might be problems.

Flush the toilet. Does it take too long to flush? Does it leak on the floor? Is the water discolored? If so, the pipes may be rusty or unclean.

If the water is connected, fill a sink with hot and cold water. Turn the faucets on all the way, and listen for vibrating or knocking sounds in the pipes. See if the water in the sink is discolored. Drain the sink, and see if it takes too long for the water to run out.

c. Check the BATHROOM

The State Housing Law requires that every apartment and house have at least one working toilet, wash basin, and bathtub (or shower) in it. The toilet and bathtub (or shower) must be in a room which gives privacy to the occupant and which is ventilated. All of these facilities must be installed and maintained in a safe and sanitary condition.

d. Check the KITCHEN

The State Housing Law requires that every apartment and house have a kitchen. The kitchen must have a kitchen sink, which cannot be made of wood or other absorbent material.

e. Check the HOT WATER

The landlord must see that you have both hot and cold running water (although he can require you to pay the water and gas bills). "Hot" water means a temperature of not less than 120 degrees F.

f. Check the HEAT

The landlord must provide adequate heating facilities. Unvented fuel-burning heaters are not permitted.

g. Check the LIGHT AND VENTILATION

All rooms you live in must have natural light through windows or skylights, which must have an area not less than one-tenth of the floor area of the room, with a minimum of 12 square feet (3 square feet for bathroom windows). The windows must be openable at least half way for venti-lation, unless mechanical ventilation is provided.

Hallways and stairs in the building must be lighted at all times.

h. Check for signs of INSECTS, VERMIN AND RODENTS

The landlord must provide facilities to prevent insect and rodent infestation and, if there is infestation, provide for extermination services.

These pests can be hard to notice. Remember, however, that they are very shy and stay out of sight. Therefore, if you see any fresh signs of them, they are probably very numerous and will bother you later on. Also, these pests travel from house to house. If your neighbors have them, they will probably get to you.

Check for rodent trails and excrement. Rats and mice travel the same path day after day and leave a gray coloring along the floor and baseboards. Look at the kitchen carefully, for rodents go there for food supplies. Check in closets, cupboards, and behind appliances for cockroaches.

Check for possible breeding grounds nearby. Stagnant water is often a source of pests. So are garages and basements that have piles of litter or old couches.

As mentioned before, cracks and holes in the walls and floors can be entry-points for pests.

i. Check the WIRING AND ELECTRICITY

Loose or exposed wiring can be dangerous, leading to shock or fires. The landlord must provide safe and proper wiring.

If electrical power is available in the area, the place must be connected to it. Every room you live in must have at least two outlets (or one outlet and one light fixture). Every bathroom must have at least one light fixture.

j. Check for FIRE SAFETY

The landlord must provide safe exits leading to a street or hallway. Hallways, stairways and exits must be free from litter. Storage rooms, garages, and basements must not contain combustible materials. Many cities require smoke detectors.

k. Check for adequate TRASH AND GARBAGE RECEPTACLES

The landlord must provide adequate garbage and trash storage and removal facilities. Garbage cans must have tight-fitting covers.

l. Check the general CLEANLINESS OF THE AREA

The landlord must keep those parts of the building which he controls (hallways, stairs, yards, basement, driveway, etc.) in a clean, sanitary, and safe condition.

3. What If the Place Does Not Meet the Above Standards?

If the place has serious problems, you should probably not rent it if you can possibly avoid it. A landlord who would even show you such a place probably won't or can't make the needed repairs. If the landlord promises to fix it up, be careful. First, ask other tenants how good the landlord is at keeping promises. Second, make him put his promises in writing and sign it, as illustrated in Section G of this chapter. Be sure he also puts down dates on which certain repairs will be completed. Also, get him to write down that you will not have to pay your rent if he fails to meet the completion dates. If he doesn't want to agree to these things, he probably isn't taking his obligation to repair very seriously.

If you like the place but it has a few problems, simply ask the landlord to promise to make the necessary repairs. You might point out to him that he is required to make such repairs before renting, under the State Housing Law, but you will rent the place and let him repair it later, if he makes his promise (with dates) in writing and signs it.

If the landlord refuses to make the repairs, or if the place is so bad you don't trust his promises to make repairs, you should not rent the place, but you should report him to your city or county Building Inspection Department. He is violating the law (the State Housing Law), so this is your duty as a citizen. Also, you may be helping the tenant who ends up having to take the place.

F. How to Bargain for the Best Deal

Once you decide that you might like to rent a particular place, then negotiate the terms of the rental with the landlord or his agent. Often you will be presented with a "take it or leave it" proposition, where the landlord is not open to making changes. Many times, however, landlords will be open to reasonable changes. Whether it be the rent that you are trying to change, or particular terms in the contract, it never hurts to try.

In your first negotiation, it is good to remember that if the landlord is impressed with you, she will be more likely to want you as a tenant. Take a moment to consider what sort of folks you would like to rent to if you were a landlord. In fact, you might think over the information in Chapter 1 about your landlord and his situation. Certainly, a good first impression can be made on the application form. Most landlords ask you to fill out an application listing your jobs, bank, cars, income and references. It is a good idea to make up your own form in advance, much as you would write a job resume. It's a good idea to photocopy your application. If you don't get the first place, it will be available to submit when you apply for other units.

How good a deal you can get from a landlord depends on how badly he wants you. If there are very few places available at the rent he is asking and a lot of people are looking, which is usually the case these days, he may tell you to take his deal (rent, security deposit and form lease) or forget the whole thing. Even an attempt to bargain may make the landlord reluctant to rent to you.

If you are in an area where there are lots of places for rent and not too many people looking (say a university area in the spring), you will have more bargaining power. The landlord wants to rent the place soon (to get the rent) and may be afraid of losing you to another landlord.

If you can, try to talk to the last tenant that lived in the place. She might give you some very valuable information on how to deal with the landlord, what is wrong with the place, and generally what it is like to live there. Other tenants or neighbors in the area might also be helpful on this.

The more you look like a responsible tenant, the more bargaining power you will have. Every landlord wants "responsible" tenants who will pay rent regularly, not mess up his place, and not complain about anything. The more you appear to be this way, the better the deal you will get. The landlord won't rent to you at all unless he trusts you, and if he trusts you, he may be willing to give you things you ask for in order to keep you.

If you have any bargaining power, try to use it. You are investing a lot of your money and energy for a long time to come, and you are entitled to shop around and bargain to get the best deal you can. Some people don't like to bargain, because they think others will think they are cheap. But don't forget that the landlord is trying to get as much as he can out of his tenants, and he is not considered cheap, but a "good businessman." You should be a "good consumer" and get as much as you can for a reasonable price.

Even if the rent is fair and the landlord won't budge on that, there are other things he might give you if you ask. He may have a better refrigerator in storage or he may be willing to eliminate some lease provisions you don't like, or he may do some other things mentioned in this Handbook.

G. Get All Promises In Writing

Your future relationship with your landlord may be very pleasant. Hope for the best and try to be open, honest and friendly. However, at the same time, sensible steps should be taken for your own self protection, just in case things take a nasty turn.

It often happens that a tenant moves into an apartment which has not been properly cleaned, or which needs painting or repairs. The landlord may say that the tenant can leave it in the same condition when he leaves, or perhaps that he can deduct money from the rent in exchange for cleaning, painting or repairs. Whatever promises the landlord makes, you should be aware that it is very common for this sort of vague, oral agreement to lead to misunderstanding, bitterness and financial loss. The time to protect yourself is at the beginning. This may be your only chance to do so.

If a landlord promises to clean, paint, build a deck, install a fence or reimburse you for material and work, or if there are any other kinds of promises you want to depend upon, get them in writing and include a date for completing the work. Asking for a promise in writing need not cause you tension or embarrassment. Just tell the landlord, politely, that you have made a simple list of what has been agreed to, and you want to go over it with him for clarification. If he agrees that the list is accurate, include a line saying that this list is made a part of the written lease or rental agreement and have him date and sign it. There should be two copies, one for the landlord and one for your own file.

The use of written contracts is standard among business people and among friends when they are in a business relationship. The purpose of such writings is to remind people of what they once agreed to do. If the landlord balks at putting things in writing, be very careful in all dealings with him.

If the landlord won't paint, clean or make repairs, be sure to list the faults as particularly and completely as you can and get him to sign and date the list. Otherwise, when you move out he may claim that you caused the damage, and refuse to refund all, or a part, of your deposit.

January 1, 19__

Landlord *Smith Realty* and Tenant *Patricia Parker* make the following agreement, which is hereby added to the lease (or rental agreement) they entered into on _____, 19__:

1. Patricia Parker agrees to buy paint and painting supplies not to exceed a cost of $120 and to paint apartment #4 at 1500 Acorn Street, Cloverdale, California, on or before February 1, 19__ and to forward all receipts for painting supplies and paint to Smith Realty;

2. Smith Realty agrees to reduce the payment due February 1, 19__ by $150 in consideration for the painting to be done by Patricia Parker and in addition to allow Patricia Parker to deduct the actual cost of paint and painting supplies (not to exceed $120) from the rent payment due February 1, 19__.

3. The premises are being rented with the following defects:

a. dent in oven door,

b. gouge over fireplace in wall.

These deficits will be fixed by Smith Realty by _____, 19__.

Smith Realty Company
By: B. C. Smith

Patricia Parker

H. Self Protection When Moving In

1. Look Around the Place

When you are about to move in, take a look around. If there is anything at all wrong with the place--if there is any dirt or damage of any kind--get a few of the most responsible of your friends to take a look at it. The reason for doing this is simple. When you move out the landlord may accuse you of having caused the problem and withhold all or part of your deposit. If this occurs, your friends can testify to the condition of the place when you moved in. Get them to write a simple little dated note (reminder) of what they saw. And, if possible, have a friend take a photograph of all defects. After the photographs are developed, the person taking them should identify each photo on the back by location, date and signature. All notes and pictures should go into your file with your other records.

If you plan to attach cupboards, shelves, bookcases, air conditioners, room dividers or anything at all to the premises, you should get something in writing from the landlord permitting you to install such things, and (if you plan it) to remove them later. By California law, anything which is nailed, screwed or bolted to the premises becomes the property of the landlord. If you remove the object when you leave, your landlord will have the right to recover compensation for any damage to the premises and may also be able to recover the value of the object removed, unless there is a written agreement to the contrary. In addition, most landlords are sensitive to having the premises altered without their consent and may get quite irritated if they discover changes after they have already been made. One way to avoid this type of problem is to install only objects designed not to be permanently attached to the dwelling. Stores which cater to apartment living stock all sorts of clever gadgets that make nails and screws seem old-fashioned.

Temporary fasteners--such as tacks to hang art that can be removed so as to leave only a small hole that at worst needs a dab of spackling paste and paint to render invisible--are not fixtures which you must leave in place when moving out, although you will be responsible for any damage to the walls that can't fairly be considered normal wear and tear.

2. Landlord-Tenant Checklist

Another good self-protection device for both landlord and tenant involves taking an inventory of the condition of the premises at the time you move in, and then again when you move out. This means no more than making a brief written record of the condition of each room and having it signed by you and your landlord. Not only does the inventory give both of you an accu-rate record of the condition of the unit, but the act of making it provides a framework for communication and the resolution of potential disputes. We include two tear-out copies of a landlord-tenant checklist in the Appendix at the back of this book.

When filling out your checklist you will want to be as specific as possible. Thus, you might state next to the stove listing: "generally good, but crack in freezer door." Be sure to note things like worn rugs, chipped enamel, holes in screens, dirty cabinets, etc. If you need more space than provided on your checklist form, make a separate writing for those items signed by both landlord and tenant and have it stapled to the checklist.

Checklist

The following is a summary of the conditions of the premises at

_____, California,

on the dates indicated below.

	Condition on Arrival	Condition on Departure
Living Room		
Floor & Floor Covering		
Drapes		
Walls & Ceilings		
Furniture (if any)		
Light Fixtures		
Windows, Screens & Doors		
Anything Else		
Kitchen		
Floor Covering		
Stove & Refrigerator		
Light Fixtures		
Windows, Screens & Doors		
Sink & Plumbing		
Cupboards		
Dining Room		
Floor & Floor Covering		
Drapes		
Walls & Ceilings		
Furniture (if any)		
Light Fixtures		
Windows, Screens & Doors		
Bathroom(s)		
Toilet(s)		
Sink(s)		
Shower(s)		
Floor, Walls & Ceiling		
Light Fixtures		
Windows, Screens & Doors		
Bedrooms		
Floors & Floor Covering		
Walls & Ceiling		
Furniture (if any)		
Light Fixtures		
Windows, Screens & Doors		
Other Areas		
Floors & Floor Covering		
Windows, Screens & Doors		
Walls & Ceilings		
Furnace		
Air Conditioning (if any)		
Lawn, Ground Covering		
Patio, Terrace, Deck, etc.		
Other		

Checklist filled out on moving in on _____, 19__, and approved by

_____ and _____.
         Landlord   Tenant

Checklist filled out on moving out on _____, 19__, and approved by

_____ and _____.
         Landlord   Tenant

I. Your Responsibilities as a Tenant

1. Comply With Your Lease or Rental Agreement

Your most important responsibility as a tenant is to comply with the provisions of your lease or rental agreement. If you do not, you may have to pay money to the landlord or you may be evicted, and sometimes both. Read your lease or agreement carefully to see what it requires you to do and prevents you from doing.

2. Pay Your Rent On Time

You must pay your rent on the day it is due. Most leases and rental agreements say rent is due on the first of the month. However, if the first falls on a Saturday or Sunday or a legal holiday, then the law says that the rent can be paid on the next business day.[5] If you do not pay your rent on time, you may have to pay a reasonable late charge, if your lease or rental agreement provides for this (see Section B31 above). Also, your landlord may serve upon you a "three-day notice" to pay your rent in three days or get out. If you do not comply with the three-day notice, he can then sue to evict you, as discussed in Chapter 11.

You are entitled to a written receipt whenever you pay your rent.[6] Be especially sure to get one if you don't pay by check, as the receipt is proof that you paid your rent. Keep your receipts in a safe place--preferably in the file that you set up for all documents relating to the rental transaction. It is common for landlords to make mistakes in their bookkeeping and conclude that you are delinquent in your rent obligation. Keeping your receipts or cancelled checks is the surest way to prevent misunderstandings of this type.

3. Keep the Place Clean

The housing codes and almost all agreements require that you keep your place clean, safe and sanitary. You must properly dispose of all garbage and trash in your premises, placing it in the containers provided by the landlord.

4. Repair Anything You Break

Anything damaged by you, other occupants or guests must be repaired at your expense, unless the damage resulted from "normal wear and tear" during ordinary use. In other words, you are responsible for the loss of broken windows, toothbrushes in the toilet and other damages you cause. If you rent a furnished unit and a chair you sit on breaks from old age, you do not have to repair or replace it. If, however, your child breaks the chair in a temper tantrum, you must pay for it.

---

[5] Code of Civil Procedure §13; Government Code § 6700 et seq.

[6] Civil Code§1499: "A debtor has a right to require from his creditor a written receipt for any property delivered in performance of his obligation."

J. Co-Signing Leases

Some landlords have begun requiring a co-signer on leases and rental agreements as a condition of renting. Normally, they ask the co-signer to sign a contract saying that he will pay for any rent or damage losses that the tenants fail to pay. Several landlords have told us that inclusion of this sort of provision is mostly psychological and that they don't often sue the co-signer, even if the original tenant defaults. Psychological or not, it is possible that a co-signer will be sued if the tenant defaults, so don't co-sign if you are not fully ready to pay.

Important: Many co-signer clauses are not enforceable in court because they are so vague that they don't qualify as contracts. Also, if a landlord and tenant change the terms of their rental agreement—or even renew it—without the approval of the co-signer, she is no longer responsible.[7] Of course, any defenses that a tenant may raise (e.g., breach of the warranty of habitability because of seriously defective conditions) may also be raised by the co-signer (see Chapter 3). In addition, if a landlord sues a tenant for eviction, the co-signer can't be sued as part of the same suit. The co-signer must be sued separately in either a regular civil lawsuit or in small claims court.

---

[7]See also Civil Code § 2819; *Wexler v. McLucas*, 48 Cal. App. 3d Supp. 9 (1975).

Chapter 3:

Sharing a Home

It's more and more common for two or more unmarried people to rent a place together. Commonly a sexual relationship forms the basis of a decision to share, but often it does not. But whether or not it involves sharing a bed, sharing a home can have all sorts of legal ramifications. Of course, there are the legalities when it comes to dealing with the landlord, but sometimes the legal rules governing the relationship between the roommates are of even more importance.

A. Is It Legal to Live Together?

The answer is yes when two adults live together. And it makes no difference whether they are gay or straight, if one or both is married to someone else, or if they have or don't have a sexual relationship. There used to be laws against gay sexual conduct and against people living together when married to someone else, but since 1976 these laws no longer exist in California. Does the repeal of these laws mean that landlords must rent to gay couples or unmarried couples? Not directly, but there are other state and local laws and court decisions banning unlawful discrimination (see Chapter 5).

Three or more people used to have trouble setting up housekeeping together, even if they were all as celibate as nuns. Why? Because some communities had local zoning ordinances banning more than two unrelated persons from living together (excepting household help, of course). Usually these ordinances were in effect in conservative communities which are uptight about what they see to be "hippie communes." The California Supreme Court has ruled this sort of ordinance is unconstitutional under the California Constitution.[1] This means as far as local law is concerned that three or more unrelated people can live together anyplace in California.

But just because it's legal for three or more unrelated adults to rent a place together, does a landlord have to rent to them? In other words, can a landlord insist on renting a unit to only two people even though there is space enough for more? The answer is yes. As long as a landlord doesn't establish the number of people who can live in a unit in order to discriminate against families with children (see Chapter 5), this decision is up to her.

B. The Legal Obligations of Roommates to the Landlord

If two people--let's call them Ted and Carol--enter into a lease or rental agreement (written or oral), they are each on the hook to the landlord for all rent and all damages to the apartment (except "normal wear and tear"). It makes no difference who (or whose friends) caused the damage, or who left without paying the rent. Let's look at several common situations.

Example 1: Ted and Carol both sign a written rental agreement providing for a total monthly rent of $800 for a flat. They agree between them to pay one-half each. After three months Ted refuses to pay his half of the rent (or moves out with no notice to Carol and the landlord). In either situation, Carol is legally obligated to pay all the rent, as far as the landlord is concerned. Ted, of course, is equally liable, but if he is unreachable or out of work, the landlord will almost surely come after Carol for the whole amount. Since Ted and Carol have rented under a month-to-month written rental agreement, Carol can cut her losses by giving the landlord a 30-day written notice of intention to move. She can do this even if Ted is lying around the place, refusing to pay or get out.

Important: If Carol ends up paying the landlord more than her agreed share of the rent, she has a right to recover from Ted. If payment is not made voluntarily, Carol can sue Ted in Small Claims Court.[2]

Example 2: The same fact situation as Example 1, except that this time there is a lease for one year. Again, both partners are independently liable for the whole rent. If one refuses to pay, the other is still liable, unless a third person can be found to take over the lease, in which case both partners are off the hook from the day that a new tenant takes over. As we discuss in Chapter 10, because of the housing shortage in most parts of the state, it is often easy for a tenant to get out of a lease at little or no cost, simply by finding an acceptable new tenant and steering him or her to the landlord. A newspaper ad will usually do it. The landlord has an obligation to limit his damages (called "mitigation of damages" in legal lingo) by renting to a suitable new tenant as soon as possible. Should the landlord fail to do this, he loses the legal right to collect damages from the original tenants.

---

[1] *City of Santa Barbara v. Adamson*, 27 Cal. 3d 123 (1980).
[2] See *Everybody's Guide to Small Claims Court*, Warner (Nolo Press).

C. The Legal Obligations of Roommates to Each Other

People sharing a home usually have certain expectations of each other. Sometimes it helps to write these down. After all, you expect to write things down with the landlord almost as a matter of course, so why not do the same with each other? Nothing that Carol and Ted agree to among themselves has any effect as far as the landlord is concerned, but it still may be helpful to have something to refresh their memories, especially if the relationship gets a little rocky. Here we have a sample agreement. Of course, there are many other terms that could be included in this type of agreement and you will probably wish to make some modifications.[3]

[3]If you are interested in a comprehensive living together agreement, see *The Living Together Kit*, Ihara & Warner (Nolo Press), or *A Legal Guide for Lesbian and Gay Couples*, Curry & Clifford (Nolo Press).

AGREEMENT

Carol Pladsen and Ted Kelly, upon renting an apartment at 1500 Redwood Street, #4, Philo, California agree as follows:

1. Carol and Ted are each obligated to pay one-half of the rent and one-half of the utilities, including the basic monthly telephone charge. Each person will keep track of and pay for his or her long distance calls. Rent shall be paid on the first of each month, utilities within ten days of the day the bill is received.

2. If either Carol or Ted wants to move out, the one moving will give the other person 30 days' notice and will pay his/her share of the rent for the entire 30-day period even if he/she moves out sooner. If both Carol and Ted wish to move, they will be jointly responsible for giving the landlord 30 days' notice.

3. No third persons will be invited to stay in the apartment without the mutual agreement of both Carol and Ted.

4. If both Carol and Ted want to keep the apartment but one or the other or both no longer wishes to live together, they will have a third party flip a coin to see who gets to stay. The loser will move out within 30 days and will pay all of his/her obligations for rent, utilities and for any damage to the apartment.

Here is an alternative for number 4.

4. If both Carol and Ted want to keep the apartment but no longer wish to live together, the apartment shall be retained by the person who needs it most. Need shall be determined by taking into consideration the relative financial condition of each party, proximity to work, the needs of minor children, if any, and (list any other factors important to you). If Carol and Ted can't decide this issue by themselves or with the help of a mutually agreed upon mediator, the determination shall be made by a third party (the arbitrator). If it is not possible for Carol and Ted to agree on an arbitrator, the arbitrator will be chosen by (fill in name). The arbitrator shall be paid by the person who gets to keep the apartment. The determination shall be made within ten days after either party informs the other that he or she wishes to separate, and after the arbitrator has listened to each person present his or her case. The arbitration award shall be conclusive on the parties, and shall be prepared in such a way that a formal judgment can be entered thereon in any court having jurisdiction over the dispute if either party so desires. After the determination is made, the person who is to leave shall have an additional ten days to do so. The person who leaves is obligated for all rent, utilities and any damage costs for 30 days from the day that the original determination to separate is made.

_____	_____
Date	Carol Pladsen
_____	_____
Date	Ted Kelly

D. Having a Friend Move In

Perhaps just as common as two or more people renting a home together is for one person to move into a place already rented and occupied by another. This is often simple and smooth when the landlord is cooperative, but can raise some tricky legal questions if the landlord raises objections.

In some situations, where the landlord is not in the area or is not likely to make waves, it may be sensible to simply have the second person move in and worry about the consequences later. But is this legal? Is a tenant required to tell his landlord when a second person moves in? It depends on the lease or rental agreement. If no mention is made as to the number of persons allowed in the apartment, use your own discretion and knowledge of your landlord. Some don't care, but most probably do. We suspect that as a general rule, even in the absence of a lease or rental agreement provision dealing with the area, moving someone in without the consent of a landlord is not the most sensible thing to do. The landlord will probably figure out what is going on before long and may resent your sneakiness more than she resents your roommate. We advise you to:

• Read the lease or rental agreement to see how many people are allowed to live on the prmises and if there are any restrictions on additional people. Sometimes additional people will be allowed for a slight increase in rent.[4] Many landlords will not care whether you are married, living toge-ther or joined by the toes with rubber bands, but will expect to collect more money if more people live in their rental unit.

• Contact the landlord to explain what is happening. If you can't do this in person, you might send a letter such as this:

1500 Redwood Street #4
Philo, California
June 27, 19__

Smith Realty
10 Ocean Street
Elk, California

I live at the above address, and regularly pay rent to your office. As of July 1, 19__, there will be a second person living in my apartment. As set forth in my lease, I enclose the increased rent due which now comes to a total of $800. I will continue to make payments in this amount as long as two people occupy the apartment.

Should you wish to sign a new lease specifically to cover two people, please let me know. My friend, Carol Pladsen, is regularly employed and has an excellent credit rating.

Very truly yours,

Ted Kelly

---

[4]If you live in a rent control area, your local ordinance may restrict how much rent can be increased in this situation.

Remember: Under state law, a written rental agreement may be terminated on thirty days' notice without the necessity of the landlord giving a reason.[5] Thus, a landlord who wants to get rid of you can normally do so without too much trouble if you don't have a lease. So it pays to be reasonable when moving roommates in and out.

If you have a lease, you are probably in a little better position to bargain with the landlord if a friend moves in. This is because, to get you out before the lease expires, he would have to establish that you have violated one or more lease terms. If your lease has a provision allowing occupancy only by one person, your landlord probably has the right to terminate your tenancy if a second person moves in without his permission. However, if the landlord accepts rent with the knowledge that you are living with someone, many courts would hold that he can no longer enforce that right. Of course, if you cause the landlord too much grief, he can simply refuse to renew your lease when it runs out. Again, you will probably come out ahead by being reasonable and cooperative.

1. What Is the Legal Relationship Between the Person Moving In and the Landlord?

If Carol moves into Ted's apartment, what is the relationship between Carol and Ted's landlord? Is Carol obligated to pay rent if Ted fails to pay? What if Ted moves out, but Carol wants to remain? If Ted ruins the paint or breaks the furniture, does Carol have any obligation to pay for the damage?

The answer to these questions is that Carol starts with no legal rights or obligations to the landlord (but possibly to Ted) regarding the rent, or the right to live in the apartment. She has entered into no contract with the landlord. Of course, if she damages the property, she is liable just as a visitor, a trespasser, or a thief who caused damage would be liable. Ted is completely liable for the rent and also for damage to the premises whether caused by Carol or himself, because he has entered into a contract which may be in the form of a lease, written rental agreement or oral rental agreement. If Ted leaves, Carol has no right to take over his lease without the landlord's consent.

Carol can, of course, enter into a lease or rental agreement contract with the landlord which would give her the rights and responsibilities of a tenant. This can be done by:

• Signing a new lease or rental agreement which specifically includes both Ted and Carol as tenants.

• Making an oral rental agreement with the landlord. Be careful of this one, as an oral agreement can consist of no more than a conversation between Carol and the landlord in which she says she will pay the rent and keep the place clean and he says OK. There may be some legal question as to whether an oral agreement between Carol and the landlord is enforceable if there is still a written lease or rental agreement between the landlord and Ted which doesn't include Carol, but it

---

[5]In several populous areas, including San Francisco, Los Angeles, Berkeley, and Santa Monica (see Chapter 15 for a complete list), this rule has been changed by local rent control ordinances which prevent evictions except for reasons specified in the various enactments. These "just cause" for eviction rules are discussed in Chapter 15. Also, the eviction can't be for an improper reason, such as the type of discrimination prohibited under California law (see Chapter 5) or as retaliation for the tenant's exercise of certain rights.

is our belief that most judges would bend over backwards to give Carol the rights and responsibilities of a tenant if she seemed to be exercising them.

• The actual payment of rent by Carol and its acceptance by the landlord, especially if it is done on a fairly regular basis. As in the preceding paragraph, this would set up a month-to-month tenancy between Carol and the landlord and would mean that either could end the tenancy by giving the other a 30 day written notice of intention to end the tenancy.

Should the situation ever arise that Ted wants to move out and Carol remain, it is important that the legal relationships be clarified. Ted should give the landlord a written notice of what he intends to do at least 30 days before he leaves. If he does this, he is off the hook completely in a written or oral rental agreement situation. If a lease is involved and Ted is leaving before it runs out, he might still be OK, because the landlord has a legal duty to take steps to limit her loss as much as possible (mitigate damages--see Chapter 9). This means finding a new tenant to pay the rent. In our example, as long as Carol is a reasonably solvent and non-destructive person, the landlord would suffer no loss by accepting her as a tenant to fill out the rest of Ted's lease. If the landlord refuses Carol without good reason, Ted will probably be legally absolved of future responsibility and any loss is legally the landlord's problem, not his (again, see Chapter 9 for details).

Rent Control Note: If Carol has attained the status of a tenant, the landlord will probably not be able to raise the rent after Ted leaves, except as otherwise permitted by the ordinance. If, on the other hand, Carol has not become a tenant, the rent probably can be raised in most areas covered by rent control which contain a provision called "vacancy decontrol," which allows a landlord to raise rent as much as he wants when a tenant moves out. Berkeley, Santa Monica, and several smaller cities are exceptions to this rule, since in those areas rents are controlled regardless of who is living in the premises. When more than one tenant shares an apartment or house, the rule in some cities with vacancy-decontrol (such as San Francisco) is that the rent can't be raised more than the annual increase allowed by the ordinance until all of the original tenants whose names were on the lease or rental agreement leave. At this point, the landlord can raise the rent as much as he wants under the "vacancy-decontrol" provision. But please be aware that since this rule is subject to a number of different interpretations, depending both on the city and the precise fact situation, it's up to you to check locally.

For use if you have a *rental agreement:*

1500 Redwood Street #4
Philo, California
June 27, 19__

Smith Realty
10 Ocean Street
Elk, California

I live at the above address and regularly pay rent to your office. On July 31, 19__, I will be moving out. As you know, my friend, Carol Pladsen, also resides here. She wishes to remain and will continue to pay rent to your office on the first of each month.

We will be contacting you soon to arrange for the return of my security deposits of $500, at which time Carol will give you a similar deposit. If you have any questions, or if there is anything we can do to make the transition easier for you, please let us know.

Very truly yours,
_____
Ted Kelly

For use if you have a *lease:*

1500 Redwood Street #4
Philo, California
June 27, 19__

Smith Realty
10 Ocean Street
Elk, California

I live at the above address under a lease which expires on October 30, 19__. A change in my job makes it necessary that I leave the last day of February. As you know, for the last six months my friend, Carol Pladsen, has been sharing this apartment. Carol wishes either to take over my lease or enter into a new one with you for the remainder of my lease term. She is employed, has a stable income, and will, of course, be a responsible tenant.

We will soon be contacting your office to work out the details of the transfer. If you have any concerns about this proposal, please give us a call.

Very truly yours,
_____
Ted Kelly

2. What Is the Legal Relationship Between the Person Moving In and the Person Already There?

Alas, it seems all too common that big-brained monkeys go through violent changes in emotional feelings. A relationship that is all sunshine and roses one minute may be more like a skunk cabbage in a hurricane the next. Sometimes, when feelings change, memories blur as to promises made in happier times and the nicest people become paranoid and nasty. Suddenly, questions such as "Whose apartment is this, anyway?" may turn into serious disputes. We suggest that when feelings are relaxed (preferably at the time that the living arrangement is set up), both people make a little note as to their mutual understandings, either as part of a comprehensive living together arrangement or in a separate agreement. If this is done in a spirit of making a writing to aid the all too fallible human memory, it need not be a heavy experience. We include here an example that you might want to change to fit your circumstances.

AGREEMENT

Carol Pladsen and Ted Kelly make the following agreement:

1. Ted will move into Carol's apartment and will give Carol one-half of the monthly rent ($400) on the first of each month. Carol will continue paying the landlord under her lease and Ted will have no obligation under the lease.

2. Ted will pay one-half of the electric, gas, water, garbage and monthly telephone service charges to Carol on the first of each month; Carol will pay the bills.

3. Should Ted wish to move out, he will give Carol as much written notice as possible and will be liable for one-half the rent for two weeks from the time he gives Carol written notice. Should Carol wish Ted to move out, she will give him as much written notice as possible, in no case less than two weeks. In any case of serious dispute, it is understood that Carol has first choice to remain in the apartment and Ted must leave on her request.

_____	_____
Date	Carol Pladsen
_____	_____
Date	Ted Kelly

Important: If you get into a serious dispute with your friend involving your shared home and have no agreements to fall back on, you will have to do the best you can to muddle through to a fair solution. Here are a few ideas to guide your thinking.

• If you live in San Francisco, your living relationship may be covered by the city's rent control ordinance, which recognizes the concept of the "master tenant." A master tenant is a tenant with a formal relationship with the landlord (lease or written rental agreement). Other tenants can be evicted without a need to demonstrate "just cause" by the master tenant, who can also charge the others a disproportionate amount of the rent-controlled rental amount.

• Outside of San Francisco, if only one of you has signed the agreement with the landlord and that person pays all the rent, then that person probably should have the first claim on the apartment, especially if that person occupied the apartment first. The other should be given a reasonable period of time to find another place, especially if she has been contributing to the rent and/or has been living in the home for any considerable period of time.

• If you both signed a lease or rental agreement and/or both regularly pay rent to the landlord, your rights to the apartment are probably legally equal, even if one of you got there first. Try to talk out your situation, letting the person stay who genuinely needs the place the most. Some people find it helpful to set up an informal mediation proceeding with a third person helping the parties arrive at their own solution. If this doesn't work, you may wish to locate a neutral third party arbitrator to hear the facts and make a decision.[6] If you do this, make sure that the arbitrator is not a close friend, as the person who loses is likely to have hard feelings. Lean over backwards to be fair about adjusting money details concerning such things as last month's rent and damage deposits. Allow the person moving out a reasonable period of time to find another place. *We have found that the best compromises are made when both people feel that they have gone more than half way.*

• Each person has the right to his or her belongings. This is true even if they are behind in their share of the rent. Never lock up the other person's property.

• It is a bad idea to deny a person access to his home except in extreme circumstances. If you are going to lock out a person, you should also be ready to sign a formal police complaint or go to court and get a restraining order under California's Domestic Violence Prevention Act (C.C.P.§ 541). You can get more information about this procedure from your county clerk's office. In many instances, locking out a person is not legal and you can be sued for damages.

---

[6]A number of California cities and counties have free or low cost landlord-tenant mediation and arbitration services. In addition, the nonprofit Community Board program offers excellent mediation services in many San Francisco neighborhoods.

E. Guests

What about overnight guests--particularly those who stay over often? What relationship, if any, do these people have with the landlord? More important, is the landlord entitled to any legal recourse if you have a "regular" guest? The answer to this question often depends on what it says in a lease or written rental agreement or written tenant rules authorized by one of these documents (see Chapter 2B). Many restrict the right to have overnight guests to a certain number of days per year and require registration if a guest will stay more than a few days. While these sorts of lease provisions aren't often strictly enforced, they are legal and, in the case of persistent or serious violations, can be grounds for a landlord evicting a tenant with a lease. Even in rent control areas which require just cause for eviction, a tenant who violates guest rules may be evicted, but under the terms of many ordinances, the tenant must first be given a written notice to correct the violation (i.e., to follow the "guest" provision of the lease or written rental agreement).

Absent a specific lease or rental agreement provision dealing with the area, there is no precise line between guests and roommates. A person may be a frequent overnight visitor--four or five times a week--but still qualify as a guest, whereas a roommate may be in residence only a couple of days a week, as is common with flight attendants. A person's status as guest might be considerably enhanced by a showing that she maintains a separate residence complete with furniture and mailing address. However, to the landlord who sees the person on the premises more than the actual tenant, this might not prove persuasive.

Where the landlord is seeking to evict on the basis of a lease provision which prohibits occupancy of more than a certain number, he must (absent a provision limiting the number of days a guest can stay in the premises) prove that the extra occupant is in fact a resident. However, as we mentioned earlier in this chapter (Section D), in many parts of the state the landlord can evict for no reason at all if you have no lease. Accordingly, unless you live in an area covered by a "just cause" for eviction rent control ordinance (see Chapter 11), or have a lease, it might be a good idea to clarify your guest's status with your landlord at the outset instead of leaving things to his imagination.

Chapter 4:

All About Rent

Today, most tenants pay 35% or more of their incomes on rent--sometimes over $1,000 a month. This money obviously means a lot to you, so you should understand your rights regarding when to pay, how much to pay, and whether the landlord can increase the rent. Rent is also very important to the landlord, who usually wants to get as much as she can get as soon as she can get it. Because rent is so important to both parties, and because its non-payment is taken very seriously by the courts, it's important that you know your rights.

A. When Is Rent Due?

Under state law, rent is due at the end of the term of the tenancy (e.g., at the end of the month, in a month-to-month tenancy)--unless the lease or rental agreement provide otherwise. Civil Code § 1947. Almost every lease and rental agreement (whether written or oral) does provide otherwise, however. Most require payment at the beginning of the term. Thus, rent for use of the place in March would be due on March 1 under the terms of the agreement.

If you fail to pay your rent on the date it is due, the landlord may not throw you out or sue to evict you the next day. He must first serve you with a written notice demanding that you pay the rent or get out in three days. If the third day falls on a Saturday, Sunday, or holiday, you get until the next business day to pay the rent. Only after that day can he file a lawsuit to evict you.

If you run into trouble paying your rent on time, three days isn't much time to come up with it. You might expect such trouble if your income is from alimony and child support, or a job which might involve lay-offs or strikes. If you know this might happen, you might wish to ask the landlord to put in the lease or rental agreement a provision that she will not serve a "three-day notice" on you until some time (like 10 days or 20 days) after the first of the month. If she objects, next suggest the provision be written so that it gives you the extra time only if your income is temporarily cut off or delayed.

Both the tear-out Model Lease and the Model Rental Agreement in the Appendix at the back of this book contain a special provision (Section 14) which tries to deal with this problem in a fair way. It provides that the tenant may notify the landlord on or before the due date that he will be unable to pay the rent, and then the parties will try to work out a procedure for rent payment as soon as possible. If they can't do so within 10 days, then the landlord may serve a 3-day notice to pay rent or quit on the tenant.

Ask the landlord to use the Model Lease or Model Rental Agreement. If he won't, then he might at least allow you to include Section 14 in the forms he wants to use.

B. Late Charges

A fairly common landlord practice is to assess tenants who are late with their rent an extra late fee or charge. Some cities with rent control ordinances regulate the amount of these extra charges. Check any rent control ordinance applicable to your properties. In the great majority of California cities and unincorporated areas, however, there are no written regulations as to what you can charge.

Unfortunately, many landlords try to charge excessive late fees. This is not legal. Late charges must be reasonably related to the amount of money it costs the landlord to deal with your lateness. Rental agreements and lease clauses that provide for unreasonably high late charges are not enforceable.[1]

While there are no statutory guidelines as to how much a landlord can reasonably charge as a late fee, here are some guidelines which will help you decide if the amount is excessive:

• A reasonable late charge might be a flat charge of no more than $10-$35, depending on the amount of rent. It is common for a landlord to give a tenant a grace period of from one to five days, but this isn't required. A late charge that is out of proportion to the rent (say $50 for being one date late with rent on a $450 per month apartment) would probably not be upheld in court.

• If your landlord imposes a late charge which increases with each additional date of lateness, it should be moderate and have an upper limit. For example, $5 for the first day rent is late, plus $2 for each additional day, with a maximum late charge of $25-$35, would probably be acceptable to

---

[1]See *Fox v. Federated Department Stores* (1979) 94 Cal. App. 3d 867, 156 Cal. Rptr. 893, where the court held invalid a late charge clause in a promissory note because the charge exceeded reasonable administrative costs.

a judge, unless the property carries a high rent, in which case somewhat higher amounts might be allowed.

Some landlords try to disguise excessive late charges as a "discount" for early payment of rent. One landlord we know concluded he couldn't get away with charging a $50 late charge on a late $425 rent payment, so instead he designed a rental agreement calling for a rent of $475 with a $50 "discount" if the rent was paid before the third day after it was due. Ingenious as this sounds, it is unlikely to stand up in court, unless the discount for timely payments is very modest. This is because the effect of giving a relatively large discount is the same as charging an excessive late fee, and a judge is likely to see it as such and throw it out.

C. Partial Rent Payments

On occasion you may be short of the money to pay your full rent on time. One way to deal with this is to discuss the problem with your landlord and try to get her to accept a partial payment. Except in the unusual situation where your lease or rental agreement gives you the right to make part payments, the landlord is under no obligation to accept part of the rent on the due date along with your promise to catch up later.

Unfortunately, there is normally nothing to stop the landlord from accepting a partial rent payment on one day and serving you with a 3-day notice to pay the rest of the rent or quit the next. However, if you can get your landlord to specifically agree in writing that you can have a longer time to pay, the landlord is bound by this agreement. Here is a sample:

SAMPLE AGREEMENT

Larry Landlord and Trudie Tenant agree as follows:

1. That Trudie has paid only one-half of her $500 rent for Apartment #2 at 111 Billy St., Fair Oaks, CA, on March 1, 19__, which is the date the rent for the month of March is due.

2. That Larry agrees to accept all the remainder of the rent on or before March 15, 19__ and to hold off on any legal proceeding to evict Trudie until after that date.

_____

Larry Landlord

_____

Trudie Tenant

D. Rent Increase Notices

Subject to the provisions of any local rent control law, a landlord may raise the rent on a month-to-month tenancy by "serving" a written notice on the tenant saying that the rent will be increased in 30 days (or more). (If the tenant has a *lease*, no rent increase is appropriate until the lease ends.)

Questions often arise over the manner in which the rent increase notice is delivered. It has been our experience that most landlords simply mail notice of rent increases to their tenants. Under California law (Code of Civil Procedure § 1162), this is not technically proper service of the notice. The notice must be served as follows:

1. By handing it to the tenant personally, or

2. *If* the tenant is absent from home and work, by leaving the notice with "a person of suitable age and discretion" at home or work, *and* mailing a copy to the tenant, or

3. *If* the landlord cannot find out where the tenant lives and works, or a person of suitable age and discretion cannot be found, then the landlord may complete the service by doing all three of these things:

• Posting the notice in a conspicuous place on the property,

• Leaving a copy with someone residing in the rented premises (if such person can be found), and

• Mailing a copy to the tenant.

In other words, if you received a rent increase by mail only, it is not legally effective (unless you voluntarily comply with it). In this situation you are within your rights to tell the landlord that because his notice is ineffective, you are not going to pay the increase. Obviously, however, if the amount of the increase seems fair and you have a good relationship with the landlord, you may want to simply pay the increase and not question the way in which you were served the notice.

E. May the Landlord Increase the Rent? General Law

Rent may not be increased during a fixed-term lease unless the lease so provides.

If you live in public housing or "Section 8" housing, in most cases the rent may not be increased to an amount more than 30% of your income (after certain deductions are taken).A rent increase is invalid if you live in an area covered by rent control and it exceeds the amount allowed by the rent control ordinance--we discuss rent control in the rest of this chapter.

A rent increase is invalid if the landlord imposed it in order to retaliate against you because you exercised some legal right, such as complaining about the condition of the building or organizing a tenants' union. See Chapter 7B(3) for more on retaliation.

A rent increase is invalid if the landlord imposed it in order to discriminate against you on the basis of race, sex, children, or any other prohibited reason mentioned in Chapter 5.

Other than these restrictions, there is nothing in state law to prevent the landlord from doubling the rent or even tripling the rent. Again, you are legally protected against such acts only if you are lucky enough to live in a city or county which has a local rent control ordinance.

F. Rent Control

Rent control is a local phenomenon, established either through the initiative process or by the act of a city council or a county board of supervisors.[2]

Some form of rent regulation now exists in a number of California communities, including Los Angeles, San Jose, and San Francisco (see chart below). Before we describe how such regulation works, a few words of caution:

• Rent control is a rapidly changing field. Hardly a month goes by without one or another city changing an ordinance. And various rent control provisions are often subjected to interpretations by the courts. In short, you should read the material here only to get a general idea of the field. It is absolutely necessary that you also contact your city or county to find out whether rent control presently exists, and if it does, to get a copy of current ordinances and any regulations interpreting it.

• State law requires local rent control agencies in cities that require registration of rents to provide, upon request of the landlord or tenant, a certificate setting out the permissible rent for a particular unit. Civil Code § 1947.8. The landlord or tenant may appeal the rent determination to the rent control agency within 15 days. If no appeal is filed, the rent determination is binding on the agency. If an appeal is filed, the agency must provide a written decision in 60 days.

• No two rent control ordinances are exactly alike. Some cities have elected or appointed boards which have the power to adjust rents; others allow a certain percentage increase each year as part of their ordinances. Some cities have enlightened ordinances with "just cause" for eviction provisions which require landlords to give and prove valid reasons for terminating month-to-month tenancies, while other cities in effect encourage landlords to evict by allowing unlimited rent increases on units when they are vacated (see Chapter 11D) and not protecting existing tenants by requiring just cause for eviction. In order to summarize how each ordinance works, we

---

[2]The California Supreme Court upheld the right of cities and counties to enact rent control ordinances in *Birkenfeld v. City of Berkeley*, 17 Cal. 3d 129 (1976). The U. S. Supreme Court agreed with that decision in *Fisher v. City of Berkeley*, 475 U. S. 260, 106 S. Ct. 1045 (1986).

have prepared a "Rent Control Chart" which outlines the major points of each ordinance. We don't have the space to develop all of the details of all the various ordinances, so again it will be up to you to contact your city or county clerk to get a copy of the entire ordinance in your area.

G. General Types of Rent Control Laws

As noted above, although no two cities' rent control laws are identical, they can be broadly categorized into three types. Obviously, this sort of gross classification isn't perfect, but it should help you place your city in the scheme of things.

1. Weak Rent Regulations

Let's start with the Bay Area cities of San Jose, Oakland, Hayward and Los Gatos, all of which have weak rent control ordinances. Although the rent control ordinances of these areas set forth a certain formula (usually overly generous to landlords given present rates of inflation) by which rents can be increased each year, it is possible for a landlord to raise the rent above this figure and still stay within the law. This is because each of these cities' ordinances require a tenant whose rent is increased above the formula level to petition the board within a certain period (usually 30 days) and protest the increase. If you do not protest the increase within the time allowed, the increase is effective, even though it is higher than the formula increase allowed. If the increase is protested, a hearing is held, at which the board decides if the entire increase should be allowed.

In addition, except in Hayward, the rent control ordinances in these cities do not require the landlord to show "just cause" for eviction. In other words, your landlord can evict you following normal procedures under state law. This means, of course, that this sort of rent control ordinance is so weak that it's almost gutless. It is, however, illegal for landlords in these cities to encourage this type of fear by threatening retaliation against tenants who protest rent increases.

Finally, all these cities have "vacancy decontrol," none of their ordinances require landlords to register their units with the board, and only Oakland's applies to single-family homes.

2. Strict Rent Control

California's best rent control laws (from a tenant's point of view) are found in the cities of Berkeley, Cotati, Santa Monica and West Hollywood. Even single-family rentals are covered by these cities' laws, unless a rental property has two or fewer units and the landlord lives on the property. Landlords must register their units with the board, which decides on the amount of the across-the-board rent increase allowed citywide each year. Because inflation is presently low, this increase also tends to be low. A landlord who increases rent by a greater percentage faces civil penalties, unless the board has allowed an additional increase following the landlord's application. The burden of justifying a higher than routinely-allowable rent increase is entirely on the landlord. In addition, these ordinances provide for reducing rents on application of a tenant who contends that the landlord has poorly-maintained the property.

Finally, as you might have guessed, there is no vacancy decontrol. Again, this means that even if a tenant moves out, the maximum rent for a property remains fixed. A landlord must show just cause for eviction to evict a tenant in all "strict" rent control cities.

3. Moderate Rent Control

The rent control laws of Los Angeles, San Francisco, Beverly Hills and Palm Springs are somewhere between strict and weak, and for lack of a better term we call them "moderate."Although these moderate laws differ somewhat from city to city, they all require landlords who wish to increase the rent by more than a fixed formula amount to petition the board for a higher increase. In addition, all of them (except Palm Springs) provide for some form of vacancy decontrol and require "just cause" for eviction. As you will remember, vacancy decontrol means that when a tenant moves out voluntarily (or is asked to leave for a "just cause"), the unit can be re-rented at the market rate. But what happens if a property is rented to several tenants and one moves out, but the others stay? The rule in most cities with vacancy decontrol is that the unit is covered by rent control as long as any of the original tenants who signed a lease or rental agreement remains, and the rent can't be raised above the amount allowed by the annual increase until all original tenants leave. There is a lot of confusion about this rule in several cities, however, and the law is in a state of flux, so check locally.

Otherwise, there is little similarity in the rent control laws of these cities. For more detailed information, consult the Rent Control Chart in Section I, below.

Note: Decreases in Services as Illegal Rent Increases. If for some reason you're not getting all the use out of your apartment that you were promised when you moved in, the rent board may determine that you've been given an illegal rent increase. In one San Francisco case, elderly tenants successfully argued that their services had been decreased when the landlord moved their garbage cans up a flight of stairs.

H. Hearings

Almost all cities with rent control provide for a hearing procedure to deal with certain types of complaints and requests for rent adjustments. In cities with "weak" rent control, a tenant's protest of a rent increase higher than that allowed by the applicable rent increase formula will result in a hearing at which the landlord must justify the increase. In other rent control cities, the landlord must request a hearing in order to increase rent above the formula amount. Finally, a few cities--such as Santa Monica and Berkeley--allow tenants to initiate hearings to decrease rents on the basis of the landlord's alleged neglect or lack of maintenance on the property.

In the first two types of hearings above, whether initiated by a tenant who protests a rent increase over the formula amount in a "weak" rent control city, or by a landlord in a city that requires him to first obtain permission before exceeding the formula increase, the landlord must demonstrate at the hearing that he needs a rent increase higher than that normally allowed in order to obtain a fair return on his investment. This most often means establishing that taxes, maintenance costs, utility charges, or other business expenses, as well as the amortized cost of any capital improvements, make it difficult to obtain a fair return on one's investment, given the existing level of rent.

1. Initiating the Hearing

A hearing is normally initiated by the filing of a "petition" or "application" with the rent board. In describing this process, let's assume that a landlord is filing a petition in a "strict" or "moderate" rent control city that requires her to obtain permission before raising rents above the formula increase allowed. You, the tenant, wish to protest the increase. Remember, this process is approximately reversed in "weak" rent control cities that require the tenant to protest such an increase.

In some cities, including Los Angeles and San Francisco, there are two types of petitions a landlord seeking an above-formula rent increase can file. If an increase is sought on account of recent capital improvements the landlord has made, a "petition for certification" of such improvements is filed. If a rent increase is sought on other grounds, a "petition for arbitration" is filed.

2. Preparing for the Hearing

As a general rule, you will greatly increase your chances of prevailing if you appear at the hearing fully prepared. The hearing officer will be much better disposed to listen to your concerns if you are thoroughly familiar with the issues and make your presentation in an organized way. Possibly, the landlord (if he appears) will not be well-prepared, which should make you look good.

As part of planning your preparation, first obtain a copy of the ordinance and any applicable regulations for the area in which your property is located. Then determine which factors the hearing officer must weigh in considering whether to give the landlord an upward individual adjustment from the formula increase. Your job is to show that the increase being requested is either not justified at all, or too high. To do this you will need to carefully review the landlord's claimed expenses and compare them to what is allowed under the ordinance. For example, San Francisco's ordinance allows the consideration of the cost of capital improvements, energy conservation measures, utilities, taxes, janitorial, security, and maintenance services. Increased mortgage payments resulting from a recent purchase of the property by a new owner may be passed along in some, but not all, circumstances.[3]

You should also be prepared to produce a witness who is familiar with any items which you think might be contested. If for some reason your witness cannot appear in person, you may present a written statement from that person. The statement should be as specific as possible. At the end, the words, "I declare under penalty of perjury under the laws of California that the foregoing is true and correct," should appear, followed by the date and the person's signature.

Before the date set for your hearing, go and watch someone else's. (Most cities' hearings are open to the public, and even if they are sometimes closed, you can almost always arrange to attend as an observer if you call ahead.) Seeing another hearing may even make the difference between winning and losing at yours. This is because both your confidence and your capabilities will grow as you understand what the hearing officers are interested in and how they conduct the hearing. By watching a hearing, you will learn that while they are relatively informal, all follow some procedural rules. It is a great help to know what these are so you can swim with the current, not against it.

You are permitted to have an attorney or any other person, such as an employee or volunteer from a local tenants' rights group, represent you at a rent-adjustment hearing. (Many landlords are represented at such hearings by their apartment managers or management companies.) Hiring someone to speak for you is probably not necessary. If you do a careful job in preparing your case, you will probably do as well alone as with a lawyer or other representative. One good alternative is for a group of tenants similarly situated to chip in and consult with an attorney or someone else thoroughly familiar with rent-board hearings to discuss strategy, but handle the hearing yourself.

3. The Actual Hearing

Arrive at the hearing room at least a few minutes before it is set to begin. Go to the clerk or other official and establish who you are. Ask to see the file which contains the papers relevant to the application (either yours or the landlord's, depending on the type of ordinance). Go through this material to see if there are any comments by office workers, rent-board investigators, your landlord, or other tenants. Read the latter very closely and prepare to answer questions from the hearing officer on any of these points.

As you sit in the hearing room, you will probably see a long table, with the hearing officer seated at the head. (In a few cities, the hearing is held before several members of the rent board, and they may sit more formally on a dais or raised platform.) In any event, you, the landlord, your representatives (if any), and any witnesses will be asked to sit at a table or come to the front of the room. A clerk or other employee may make summary notes of testimony given at the hearing. Or, in some cities, hearings are tape recorded. If, under the procedure followed in your city, no record is kept, you have the right to have the proceedings transcribed or tape-recorded, though at your own expense.

---

[3]Some cities have anti-speculation ordinances which do not allow increases in mortgage rates to be passed through to tenants if a building is sold and resold frequently. Check your rent control ordinance on this point.

The hearing officer or chairperson of the rent board will introduce herself and the other people in the room. If you have witnesses, tell the hearing officer. The hearing officer, or sometimes an employee of the rent board, will usually summarize the issues involved in the hearing. At some point, you will be sworn to tell the truth (it is perjury to lie at the hearing). When these preliminaries are complete, you and your landlord will have an opportunity to present your cases.

Note on Hearing Officers: Many hearing officers, rent board employees and members of rent boards tend to be sympathetic to tenants. This is not the same thing as saying that they will bend over backwards to help you. Like most judges (who on balance are probably more sympathetic to landlords), most make an honest effort to follow the law. In other words, your job is to work to make your legal position as unassailable as possible.

A rent adjustment hearing is not like a court hearing. There are no formal rules of evidence. Hearing officers will usually allow you to bring in any information that may be important, though in a court of law it might not be admissible. Relax and just be yourself.

Present your points clearly, but not in an argumentative way. Sometimes an outline on a 3 x 5 card is a help to focusing. Don't get carried away in unnecessary detail. You probably won't be given much time, so be prepared and get to the point quickly. The hearing officer may well ask you questions to help you explain your position. Make sure you present all documentary evidence and witnesses necessary to back up your contentions. Later, the hearing officer will give the landlord or his representative a chance to present his case and to ask you questions. Answer the questions quietly. It is almost always counterproductive to get into an argument. Even if you feel the landlord is lying or misleading, don't interrupt. You will be given time later to rebut the testimony. Direct all your argument to the hearing officer, not to the landlord or her representative.

When your witnesses are given the opportunity to testify, the normal procedure is simply to let them have their say. You may ask questions if the witness forgets something important, but remember, this is not a court and you don't want to come on like a lawyer. Very likely, the hearing officer will also ask your witnesses questions. The landlord has the right to ask the witnesses questions as well.

In rare instances, you may get a hearing officer or rent board chairperson who dominates the hearing or seems to be hostile to you, or perhaps to tenants in general. If so, you will want to stand up for your rights at the same time that you take care not to needlessly confront the hearing officer. Obviously, this can be a tricky business, but if you know your legal rights and put them forth in a polite, but direct way, you should do fine. If you feel that the hearing officer is simply not listening to you, politely insist that you be given your right to complete your statement and question your witnesses.

Just before the hearing is to end, the hearing officer should ask if you have any final comments to make. Don't repeat what you have already said, but make sure all your points have been covered and heard.

The final words from the hearing officer will usually be to thank everyone for coming and to tell you when you can expect the decision. Most put this in the mail within a few days or weeks of the hearing.

4. The Decision

Depending on the city and the hearing procedure, you may or may not end up with a written decision and an explanation of why it was so decided.

In most cities, if a landlord's application for an increase was heard by a hearing officer, you have the right to appeal to the full rent board if the increase is allowed and you still feel it is improper. Your landlord has this same right if you prevail. To appeal, you must file within a certain time and state your reason for the appeal. You may or may not have the opportunity to appear in person.

The rent board will probably take the facts as found by the hearing officer as being true and limit its role to deciding whether the hearing officer applied the law to these facts correctly.[4] In addition, the board will not usually consider any facts you raise in your statement which you could have brought up at the earlier hearing, but didn't. If a new piece of information not known at the time of the first hearing has just been discovered, however, they might consider it. (If it's your landlord who is appealing and you are satisfied with the earlier decision, you will want to emphasize the thoroughness and integrity of the earlier procedure and be ready to present detailed information only if it seems to be needed.) On the other hand, the rent boards of some cities (including Los Angeles) will allow the entire hearing to be held all over again. (This is sometimes called a "de novo" hearing.)

The entire rent board may have more discretion to make a decision than does a single hearing officer. If your case is unique, the hearing officer may even decide to sidestep it and let the entire board consider the implications of establishing a new legal rule or interpretation. If you again lose your decision before the entire board, or if your city permits only one hearing in the first place and you have availed yourself of it, you may be able to take your case to court, if you are convinced the rent board or hearing board failed to follow either the law or their own procedures. However, if yours is a situation where the hearing officer or board has broad discretion to decide issues such as the one you presented, you are unlikely to get the decision overturned in court. Speak to an attorney about this as soon as possible, as there is a time limit (usually 30 days) on how long you can take to file an appeal. To appeal a rent board decision, you must have a transcript of the hearing to give to the court. *Buckhart v. San Francisco Rent Stabilization and Arbitration Board*, 197 Cal. App. 3d 1032 (1988).

I. Rent Control Chart

The following Rent Control Chart summarizes the major features of California's local rent control laws. However, for more specifics and any recent changes not reflected in this book, it is absolutely essential that you obtain a copy of your local ordinance.

Here are brief explanations of the headings we use in the chart.

---

[4]There is an exception to this general rule in some cities. If you arranged for a typed transcript of the original hearing at your expense or have paid to have the tape recording of the hearing made by the hearing officer typed, the rent board may review it.

Exemptions: Ordinances don't cover all rental housing within the locality. Commonly, owner occupied buildings with four (or sometimes two or three) units or less and new construction are exempted from rent control ordinances.[5] Some cities also exempt luxury units, single family dwellings, etc.

Registration: Some cities having rent control require the owners of controlled units to register their units with the agency which administers the rent control ordinance. This allows the agency to keep track of the city's rental units and obtain operating funds from the registration fees. Berkeley and Santa Monica allow tenants to withhold rent payments if a landlord fails to register. Some other cities require no registration at all.

Administration: Most rent control ordinances are administered by rent control boards whose members are appointed (elected in Santa Monica and Berkeley) by the mayor, city council, or board of supervisors. The formal name, address and phone number of the board is given.

Annual General Rent Increase and **Individual Adjustments:** Here you will find a brief summary of the mechanism each city follows to allow rent increases. Most cities have two principal ways of doing this. First, general percentage increases are allowed periodically, either by action of the boards (as in Santa Monica and Berkeley) or by allowing specified increases over time periods (San Francisco, San Jose, and Los Angeles). Second, in most cities, landlords (and sometimes tenants) may petition the board for higher (or lower) rents based on certain criteria.

Vacancy Decontrol: This means that if the unit becomes vacant, the rent becomes "decontrolled" until a new tenant moves in. For example, Tom rents an apartment in San Francisco for $400 a month. While Tom is there, his landlord may raise the rent only as much as the city's rent control law currently allows (e.g., 4% a year). When Tom moves out and Tina then becomes the tenant, the landlord may charge Tina an initial rent of $500, $5,000, or anything he likes! With this new starting point, further increases to Tina will be limited by the rent control law. But when Tina moves out, the landlord will once again be able to raise the rent as much as the market will tolerate. (If you think this gives the landlord a strong incentive to evict tenants, you are right.)

"Vacancy decontrol" really weakens the protections which rent control can give tenants. (A study in Los Angeles showed that, overall, rents there went up just about as much as in surrounding cities--even though Los Angeles had rent control and the other cities did not! This was because Los Angeles has "vacancy decontrol.")

In cities without "vacancy decontrol" (such as Santa Monica, Berkeley and West Hollywood), the limits on rent increases apply even when a tenant moves out and a new tenant moves in. The landlord gets a fair increase, a fair rent, and a fair profit, but she can't exploit a new tenant just because he is new. We think this is a better way to do it.

Eviction Protection (Just Cause for Eviction): If a city has a "vacancy decontrol" provision (in other words, the rent can be raised when a tenant moves), it is essential to the success of the ordinance that a tenant can be evicted only for "just cause."This is because if the rents can be raised as much as the landlord wants when a tenant leaves, landlords will have a motive to avoid rent control by giving a 30-day notice to a month-to-month tenant whose rents

---

[5]One hearing officer for the San Francisco rent board estimates that the majority of illegal evictions there involve landlords falsely claiming to occupy the building.

are controlled. What constitutes "just cause to evict" is discussed in some detail in Chapter 11D and for reasons of space is not repeated here.

Berkeley

Ordinance Adoption Date:	6/3/80; latest amendment 6/8/82.
Exemptions:	Units constructed after 6/3/80, owner-occupied single-family residences and duplexes. [Sec. 5.]
Administration:	Elected 9-member Rent Stabilization Board, 2180 Milvia Street, Berkeley, CA 94704, (415) 644-6128.
Registration:	Required, or landlord can't raise rents, and tenants can withhold current rents (but may have to pay all or part of withheld rent to landlord after registration). Stiff penalties for non-cooperation. [Secs. 8, 11.f.4, 11.g.]
Annual General Rent Increase:	Annual adjustments by Board after survey and hearings. Call the city to check amount.
Individual Adjustments:	Landlord may petition for further increase based on increased taxes, unavoidable increases in utility or maintenance costs, and on costs of capital improvements necessary to bring property up to minimum legal requirements. Increase not allowed based on increased debt service cost due to recent purchase. If tenant agrees to join in landlord's request, "fast track" petition method, under which a decision will be made within 30 days and without a formal hearing, may be used. Tenant may apply for rent reduction based on poor maintenance. [Sec. 12.]
Vacancy Decontrol:	No increase allowed upon vacancy.
Eviction Protection:	Landlord must show "just cause" to evict.
Penalties:	Violation of ordinance is misdemeanor punishable by maximums of $500 fine and 90 days imprisonment (1st offense) and $3000 fine and one year imprisonment (2nd offense). [Sec. 19.] Tenant may sue for excess rent collected plus up to $750. [Sec. 15.a]
Other Features:	Landlord must place security deposits in interest-bearing savings and loan account and credit interest against rents each December, as well as when tenant vacates. [Sec. 7, Regulation Secs. 701, 702.]

Beverly Hills

Ordinance Adoption Date:	(Beverly Hills Municipal Code, Titles 11 and 12) 4/27/79; latest amendment 7/21/88.
Exemptions:	Units constructed after 10/20/78, units that rented for more than $600 on 5/31/78, single-family residences, rented condominium units [Sec. 11-1.02.]
Administration:	Appointed 7-member Rent Adjustments Board 336 N. Foothill Blvd., Room 103, Beverly Hills, CA 90212, (213) 285-1035.
Registration:	Not required.

Annual General Rent Increase:	On units that rented for more than $600 as of 5/31/78, rent increases are limited to 10% within any 12-month period, and 60 days' notice of the increase must be given. For other units, except for specific "surcharges" which must be justified and the rent-increase notice (see below), rents may not be increased in any 12-month period by more than 8% or a percentage based on the "Urban All Items Consumer Price Index for Los Angeles," whichever is less. (The CPI-based figure is calculated by adding the monthly CPI figures for the most recently-published 12-month period, subtracting from that a second CPI sum based on for the 12-month period before that, and dividing the difference by the lesser of the two sums.) To this permitted increase, the landlord may add a "capital expenditure surcharge" so as to additionally increase the rent by up to 4% more (calculated by amortizing capital improvement costs), a "utility expense surcharge" based on owner-paid utility cost increases in excess of the allowed annual percentage increase, and a 10% surcharge for each adult tenant occupying the unit over and above any maximum number of adult occupants specified in the lease. The landlord may also pass through the amortized cost of any legally-required improvements. [Secs. 11-3.02 - 11-3.07.]
Individual Adjustments:	Tenant who contests validity of any capital improvement surcharge or utility surcharge over and above the annual increase percentage may petition Board to request non-allowance of the surcharge. Landlord seeking increases above annual percentage increase and allowed surcharges may apply to Board for higher "hardship" increase. (Ordinance is silent on fcators to be considered, but does not preclude hardship increase based on high debt service costs due to recent purchase.) [Sec. 11-4.02.]
Notice requirements:	Landlord must post in the lobby, hallway, or other "public" location on the property a notice stating the name, address, and telephone number of the owner or authorized agent, and must give each tenant a copy of the notice; failure to comply with this requirement precludes increase of rents. Rent-increase notice must state the basis justifying the rent increase and advise the tenant that records and documentation verifying it will be made available for inspection by the tenant or the tenant's representative. [Sec. 11-3.09.] The justification should break down the increase into portions allowed under annual adjustment and individual surcharges.
Vacancy Decontrol:	Landlord may charge any rent after a tenant vacates voluntarily, but not when landlord terminates tenancy. Once the property is rerented, it is subject to rent control based on the higher rent. [Sec. 11-3.10.]
Eviction:	Landlord must show "just cause" to evict.

Penalties: Violation of ordinance is a misdemeanor punishable by maximums of $500 fine and 6 months imprisonment. [Sec. 11-7. 06.] Tenant may sue for three times any rent in excess of legal rent collected ($500 minimum), plus attorney's fees. [Sec. 11-7.05.]

Campbell

Ordinance Adoption Date: (Campbell Municipal Code, Chapter 6.09), 1983.

Exemptions: Single-family residences, duplexes, and triplexes. [Sec. 6.09.030(1).]

Administration: Campbell Rent Mediation program, 3275 Stevens Creek Blvd., Suite 310, San Jose, CA 95117, (408) 243-8565.

Registration: Not required.

Annual General Rent Increase: No fixed formula; rent increases must be "reasonable." [Sec. 6. 09.150.]

Individual Adjustments: Tenants in 25% of the units (but at least 3 units) affected by an increase can contest it by filing a petition within 37 days, or lose the right to object to the increase. Disputes raised by tenant petition are first subject to "conciliation," then mediation. If those fail, either party may file written request for arbitration by city "Fact Finding Committee." Committee determines whether increase is "reasonable" by considering costs of capital improvements, repairs, maintenance, and debt service, and past history of rent increases. However, the Committee's determination is not binding. [Secs. 6.09.050 - 6.09.150.]

Notice Requirements: On written request by a tenant, an apartment landlord must disclose in writing to that person the apartment numbers of all tenants receiving rent increases that same month. [Sec. 6.09.040.]

Vacancy Decontrol: No restriction on raises after vacancy.

Eviction Features: Ordinance does not require showing of "just cause" to evict, so 3-day and 30-day notice requirements and unlawful detainer procedures are governed solely by state law.

Note: Because this ordinance does not provide for binding arbitration of any rent-increase dispute, it is not truly a rent-control ordinance. Compliance with any decision appears to be voluntary only.

Cotati

Ordinance Adoption Date: (Cotati Municipal Code, Chapter 19. 19), 9/23/80; latest amendment 2/7/84.

Exemptions: Units constructed after 9/23/80 (Board has authority to remove exemption), owner-occupied single-family residences, duplexes, and triplexes. [Sec. 19.12.020.D.]

Administration: Appointed 5-member Rent Appeals Board, 201 W. Sierra, Cotati, CA 94928, (707) 795-5478.

Registration: Required, or landlord can't raise rents, and tenants can seek Board permission to withhold current rents (but

	may have to pay all or part of withheld rent to landlord after regis-tration). [Sec. 19.12.030 O.]
Annual General Rent Increase:	9/23/80 freeze at 6/1/79 levels, plus annual "general adjustments" by Board after investigation and hearings. [Sec. 19.12.050.] Annual general adjustment is to be adequate to cover operating cost increases and to permit net operating income to increase at 66% of the rate of increase in the CPI [Consumer Price Index (all items) for urban consumers, San Francisco-Oakland]. [Regulation Secs. 3000-3002.]
Individual Adjustments:	Within 30 days after Board determines annual general adjustment, landlord may petition for further increase based on increased taxes or unavoidable increases in utility or maintenance costs, and on costs of capital improvements necessary to bring property up to mini-mum legal requirements. Increase not allowed based on increased debt service cost due to recent purchase. Tenant may apply for rent reduction based on poor maintenance. [Secs. 19.12.060, 19.12.070, Reg. Secs. 4001-4052.] Landlord can charge extra 10% (15% if landlord pays utilities) if tenant brings in new tenant not mentioned in rental agreement.
Notice Requirements:	None in addition to state law.
Vacancy Decontrol:	None. [Ordinance Sec. 19.12.030. P allows Board to decontrol only of a category of housing whose rental unit vacancy rate exceeds 5%; this is highly unlikely.]
Eviction:	Landlord must show "just cause" to evict.
Penalties:	Tenant may sue for three times any excess rent collected ($500 minimum) plus attorney's fees, or tenant may simply credit any excess payments against future rent payments. [Sec. 19.12.110.]
Other Features:	Landlord must place security deposits in interest-bearing savings and loan account and credit interest to tenant when she vacates. [Sec. 19.12.150.]

East Palo Alto

Ordinance Adoption Date:	11/23/83; latest amendment 4/88.
Exemptions:	Units constructed after 11/23/83, units owned by land-lords owning 4 or fewer units in city, property "substantially rehabilitated" as determined by the Board.
Administration:	Appointed 7-member Rent Stabilization Board, 2415 University Ave., East Palo Alto, CA 94303, (415) 853-3100.
Registration:	Required, or landlord can't raise rents, and tenants can apply to Board for permission to withhold current rents (but may have to pay all or part of withheld rent to landlord after registration). [Secs. 8, 11.E.4, 15.A.1.]
Annual General Rent Increase:	11/23/83 freeze at 4/1/83 levels, plus annual adjustments by Board equal to the lesser of the All-Urban-Consumers or Rent-Residential Consumer Price Index

for the San Francisco/Oakland Metropolitan area. [Secs. 10, 11.]

Individual Adjustments: Landlord may apply for further increase based on increased taxes or unavoidable increases in utility or maintenance costs, and on costs of capital improvements necessary to bring property up to minimum legal requirements. Increase not allowed based on increased debt service due to recent purchase. Tenant may apply for rent reduction based on poor maintenance. [Sec. 12.]

Notice Requirements: Notices requesting increases of more than that allowed under annual across-the-board adjustment must list Board address and telephone number. Board certifies rents each year with notices to landlord and tenant, and advises of petition or appeal rights.

Vacancy Decontrol: No increases allowed upon vacancy.

Eviction: Landlord must show "just cause" to evict.

Penalties: Violation of ordinance is misdemeanor punishable by maximums of $500 fine and 90 days imprisonment (1st offense) and $3000 fine and one year imprisonment (2nd offense). [Sec. 19.] Tenant may sue landlord for excess rent unlawfully collected plus up to $500. [Sec. 15.A.4.]

Other Features: Landlord must place security deposits in interest-bearing Savings and loan account and credit interest against rents each December, as well as when tenant vacates. [Sec. 7.]

Hayward

Ordinance Adoption Date: 9/13/83; latest amendment 2/24/87.

Exemptions: Units first occupied after 7/1/79, units owned by landlord owning 4 or fewer rental units in the city. [Sec. 2(l).]

Administration: Administered by city-manager-appointed employees of Rent Review Office, 22300 Foothill Blvd., Hayward, CA 94541, (415) 581-2345 ext. 5214.

Registration: Not required.

Annual General Rent Increase: Annual rent increases limited in any 12-month period to 7%, plus increased utility costs if documented as specified. [Sec. 3(c),(d).]

Individual Adjustments: The tenant can contest an increase over 7% by first contacting the person specified in the notice (see notice requirements, below) for an explanation of the increase. Tenant then must file petition with the Rent Review Office before the increase takes effect (30 days) or lose the right to object to it. If a building has more than 10 units, a tenant can petition only if at least 25% of the tenants affected sign the petition. Disputes raised in tenant petition are heard by a hearing officer. Landlord may be allowed to pass on increased utility and maintenance costs and "amortize" (spread out) capital expenditures. [Sec. 5.]

Notice Requirements: Landlord must give tenant a copy of ordinance or city-prepared booklet summary of it at the beginning of the tenancy, and with a document which gives the unit's rent history [Sec. 4(a)], lists improvements to the unit, and states that the previous tenant's security deposit was not used for any improper purpose [Sec. 7(d)]. Rent-increase notices must be accompanied by a blank tenant petition form and also by a second notice either stating that the increase is allowed under the 5%-increase limitation, or giving specific reasons for an increase above 5%. The notice must also include the name, address, and telephone number of the landlord or other person able to explain the increase. [Sec. 4(b).] If the building has more than 10 units, the notice must state which tenants are affected by the increase.

Vacancy Decontrol: Rent controls are permanently removed from each unit following a voluntary vacancy (without any legal action by or notices from the landlord, even for cause), the expenditure of at least $200 (1-bedroom units), $400 (2-bedroom), or $500 (3-bedroom) in improvements by the landlord afterward, and city certification of compliance with city Housing Code. [Sec. 8.]

Eviction: Landlord must show "just cause" to evict.

Penalties: Failure to provide required information to tenant is an infraction (petty offense) punishable on first, second, or third offense within 12-month period by fines of up to $50, $100, and $250, respectively. Fourth offense within 12 months is misdemeanor punishable by maximums of $500 fine and 6 months imprisonment. [Sec. 20.b.] Tenant may sue for excess rent collected, treble that amount or $500 (whichever is greater), and attorney's fees. [Sec. 20.a.]

Other Features: Ordinance requires landlords holding security deposits longer than a year to pay 6. 5% interest, credited against the tenant's rent on his anniversary date; no requirement for separate account, however.

Los Angeles

Ordinance Adoption Date: (Los Angeles Municipal Code, Chapter XV), 4/21/79; latest amendment 1989.

Exemptions: Units constructed (or substantially renovated with at least $10,000 in improvements) after 10/1/78, "luxury" units (defined as 0,1,2,3, or 4+ - bedroom units renting for at least $302, $420, $588, $756, or $823, respectively, as of 5/31/78), single-family residences, except where 3 or more houses are located on the same lot. [Sec. 151.02.G,M.]

Administration: Appointed 7-member Rent Adjustment Commission acts as Appeals Board; ordinance is administered by Community Development Department, 215 West 6th St., Room 800, Los Angeles, CA 90014, (213) 485-4727.

Call (213) 624-7368 if you have questions about the rent control ordinance.

Registration: Required, or tenants can withhold rents. (However, once the landlord registers the property, the tenants must pay all the rent withheld. [Sec. 151.11.B.] Tenant may also defend any unlawful detainer action on the basis of the landlord's failure to register the property [Sec. 151.09.F].

Annual General Rent Increase: Annual rent increase amount is established each year based on a percentage of the All Urban Consumer Price Index with a 3% minimum and a 12% maximum.

Individual Adjustments: Landlord may apply to the Community Development Department for higher increase to obtain "just and reasonable return" (does not include "negative cash flow" based on recent purchase, but does include negative "operating expense" not counting landlord's mortgage payment). [Sec. 151. 07. B] Also, landlord may apply to the Department for permission to pass on to the tenant the cost of capital improvements not directly benefitting the landlord (e.g., new roof cost considered, but not cost of new swimming pool) spread out over 5 or more years [Sec. 151. 07. A]. Appeal is to Rent Adjustment Commision.

Notice Requirements: Landlord must give tenant a copy of current registration statement showing that the property is registered with the Department. Landlord who proposes to charge tenant rent higher than maximum is required to provide written justification for the difference. [Sec. 151.05.]

Vacancy Decontrol: Landlord may charge any rent after a tenant either vacates voluntarily or is evicted for nonpayment of rent or breach of a rental agreement provision. Controls remain if landlord evicts for any other reason, fails to remodel after evicting for that purpose, or terminates or fails to renew a subsidized-housing lease with the city housing authority. However, once the new rent for a vacated unit is established by the landlord and the property is rerented, it is subject to rent control based on the higher rent. [Sec. 151.06.C.]

Eviction: Landlord must show "just cause" to evict.

Penalties: Violation of ordinance, including failing to include proper information in eviction notices, is a misdemeanor punishable by maximums of $500 fine and 6 months imprisonment. [Sec. 151.10.B.] Tenant may sue for three times any rent in excess of legal rent collected, plus attorney's fees. [Sec. 151.10.A.]

Los Gatos

Ordinance Adoption Date: (Los Gatos Town Code, Chapter 24), 10/27/80; latest amendment 12/5/83.

Exemptions: Property on lots with 2 or fewer units; single-family residences; rented condominium units. [Sec. 24 20.015.]

Administration: Los Gatos Rent Mediation program, 3275 Stevens Creek Blvd., Suite 310, San Jose, CA 95117, (408) 243-8565.

Registration: Not required. (However, a "regulatory fee" to pay for program is added to annual business license fee, when business license is required.)

Annual General Rent Increase: Rents may not be increased more than once within 12-month period (except to pass through regulatory fee), and are limited to 5% or 7% of the All Urban Consumers Consumer Price Index for the San Francisco-Oakland area. [Secs. 24.30.010, 24.70.015(3).]

Individual Adjustments: Tenants in 25% of the units affected by an increase above the formula above can contest itby filing a petition within 30 days, or will lose the right to object to the increase. Disputes initiated by tenant petition are first attempted to be resolved by "conciliation." If that fails, either party may file a written request for mediation, and, if that fails, binding arbitration. [Secs. 24.40.010 - 24.40.050.] Mediator/arbitrator may consider costs of capital improvements, repairs, maintenance, and debt service, and past history of rent increases. [Regulation Secs. 2.03 - 2.05.] (Landlord may also file petition to ask for rent increase over allowed percentage, but why bother if burden is on tenant to contest any increase?).

Notice Requirements: Rent-increase notice (or separate statement served with it) must state, "You have the right to use the Rental Dispute Mediation and Arbitration Hearing Process. For further information contact Los Gatos Rent Mediation Program," giving program's address and telephone number. On written request by a tenant, an apartment landlord must disclose in writing to that person the apartment numbers of all tenants receiving rent increases that same month. [Sec. 24.30.030.]

Vacancy Decontrol: Landlord may charge any rent after a tenant vacates voluntarily or is evicted following 3-day notice for nonpayment of rent or other breach of the rental agreement. Once the property is rerented, it is subject to rent control based on the higher rent. [Sec. 24.70.015(1).]

Eviction: Ordinance does not require showing of "just cause" to evict, but tenant has other defenses.

Other Features: Mediation/arbitration process applies not only to rent increases and evictions, but also to provision of "housing services". [Sec. 24.40.010.] Since ordinance deems every lease and rental agreement to include a provision to agree to binding arbitration under the ordinance Sec. 24.40.040], a party invoking the process can in effect keep a "housing services" dispute out of the courts, which will do nothing other than enforce any final binding arbitration award.

Oakland

Ordinance Adoption Date: 10/7/80; latest amendment 1987.

Exemptions:	Units constructed after 1/1/83, buildings "substantially rehabilitated" at cost of 50% of that of new construction, as determined by Chief Building Inspector. [Sec. 2.i].
Administration:	Appointed 7-member Residential Rent Arbitration Board, 1417 Clay St., Third Floor, Oakland, CA 94612, (415) 273-3721.
Registration:	Not required.
Annual General Rent Increase:	Rents may not be increased more than 6% in any 12-month period for occupied units, and 12% in any 12-month period for units vacated after the landlord terminated the tenancy." [Sec. 5.]
Individual Adjustments:	Tenant may contest an increase in excess of that allowed (but only if his rent is current) by filing a petition with the Board. The petition must be filed within 30 days. Hearing officer may consider costs of capital improvements, repairs, maintenance, and debt service, and past history of rent increases. [Sec. 5.c.]
Notice Requirements:	Landlords are required to notify tenants of the Residential Rent Arbitration Board at outset of the tenancy, in an addendum to the lease or rental agreement. [Sec. 5.d.]
Vacancy Decontrol:	Landlord may charge any rent after a tenant vacates voluntarily. Controls remain if tenant vacates "involuntarily," though 12-month rent-increase ceiling increases to 12% from 8%. Once the property is rerented, it is subject to rent control based on the higher rent. [Sec. 5.b] Controls may be permanently removed if landlord spends at least 50% of new-construction cost to "substantially rehabilitate" property.
Eviction:	Ordinance does not require showing of "just cause" to evict, but there are other requirements.
Penalties:	Violation of ordinance is infraction (petty offense) punishable on first, second, and third offenses within 12-month period by fines of up to $50, $100, and $250, respectively. A fourth offense within 12 months is a misdemeanor punishable by maximums of a $500 fine and 6 months imprisonment. [Sec. 9.1.]

Palm Springs

Ordinance Adoption Date:	(Palm Springs Municipal Code, Title 4), 9/1/79; latest amendment 6/88.
Exemptions:	Units constructed after 4/1/79; owner-occupied single-family residences, duplexes, triplexes, and 4-plexes; units where rent was $450 or more as of 9/1/79. [Secs. 4.02.010, 4.02.030.]
Administration:	Appointed 5-member Rent Review Commission, 3200 E. Tahquitz McCallum Way, Palm Springs, Calif., (619) 323-8211.
Registration:	Required, or landlord can't raise rents. [Sec. 4.02.080.]
Annual General Rent Increase:	Rent as of 9/1/79, plus annual increases not exceeding 75% of the annual All Urban Consumers Consumer Price

Index for the Los Angeles/Long Beach/Anaheim metropolitan area. (Step-by-step calculation procedure is set forth in ordinance.) [Secs. 4.02.040, 4.02.050.]

Individual Adjustments: Landlord may petition for further increases based on "hardship." Commission consent for increase is not necessary if tenant agrees in writing, but landlord may not coerce consent under threat of eviction or nonrenewal of lease, and may not include general waiver in lease or rental agreement. [Secs. 4.02.060, 4.02.065.]

Notice Requirements: Before raising rent, landlord must notify tenant in writing of the base rent charged on 9/1/79, the present rent, and the date of the last previous rent increase. [Sec. 4.02.080 (d)(2).] This information can be included on the rent-increase notice. Ninety days' notice is required.

Vacancy Decontrol: No increases allowed when vacancy occurs.

Eviction: "Just cause" to evict is not required, but there may be other restrictions.

Penalties: Tenant may sue for any excess rent collected, attorney's fees, and a penalty of up to $300. [Sec. 4.02.090.] Tenant may also seek the $300-plus-attorney's-fees penalty against landlord who coerces consent to rent increase. [Sec. 4.02.060(c).]

San Francisco

Ordinance Adoption Date: (San Francisco Administrative Code, Chapter 37), 6/79; latest amendment 9/13/87.

Exemptions: Units constructed after 6/79; buildings over 50 years old and "substantially rehabilitated" since 6/79; owner-occupied duplexes, triplexes, and 4-plexes. [Sec. 37.2(o).]

Administration: Appointed 5-member Residential Rent Stabilization and Arbitration Board, [Sec. 37.4], 170 Fell St., Room 16, San Francisco, CA 94102, (415) 621-RENT.

Registration: Not required.

Annual General Rent Increase: Rents may not be increased by more than a 4%-to-7% percentage based on the "All Urban Consumers Consumer Price Index" for the San Francisco-Oakland Metropolitan Area. The figure is published each year by the Board. Landlord may also pass through increased utility costs without permission from the Board [Sec. 37.3], and may apply to the Board for certification of capital improvements the amortized cost of which may also be passed through to the tenant [Sec. 37.7.]

Individual Adjustments: Landlord may apply to Board for higher increase based on increased costs. Hearing officer decides case based on various factors, including operating and maintenance expenses, but not "negative cash flow" based on recent purchase. Hearing officer may also consider rent-increase history, failure to make repairs, or any decrease in services. Tenant may contest any claimed passthrough of utility costs, or to request rent reduction based on decrease of services or poor maintenance. [Secs. 37.8.]

Notice Requirements: Where rent increase includes utility or capital-improvement passthroughs or banked (accumulated) previous across-the-board increases (all of which may be applied without Board permission), landlord must give tenant written itemized breakdown of such increases, on or before the date of service of the rent-increase notice. [Regulation Sec. 4.10.]

Vacancy Decontrol: Landlord may charge any rent after a tenant vacates voluntarily or is evicted for good cause. Once the property is rerented, it is subject to rent control based on the higher rent. [Sec. 37.3(a).]

Eviction: Landlord must show "just cause" to evict.

Penalties: Violation of ordinance, including wrongful eviction or eviction attempts, is a misdemeanor punishable by maximums of a $2000 fine and 6 months imprisonment. [Sec. 37. 10.]

San Jose

Ordinance Adoption Date: (San Jose Municipal Code, Title 17, Chapter 17), 7/7/79; latest amendment 7/15/88.

Exemptions: Units constructed after 9/7/79, single-family residences, townhouses, duplexes, and condominium units. [Sec. 17.23.150.]

Administration: Appointed 7-member Advisory Commission on Rents, 4 N. Second Street, Suite 950, San Jose, CA 95113, (408) 277-5431.

Registration: Not required.

Annual General Rent Increase: Rents may not be increased more than 8% in any 12-month period, and may not be increased more than once within the 12 months. However, a landlord who has not raised the rent for 24 months is entitled to a 21% increase. [Secs. 17.23.180, 17.23.210.].

Individual Adjustments: Tenant can contest an increase in excess of that allowed by filing a petition before rent increase takes effect (30 days), or lose the right to object. Disputes initiated by tenant petition are heard by a mediation hearing officer, who may consider costs of capital improvements, repairs, maintenance, and debt service, past history of rent increases and hardship to the tenant [*Pennell v. City of San Jose* (1988, U. S. Sup. Ct.)]. Either party may appeal mediator's decision and invoke binding arbitration. (Landlord may also file petit-ion to ask for rent increase over allowed percentage, but why bother if burden is on tenant to contest any increase?) [Secs. 17.23.220 - 17.23.440.]

Notice Requirements: Where rent increase exceeds 8%, rent-increase notice must advise tenant of her right to utilize the Rental Dispute Mediation and Arbitration Hearing Process, giving the address and telephone number of the city's rent office. The notice must also indicate the time limit within which the tenant may do this. [Sec. 17.23.270.]

Vacancy Decontrol: Landlord may charge any rent after a tenant vacates voluntarily or is evicted following 3-day notice for nonpayment of rent or other breach of the rental agreement. Once the property is rerented, it is subject to rent control based on the higher rent. [Sec. 17.23.190.]

Eviction: Ordinance does not require showing of "just cause" to evict.

Penalties: Violation of ordinance by charging rent in excess of that allowed following mediation/arbitration, by retaliation against the tenant for asserting his rights, or by attempting to have tenant waive rights under ordinance is a misdemeanor punishable by maximums of a $500 fine and 6 months imprisonment. [Secs. 17.23.515 - 17.23.530.] Tenant may sue landlord for excess rents charged, plus treble damages or $500 (whichever is greater) [Sec. 17.23.540.]

Santa Monica

Ordinance Adoption Date: (City Charter Article XVIII), 4/10/79; latest amendment 11/4/84.

Exemptions: Units constructed after 4/10/79; owner-occupied single-family residences, duplexes, and triplexes; single-family dwellings not rented on 7/1/84. [Charter Amendment (C.A.) Secs. 1801(c), 1815, Regulation (Reg.) Secs. 2000+, 12000+.] However, rental units other than single-family dwellings not rented on 7/1/84 must be registered and the exemption applied for.

Administration: Elected 5-member Rent Control Board, 1685 Main Street, Santa Monica, CA 90401, (213) 458-8751.

Registration: Required, or landlord can't raise rents, and tenants can request permission from Board to withhold rents. [C.A. Secs. 1803(q), 1805(h).]

Annual General Rent Increase: 4/10/79 freeze at 4/10/78 levels, plus annual adjustments by Board after investigation and hearings. [C.A. Secs. 1804, 1805(a),(b), Reg. Secs. 3000+.]

Individual Adjustments: Landlord may apply for further increase based on increased taxes or unavoidable increases in utility or maintenance costs, capital improvements, but not "negative cash flow" due to recent purchase. Tenant may apply for rent reduction based on poor maintenance. [C.A. Sec. 1805(c)-(h), Reg. Secs. 4000+.]

Notice Requirements: Rent-increase notice must state, "The undersigned [landlord] certifies that this unit and common areas are not subject to any uncorrected citation or notices of violation of any state or local housing, health, or safety laws issued by any government official or agency." [Reg. Sec. 3007(f)(3)]. Otherwise, tenant may refuse to pay increase and successfully defend unlawful detainer action based on failure to pay increase.

Vacancy Decontrol: None. [C.A. Sec. 1803(r) allows Board to decontrol any category of property only if the rental unit vacancy rate exceeds 5%; this is a virtual impossibility.]

Eviction: Landlord must show "just cause" to evict.

Penalties: Violation of the charter amendment is a misdemeanor punishable by maximums of a $500 fine and 6 months imprisonment. Tenant may sue landlord in court or in administrative hearing for violating ordinance in any way, and may recover rents unlawfully charged and attorney's fees. [C.A. Sec. 1809(a)-(d).]

Other Features: Landlord must place security deposits in interest-bearing savings and loan account, but landlord may use interest to "offset operating expenses"; in considering rent-increase petitions, Board may consider whether interest was actually so applied. [C.A. Sec. 1803(s).] Security deposits cannot be increased by notice of change of terms of tenancy. [Reg. Sec. 3000.]

Thousand Oaks

Ordinance Adoption Date: 7/1/80; latest amendment 3/24/87.

Exemptions: Units constructed after 6/30/80; "luxury" units (defined as 0,1,2,3, or 4+ - bedroom units renting for at least $400, $500, $600, $750, or $900, respectively, as of 6/30/80); single-family residences, duplexes, triplexes, and 4-plexes, except where 5 or more units are located on the same lot. [Sec. III.L.]

Administration: Appointed 5-member Rent Adjustment Commission, 2150 W. Hillcrest Drive, Thousand Oaks, California, (805) 497-8611.

Registration: Required. [Sec. XIV.]

Annual General Rent Increase: Rents may not be increased by more than 3% to 7% in any 12-month period, based on 75% of the Los Angeles/ Anaheim/ Riverside Regional Consumer Price Index. [Secs. III.G, H, VI.]

Individual Adjustments: Landlord may apply to the Rent Adjustment Commission for higher increase based on capital improvement costs, or to obtain "just and reasonable return" (does not include "negative cash flow" based on recent purchase.) [Sec. VII.]

Notice Requirements: Landlord must prominently post in the apartment complex a listing or map of rental units, showing which are subject to the ordinance and which are not. [Sec. VI.C.] Landlord who proposes to increase rent more than 7% (thus requesting individual adjustment increases), is required to provide written justification for the difference. [Sec. V.]

Vacancy Decontrol: Property that becomes vacant after 5/1/81 due to tenant voluntarily leaving or being evicted for nonpayment of rent is no longer subject to any provision of the ordinance. [Sec. VI.]

Eviction Features: Landlord must show "just cause" to evict.

Penalties: Tenant may sue for three times any rent in excess of legal rent collected, plus a penalty of up to $500 and attorney's fees. [Sec. IX.]

Other Features: A landlord can exempt a unit from rent control by offering a three-year lease, or a five-year lease if the tenant is over 65 or handicapped. [Sec. III N (10).]

West Hollywood

Ordinance Adoption Date: (West Hollywood Municipal Code, Article IV, Chapter 4), 6/27/85; latest amendment 5/88.

Exemptions: Units constructed after 7/1/79 ("just-cause" eviction requirements do apply, however). However, many exemptions must be applied for in registration document (see below). [Sec. 6406.]

Administration: Appointed 5-member Rent Stabilization Commission, 8611 Santa Monica Blvd., West Hollywood, CA 90069, (213) 854-7450.

Registration: Required, or landlord can't raise rents. [Sec. 6407.]

Annual General Rent Increase: 11/29/84 freeze at 4/30/84 levels, plus annual adjustments by Board after investigation and hearings. Landlords who pay for gas or electricity may increase an additional 1/2 % for each such utility. [Secs. 6408, 6409.].

Individual Adjustments: Landlord may apply for further increase based on unavoidable increases in utility or maintenance costs or taxes, and for capital improvements. Tenant may apply for rent reduction based on poor maintenance. [Sec. 6411.]

Rent-Increase Notification: Rent-increase notice must contain statement to the effect that landlord is in compliance with ordinance, including filing and payment of required registration documents and fees. [Sec. 6409.G, Regulation Sec. 40000(f).]

Vacancy Decontrol: When tenant of property other than a single-family dwelling voluntarily vacates or is evicted for cause, landlord may increase rent by additional 10%; however, no more than one such increase is permitted within any 24-month period. When tenant of single-family dwelling voluntarily vacates or is evicted for cause (other than for occupancy by owner or relative), landlord can raise rent to any level; once the single-family dwelling is rerented, it is subject to rent control at the new higher rent. In either case, landlord must file "vacancy increase certificate" with city and show she has repainted and cleaned carpets within previous six months; certificate must be filed within 30 days after tenant vacates, or landlord cannot raise rent under this provision. [Sec. 6410.]

Eviction:	Landlord must show "just cause" to evict.
Penalties:	Violation of ordinance is misdemeanor punishable by maximums of $1000 fine and 6 months imprisonment. [Sec. 6414.E.] Tenant may sue landlord for three times any rents collected or demanded in excess of legal rents, plus attorney's fees. [Sec. 6414.C.]
Other Features:	Landlord must credit 5 1/2 % interest on security deposits against rents at least once every five years, as well as when tenant vacates. [Sec. 6408.B.]

Westlake Village

Note:	This small city (population 10,000) has a rent-control ordinance that applies to apartment complexes of 5 units or more (as well as to mobilehome parks, whose specialized laws are not covered in this book.) Because the city's only apartment complex of this size has undergone conversion to condominiums, there is therefore now no property (other than mobilehome parks) to which the ordinance applies, and we don't explain the ordinance here.

J. What To Do If the Landlord Violates Rent Control Rules

• Get a copy of your local ordinance—and any regulation interpreting it—and make sure you are right;

• If you think your landlord may have made a good faith mistake, try to work the problems out informally;

• Contact any local tenants rights organization and get the benefit of their advice;

• File a formal complaint with your city rent board;

• If the landlord's conduct is extreme, talk to a lawyer. You may have a valid suit based on the intentional infliction of emotional distress, for invasion of privacy, or on some other grounds, including those provided in the ordinance itself.

K. Rent "Mediation"

In a few cities where city councils have felt tenant pressure, but not enough pressure to enact rent control ordinances, so-called voluntary rent "guidelines," or landlord-tenant "mediation" ser-vices have been adopted. The chief beneficiaries of these dubious standards and procedures seem to be the landlords, since voluntary programs have no power to stop rent increases. On rare occa-sions, however, voluntary mediation or guidelines may work, particularly with smaller landlords who are trying to be fair. If your city or county isn't on the rent control list, check to see if it has a voluntary program.

Chapter 5:

Discrimination

There was a time when a landlord could refuse to rent to just about anyone she didn't like. All sorts of groups—including blacks, Asians, Chicanos, women, unmarried couples, gays, families with children and many more—were routinely subjected to discrimination. Fortunately, our state and federal legislatures have taken steps to end these abuses.

Today it is illegal for a landlord to refuse to rent to you or engage in any other kind of discrimination on the basis of a group characteristic which is not closely related to the legitimate business needs of the landlord. To put this more specifically, a combination of statutes and cases forbid discrimination on the following grounds:

• Race

• Religion

• Ethnic Background

• Sex

• Marital status (includes discrimination against unmarried couples)

• Physical disability

• Families with children (unless the rental units are specifically designated for older citizens, as is the case with retirement communities)

In addition, the California Supreme Court has held that state law forbids landlords from *all* arbitrary discrimination. The Court indicated that discrimination against the following groups would be arbitrary: Republicans, students, welfare recipients, "entire occupations or avocations, e.g., sailors or motorcyclists," and "all homosexuals."[1]

A. Forbidden Types of Discrimination

It is illegal for a landlord to refuse to rent to a tenant, or to engage in any other kind of discrimination (such as requiring more rent or larger deposits) on the basis of a group characteristic, such as race or religion. It is legal to discriminate against people for reasons closely related to the landlord's legitimate business needs, as would be the case where a prospective tenant has a bad credit history or references (see Section B, below). State law, and in some cases federal law, absolutely forbids discrimination on the following grounds, regardless of a landlord's claim of a legi-timate business need:

Race: This is forbidden by California's Unruh Civil Rights Act [Civil Code Sections 51-53] and Fair Employment and Housing Act [Government Code Sections 12900-12996], and by the U.S. Civil Rights Act of 1866 [42 U.S.C., Section 1982—see *Jones v. Mayer Co.* (1968) 329 U.S. 409], and the Federal Fair Housing Act of 1968 [42 U.S.C., Sections 3601-3619].

Religion: This is forbidden by all the laws listed above, except the Civil Rights Act of 1866.

Ethnic Background and National Origin: Same as **Religion**, above.

Sex: Same as **Religion**, above.

---

[1]*Marina Point, Ltd. v. Wolfson* (1982) 30 Cal. 3d 72.

Marital Status (including discrimination against couples because they are unmarried): This is forbidden under California law by both the Unruh and Fair Employment and Housing Acts [see *Atkisson v. Kern County Housing Authority* (1976) 59 Cal. App. 3d 89; and *Hess v. Fair Employment and Housing Comm.* (1982) 138 Cal. App. 3d 232].

Age: This is forbidden by Civil Code 51.2.

Families with Children: Discrimination against families with children is forbidden by the federal Fair Housing Amendments Act of 1988 (42 U. S. C. § 3604) and by the Unruh Civil Rights Act [see Civil Code Section 51.2 and *Marina Point, Ltd. v. Wolfson* (1982) 30 Cal. 3d 72], except in housing reserved exclusively for senior citizens.[2] In addition, San Francisco, Berkeley, Los Angeles, Santa Monica and Santa Clara County (unincorporated areas only) have local ordinances forbidding this sort of discrimination.

Physical Disability: It is illegal for a landlord to refuse to rent to a person with a physical handicap on the same terms as if he were not handicapped. The landlord must permit the tenant to make reasonable modifications to the premises if necessary for the tenant to fully use the premises. The landlord may, however, require the tenant to restore the interior of the premises at the end of the tenancy. In addition, a landlord must rent to an otherwise qualified blind, deaf or physically-handicapped person with a properly-trained dog, even if he otherwise bans pets. Discrimination on the basis of physical disability is forbidden by California Civil Code Section 54.1, the federal Fair Housing Act and the federal Fair Housing Amendments Act of 1988 (42 U. S. C. § 3604).

Sexual Orientation: This includes homosexuality. Discrimination on this basis is forbidden by the Unruh Civil Rights Act.[3] In addition, a number of California cities specifically ban discrimination for this reason.

Smoking: Discrimination against smokers has not been tested in California courts.

Animals: Although it is generally legal to refuse to rent to people with pets, it is illegal to do so in the case of properly-trained dogs for the blind, deaf, and physically handicapped.[4]

Public Assistance: Discrimination against people on public assistance is forbidden by the Unruh Civil Rights Act [see 59 Ops. Cal. Atty. Gen. 223 (1976)].

Other Unlawful Discrimination: After reading the above list outlining the types of discrimination forbidden by California and federal law, you may assume that it is legal to discriminate for other reasons—say because a person owns a computer. Or, because none of the civil rights laws specifically prohibit discrimination against men with beards or long hair, you might conclude that such discrimination is permissible. This is not true. Although federal civil rights laws have generally been interpreted by the courts to prohibit only those types of discrimination specifically covered by their terms (i.e., discrimination based on "race, color, religion, national origin, or sex"), California's Unruh Civil Rights Act has been construed by various California appellate courts to forbid all forms of "arbitrary" discrimination which bear no

---

[2]Civil Code § 51.3 defines senior-citizen housing as that reserved for persons 62 years of age or older, or a complex of 150 or more units (35 in non-metropolitan areas) for persons older than 55 years. Under federal law, housing for older persons is housing solely occupied by persons 62 or older, or housing intended for people over 55 that has special facilities for older residents and is in fact 80% occupied by people 55 or older (42 U. S. C. § 3607).

[3]See *Hubert v. Williams* (1982) 133 Cal. App. 3d Supp. 1.

[4]Civil Code § 54.1(b)(5).

relationship to a landlord's legitimate business concerns. So, even though the Unruh Act contains only the words "sex, race, color, religion, ancestry, or national origin" to describe types of discrimination that are illegal, the courts have ruled that these categories are just examples of types of arbitrary and illegal discrimination. On this basis, the California Supreme Court has ruled that landlords can't discriminate against families with children, and has stated that discrimination against other groups, such as "Republicans, students, welfare recipients," or "entire occupations or avocations, e.g., sailors or motorcyclists"[5] is also illegal. Similarly, if you refuse to rent to a person because you don't approve of unmarried people living together, you are guilty of unlawful discrimination.

Although the most common forms of illegal discrimination in rental housing consist of refusing to rent to prospective tenants for an arbitrary reason, or offering to rent to one person on tougher terms than are offered to others with no good reason for making the distinction, these aren't the only ways a landlord can be legally liable for unlawful discrimination. A landlord's termination, or attempt to terminate a tenancy, for a discriminatory reason, or discrimination in providing services, such as the use of pool or meeting-room facilities or other common areas, is illegal and can provide the discriminated-against tenant with a defense to an eviction lawsuit as well as a basis for suing the landlord for damages (see Section D, below).

Example 1: Bill Lee rents apartments in his six-unit apartment building without regard to racial or other unlawful criteria. His tenants include a black family and a single Latina woman with children. When Constance Block buys the building from Bill, she immediately gives only these two tenants 30-day notices. Unless Constance can come up with a valid non-discriminatory reason for evicting these tenants, they can defend an eviction lawsuit Constance brings on the basis of unlawful discrimination. The tenants can also sue Constance for damages in state or federal court.

Example 2: Now, let's assume that Constance, having lost both the eviction lawsuits and the tenants' suits for damages against her, still tries to discriminate by adopting a less blatant strategy. One way she does this is by adopting an inconsistent policy of responding to late rent payments. When her Caucasian tenants without children are late with the rent, she doesn't give them a three-day notice to pay rent or quit until after a five-day "grace period," while non-white tenants receive their three-day notices the day after the rent is due. In addition, when non-white tenants request repairs or raise other issues about the condition of the premises, the speed of Constance's response mimics a turtle's walk after waking from a snooze in the sun. These more subtle (or not so subtle, depending on the situation) means of discrimination are also illegal, and Constance's tenants have grounds to sue her, as well as to defend any eviction lawsuit she brings against them.

B. Legal Reasons to Discriminate

The fact that all forms of arbitrary discrimination in rental housing are illegal does not mean that every time you are turned down for an apartment that you are being discriminated against for an illegal reason. The landlord may have had a lot of applicants and simply preferred someone else. Or the landlord may have discriminated against you for a legal reason. What are legal reasons that justify a landlord in discriminating against a prospective tenant? There is no list set out in a statute, but if a landlord discriminates against a prospective tenant because that person has objective

---

[5]See *Marina Point, Ltd., v. Wolfson* (1982) 30 Cal. 3d 72, 180 Cal. Rptr. 496.

characteristics that would tend to make him a poor tenant, the landlord is on solid legal ground. These characteristics include a bad credit history, credit references that don't check out, a past history of not paying rent or of using residential premises to run an illegal business (e.g., drugs or prostitution), and anything else that honestly and directly relates to the quality of being a good tenant.

Credit Disclosure Note: If a landlord relies on a credit report to take any action that negatively affects a tenant's (or prospective tenant's) interest, the tenant has a right to a copy of the report. Civil Code § 1787.2.

1. Landlord-Occupied Premises

A few words should be said about situations where a tenant rents part of a house or apartment in which the owner resides, sharing common kitchen and bathroom facilities. You've undoubtedly seen roommate or housesharing ads containing all sorts of restrictions like, "Young, female, non-smoking vegetarian who reads Asimov, wanted to share house," etc. Is this legal? Yes, because the California and federal civil rights laws apply only to housing rental operations that are considered to be "businesses." Although the renting of a single separate apartment or house (or even one half of an owner-occupied duplex)[6] constitutes the operation of a "business" to which these laws apply, renting out a portion of a dwelling in which the owner (or a tenant seeking a room-mate) continues to reside normally does not. In other words, an owner (or tenant) occupant who will be sharing common kitchen or bathroom facilities with the tenant (sub-tenant) may, if she wishes, discriminate arbitrarily in renting a portion of the property, without violating any civil rights laws. One exception, however, is where the owner-occupant (or tenant) rents two rooms or portions of a dwelling (such as in a single-family house with three or more bedrooms). In this situation, California's civil rights laws do apply to make discrimination illegal,[7] although we haven't heard of any lawsuits challenging people's rights to choose only non-smoker, vegetarian, single mothers or some other narrowly-restricted group in this situation. Obviously, if a landlord in this situation discriminates on the basis of race or religion, there could well be cause for legal action.

---

[6]An owner-occupant of a duplex or triplex, etc. is governed by civil rights laws in the renting of the other unit(s) in the building, even though he or she lives in one of the other units, because that person is renting out property for use as a *separate* household, where kitchen or bathroom facilities aren't shared with the tenant. See *Swann v. Burkett* (1962) 209 Cal. App. 2d 685 and 58 Ops. Cal. Atty. Gen. 608 (1975).

[7]Government Code § 12927(c).

2. Families with Children and "Overcrowding"

The fact that discrimination against families with children is illegal does not mean a landlord must rent you a one-bedroom apartment if you have a family of five. In other words, it is legal to establish reasonable space-to-people ratios. But it is not legal to use "overcrowding" as a euphem - ism justifying discrimination because a family has children, if a landlord would rent to the same number of adults.

A few landlords, realizing they are no longer able to enforce a blanket policy of excluding children, have now adopted criteria that for all practical purposes forbid children, under the guise of preventing "overcrowding." These include allowing only one person per bedroom, with a married or living-together couple counting as one person. This would allow renting a 2-bedroom unit to a husband and wife and their one child, but would allow a landlord to exclude a family with two children. Although the courts have not yet ruled on this practice, chances are they will soon find it illegal where the effect of its use is to keep all (or most) children out of a landlord's property.

Until the courts spell out just what type of overcrowding standards a landlord can legitimately apply in a situation where he refuses to rent to children, we suggest that you refer to the Uniform Housing Code (which has been adopted by most California cities) to determine whether the land- lord is requiring a lot more space per person than is reasonable.

The Uniform Housing Code [Section 503(b)] states that a unit is considered overcrowded if any bedroom has an area of less than 70 square feet for one or two occupants, plus 50 additional square feet for each additional occupant. When you think about it, this means that bedrooms can be fairly crowded. Many landlords may conclude that the code in fact allows too much crowding, and will want to adopt a somewhat stricter standard. Although it's impossible to be sure, we suspect that requiring somewhat more space per tenant will stand up should it be challenged in court. For example, if a landlord requires a sleeping area of 90 square feet for the first two occupants and 70 square feet for any additional occupant in the same bedroom, or restricts occupancy of studio apartments to one person, one-bedroom apartments to two people, and two-bedroom apartments to four people, no matter what the square-foot-to-people ratio, she will probably be on safe legal ground.

Also, look at the history of a landlord's rental policies. If he used to disallow children, before someone complained or sued about this, and then he adopted strict occupancy limits, it is likely that his intent is still to keep out children, and a court might well find his new policy illegal.

Example: A married couple and their three children seek to rent a small house. The landlord has a policy of requiring 90 square feet sleeping space for a couple and 70 square feet for any addi- tional person in the same bedroom. The house has two bedrooms, one measuring 12' x 14' (168 square feet), and a smaller one measuring 10' x 10' (100 square feet). Under even the strict stan- dards discussed above, three persons (the couple and one child) could share the larger bedroom, with 90 square feet required for the couple and 70 more, for a total of 160 square feet, for the child. The other two children could share the 10' x 10' bedroom, since its 100 square feet accommodate two people. Therefore, if a landlord claims overcrowding as an excuse not to rent to them, she is probably guilty of discriminating against children. However, if there were only two small bedrooms, overcrowding would be a legitimate criterion for refusing to rent. It is not legal for a landlord to inquire as to the age and sex difference of the two children who will be sharing the same bedroom. This is your business, not the landlord's.

Note on Afterborn Children: Often a child will be born after you have already resided in a place for some time. Is your landlord entitled to evict you if the birth of the new child would result in a seriously overcrowded situation? Legally, yes, especially if your lease or rental agreement makes it clear that the property can only be occupied by a set number of people, and the baby is one too many. However, if you face this situation and feel the landlord is in fact using the crowding issue as an excuse to get you out, carefully research the landlord's rental policies on *other* apartments. For example, if you find situations in which the landlord is allowing four adults to occupy a unit the same size as yours and moves to evict you because the birth of your second child means your unit is now occupied by four people, you clearly have a good case.

C. How to Tell If a Landlord Is Discriminating

Occasionally an apartment house manager—and rarely a landlord himself—will tell you that he will not rent to blacks, Spanish-surnamed people, Asians, etc. This does not happen often any more, because these people are learning that they can be penalized if it is proved that they are discriminating.

Today, most landlords who wish to discriminate try to be subtle about it. When you phone to see if a place is still available, the landlord might say it has been filled, if he hears a southern or Spanish accent. If he says it is vacant, then when you come to look at it and he sees that you are black, Chicano, etc., he might say it has just been rented. Or, he might say he requires a large security deposit which he "forgot to put in the ad." Or he might say that the ad misprinted the rent, which is $645, not $465. Many variations on these themes can be played.[8] If you suspect that the landlord is discriminating against you, it is important that you do some things to check it out. For example, if you think she is asking for a high rent or security deposit just to get rid of you, ask other tenants what they pay. The best way to check is to run a "test." Have someone who would not have trouble with discrimination (for example, a white male without kids) revisit the place soon after you do and ask if it is available and, if so, on what terms. If the response is better, the landlord was probably discriminating against you. Be sure that your friend's references,

---

[8]Larger landlords increasingly rely on rental agencies to take applications for them. These organizations utilize a variety of criteria to screen the prospective tenants, and are adept at choosing a legal reason (e.g., credit history) if challenged as to why one person (say a white man) got an apartment instead of another (say a black man or woman). In addition, several computerized services are offered to landlords. For a fee, firms will sell landlords information about a prospective tenant's credit history, rental history, whether the tenant has ever been sued in an unlawful detainer proceeding, etc.

type of job and life style are similar to yours, so the landlord cannot later say he took your friend and turned you down because of this difference.

If you need help with testing, contact a civil rights organization or your city's Human Relations Council.

D. What to Do About Discrimination

There are several different legal approaches to the problems raised by discrimination. Regardless of what you do, if you really want to live in the place, you must act fast, or the landlord will rent it to someone else before he can be stopped.

1. Complain to the California Department of Fair Employment and Housing

The State of California Department of Fair Employment and Housing takes complaints on discrimination in rental housing. This department enforces laws which prohibit housing discrimination. It has the power to order up to $1,000 damages for a tenant who has been discriminated against.

If you believe that you have been discriminated against, you can contact the office nearest you. You will be asked to fill out a complaint form and an investigator will be assigned to your case. You must file your complaint within 60 days of the date of the violation or the date when you first learn of the violation. The investigator will try to work the problem out through compromise and conciliation. If this fails, the Department may conduct hearings and maybe take the matter to court. However, because it has been our experience that in recent years the Department has been slack in enforcing anti-discrimination housing laws, we recommend that you consult a private attorney and consider suing the discriminating landlord.

Fresno
1963 E Street
(209) 445-5373

Los Angeles
322 West First St., Rm. 2126
(213) 620-2610

Oakland
111 Jackson Street
(415) 464-4095

San Francisco
30 Van Ness Ave.
(415) 557-2005

Sacramento
1201 I Street, 2nd Floor
(916) 323-4547

San Diego
110 West C Street, Suite 1702
(714) 237-7405

Santa Ana
28 Civic Ctr. Plaza, Suite 330
(714) 558-4159

San Jose
88 No. First, Rm. 200A
(408) 277-1264

2. Complain to the United States Department of Housing and Urban Development

You can also lodge a complaint with the U.S. Department of Housing and Urban Development (HUD) if the discrimination is based on race, religion, sex, family status or physical handicap. This federal agency has most of the same powers as does the state but must give the state agency the opportunity (30 days) to act on the case first. The HUD equal opportunity office for California is located at One Embarcadero Center in San Francisco (Phone: (415) 566-3840). HUD's power of investigation and sanctions are similar to those of the state. The experience of the authors has been that HUD is far more militant in going after discriminating landlords than is the state. However, the fact that HUD can't act until 30 days after the state has received the complaint reduces its efficiency a great deal.

3. Sue the Discriminating Landlord

We think that normally the most effective thing you can do is to see a lawyer and sue the landlord. If you have been discriminated against because of sex, race, religion, physical disability or marital status, a lawsuit may be brought in state court. Suits in federal court work only for racial, religious and sex discrimination. If you can prove your case, you will almost certainly be eligible to recover money damages. Many, if not most, attorneys have had little experience with discrimination lawsuits. This is particularly true of lawsuits brought in Federal Court. Rather than try to find an attorney at random, you would be wise to check with an organization in your area dedicated to civil rights and fighting discrimination. They will undoubtedly be able to direct you to a sympathetic attorney.

Attorneys have become more interested in taking these cases in the last few years, because the amount of money that can be recovered is now substantial. For racial, religious and sex discrimination, you may sue in federal court and collect damages to compensate you for your loss as well as substantial punitive damages and attorney's fees.[9] For discrimination based on these three areas and discrimination based on marital status, disability, having children, homosexuality, or any other "arbitrary" category, you may sue in state court and collect damages to compensate you for your loss as well as a penalty of $250 and attorney's fees.[10]

---

[9]42 U.S.C. Section 3612; *Morales v. Haines*, 486 F.2d 880 (7th Cir., 1973); *Lee v. Southern Home Sites Corp.*, 42 F.2d 290 (5th Cir. 1970).

[10]Federal Fair Housing Act of 1968 (42 U.S.C. Section 3612). For racial discrimination, you may also sue under the Civil Rights Act of 1866, which allows greater punitive damages. *Morales v. Haines*, 486 F.2d (7th Cir., 1973).

Chapter 6:

The Obnoxious Landlord and Your Right to Privacy

A. Your Rights

Some landlords can get pretty obnoxious. This is also true of plumbers, butchers, and English teachers, but since this book is for tenants, we will concentrate on just the landlords.

Typically, problems arise with those kinds of landlords who cannot stop fidgeting and fussing over their property. Normally, smaller landlords develop this problem to a greater extent than do the bigger, more commercial ones. Nosy landlords are always hanging around or coming by, trying to invite themselves in to look around and generally being pests. Sometimes you may run into a manager on a power trip.

If your landlord is difficult or unpleasant to deal with, she can make your life miserable and you may not be able to do anything about it. There is no law which protects you from a dis-agreeable personality, and, if you have no lease, you are especially unprotected from all but the most outrageous invasions of privacy or trespass. Things can get unpleasant, but if your right to privacy and peaceful occupancy are not disturbed, you may have to grin and bear it or look for another place.[1]

B. Your Landlord's Right of Entry

Section 1954 of the California Civil Code establishes the circumstances under which a landlord can enter his tenant's home, and section 1953(a)(1) provides that these circumstances cannot be expanded, or the tenant's privacy rights waived or modified, by any lease or rental agreement provision. The first thing to realize is that there are only four broad situations in which your landlord may legally enter while you are still in residence. They are:

1. To deal with an emergency;

2. To make needed repairs (or assess the need for them);

3. To show the property to prospective new tenants or purchasers; and

4. When you invite the landlord in.

In most instances (emergencies and tenant invitations excepted), a landlord can enter only during "normal business hours" and then only after "reasonable notice," presumed to be 24 hours. Because this is so important, let's examine Section 1954 of the California Civil Code carefully to make sure you thoroughly understand the details of how your right to privacy works.

1. Entry in Case of an Emergency

Under Civil Code Section 1954, your landlord or manager can enter the property without giving advance notice, in order to respond to a true emergency which threatens injury or property

---

[1]A court allowed a suit by a tenant alleging that a landlord was guilty of the intentional infliction of emotional distress. The court found that it was necessary to prove four things in this sort of suit: (1) outrageous conduct on the part of the landlord; (2) intention to cause or reckless disregard of the probability of causing emotional distress; (3) severe emotional suffering; and (4) actual suffering or emotional distress. *Newby v. Alto Riviera Apartments*, 60 Cal. App. 3d 288 (1976).

damage if not corrected immediately. For example, a fire, gas, or serious water leak is a true emer-gency which, if not corrected, will result in damage, injury, or even loss of life. On the other hand, a landlord's urge to repair an important but non-life- or property-threatening defect, say of a stopped-up drain, isn't a true emergency for which the law allows no-notice entry.

2. Entry to Make Repairs

Section 1954 allows a landlord or repairperson, contractor, etc. to enter to make and assess the need for and cost of routine repairs or alterations. In this situation, however, the landlord must enter only during normal business hours (9:00 a.m. to 5:00 p.m., Monday-Friday) and must first give "reasonable notice." Customarily, "normal business hours" means 9 a.m. to 5 p.m., Monday - Friday, but no exact hours are specified in the statute. As we noted above, Civil Code Section 1954 contains a presumption that an advance notice of at least 24 hours is reasonable. However, you should understand that if your landlord can establish a really good reason for it under the circumstances, giving a reasonable but shorter notice is legal. This is because under the wording of the statute, the 24-hour notice period raises only a presumption of reasonableness.

Example: If your landlord arranges to have a repairperson inspect a wall heater at 2 p.m. on Tuesday, she should notify you on or before 2 p.m. on Monday. But if she can't reach you until 6 p.m. (e.g., you can't be reached at home or at work), less than 24 hours' notice is probably okay. Of course, if you consent to your landlord's plan, the notice period is not a problem.

In some situations, the 24-hour notice period will not be a problem, as you will be delighted that your landlord is finally making needed repairs and will cooperate with his entry requirements. However, there are definitely situations when a landlord will be totally unreasonable, as would be the case when a repairperson simply knocks at your door with no advance notice and asks to make a non-emergency repair when you are in the middle of cooking dinner for your mother-in-law. If this occurs, you have a legal right to deny entry.

Inspection Note: Your landlord can't legally use his right to inspect your unit in order to harass you. Repeated inspections, even when 24-hour notice is given, might fall into this category. To fight back in this situation, see Section C, below.

3. Entry to Show Property

Section 1954 also allows your landlord to enter your property to show it to prospective tenants (toward the end of a tenancy) and to prospective purchasers if she wishes to sell it, as long as she complies with the "business hours" and "reasonable notice" provisions discussed above.

As noted, your landlord may show the property to prospective buyers or mortgage companies. This situation often arises when a property that is for sale is a rented single-family house or condominium unit, but can also occur where a multiple-unit building is placed on the market. Again, remember that under Section 1954, 24 hours is presumed to be reasonable notice to you.

Unfortunately, problems often occur when an overeager real estate salesperson shows up on your doorstep without warning or calls on very short notice and asks to be let in to show the place to a possible buyer. In this situation, you are within your rights to say politely but firmly, "I'm busy right now—try again in a few days after we've set a time convenient for all of us." Naturally, this type of misunderstanding is not conducive to your peace of mind, especially if you fear that the landlord or real estate person may use a pass key to enter when you are not home.

There are several ways to deal with this situation:

• You can stand on your rights and notify your landlord to follow the law or you will sue for invasion of privacy (see Section C, below); or

• You can try to work out a compromise with your landlord by which you agree to allow the unit to be shown on shorter than 24-hour notice in exchange for a reduction in the rent or other benefit. For example, you might agree in advance that two-hour notice is reasonable for up to eight house showings a month, in exchange for having your rent reduced $200 per month. This kind of tradeoff is perfectly logical—your rent pays for your right to treat your home like your castle, and any diminution of this right should be accompanied by a decrease in your rent obligation.

Lock Box Note: Under no circumstances should you allow your landlord to place a key-holding "lock box" on the door. This is a metal box that attaches to the front door and contains the key to that door. It can be opened by a master key held by area real estate salespeople. Since a lock box allows a salesperson to enter in disregard of the 24-hour notice requirement, it should not be used—period.

4. Entry with the Agreement of the Tenant

Of course, a landlord can always enter rental property, even without 24 hours' notice, if you so agree without pressure or coercion. For example, if your landlord (whom you like and feel is well motivated) has a maintenance problem that needs regular attending to (e.g., a fussy heater or temperamental plumbing), you might want to work out a detailed agreement with him allowing entry in specified circumstances.

C. What to Do About a Landlord's Improper Entry

Suppose now your landlord does violate your rights of privacy—what can you do about it?

As you probably figured out by now, it is one thing to have a right, and quite another thing to get the benefits of it. This is especially true for tenants who do not have a lease and do not live in a city where a rent control ordinance requires just cause for eviction. In this situation, if you set about aggressively demanding your rights, you may end up with a notice to vacate. It is also generally true that you can rarely accomplish good results with hard words. This doesn't mean not to be firm or determined, but rather, not to be offensive.

Here is a step-by-step approach that usually works in dealing with a landlord who is violating your right to privacy:

Step 1: Talk to the landlord (or manager) about your concerns in a friendly but firm way. If you come to an understanding, follow up with a note to confirm it.

Step 2. If this doesn't work, or if your landlord doesn't follow the agreement that you have worked out, it's time for a tougher letter. Here is a sample:

Roper Real Estate Management Co.
11 Peach Street
San Diego, CA

Dear Mr. Roper:

Several times in the last two months your employees have entered my dwelling without my being home and without notifying me in advance. In no situation was there any emergency involved. This has caused me considerable anxiety and stress, to the point that my peaceful enjoyment of my tenancy has been seriously disrupted.

This letter is to formally notify you that I value my privacy highly and insist that my legal rights to that privacy, as guaranteed to me under Section 1954 of the California Civil Code, be respected. Specifically, in non-emergency situations, I would like to have 24 hours' notice of your intent to enter my house.

I assume this notice will be sufficient to correct this matter. If you want to talk about this, please call me at 121-2121 from 9:00 a.m. to 5:00 p.m.

Step 3: If, despite this letter, the invasions of your privacy continue, document them and either see a lawyer or take your landlord to small claims court.

One difficulty with a lawsuit against a landlord guilty of trespass is that it is hard to prove much in the way of money damages. Assuming you can prove the trespass occurred, the judge will probably readily agree that you have been wronged, but he may award you very little money. Most likely, he will figure that you have not been harmed much by the fact that your landlord walked on your rug and opened and closed your door. However, if you can show a repeated pattern of trespass (and the fact that you asked the landlord to stop it) or even one clear example of out-rageous conduct, you may be able to get a substantial recovery. In this situation the landlord may be guilty of a number of "torts" (legal wrongdoings), including harassment (Code of Civil Procedure § 527.6), breach of your implied covenant of quiet enjoyment (*Guntert v. Stockton*, 55 Cal. App. 3d 131 [1976]), intentional infliction of emotional distress, and negligent infliction of emotional distress.

If your landlord comes onto your property or into your home and harms you in any way, or threatens you or damages any of your property, see an attorney. You should also report the matter to the police. Some California police departments have taken the excellent step of setting up special landlord-tenant units. The officers and legal experts in these units have been given special training in landlord-tenant law and are often helpful in compromising disputes and setting straight a landlord who has taken illegal measures against a tenant. If your city hasn't done this, why not?

Probably the time that a landlord is most likely to trespass is when the tenant has failed to pay her rent. The landlord, faced with the necessity of paying a lot of money to legally get a tenant to move out, may resort to threats or even force. While it may be understandable that a landlord in this situation should be mad at the tenant, this is no justification for illegal acts. All threats, intimidation and any physical attacks on the tenant should be reported to the police. Of course it is illegal for the landlord to come on the property and do such things as take off windows and doors, turn off the utilities or change the locks. If this is done, the tenant should see an attorney at once. Do not over-react when a landlord gets hostile. While a tenant has the right to take reasonable steps to protect himself, his family and his possessions from harm, the steps must be reasonably related to the threat. The wisest thing to do, whenever you have good reason to fear that you or your property may be harmed, is to call the police.

Note: Here's another idea for dealing with a nosy landlord who ignores repeated requests to respect your privacy: put a small chain lock (that opens with a key) on the door. This will keep him from nosing around, but not from breaking the chain if a real emergency arises.

D. Other Types of Invasions of Privacy

Entering a tenant's home without his knowledge or consent isn't the only way a landlord can interfere (however unintentionally) with the tenant's privacy. Here are a few other commonly-encountered situations, with advice on how to handle them.

1. Putting "For Sale" or "For Rent" Signs on the Property

Occasionally, friction is caused by landlords who put "For Sale" or "For Rent" signs on tenants' homes, such as a "For Sale" sign on the lawn of a rented single-family house. Although a landlord may otherwise be very conscientious about respecting your privacy when it comes to giving 24 hours' notice before showing property to prospective buyers or renters, the erection of a sale or rental sign on the property is a virtual invitation to prospective buyers or renters to disturb you with unwelcome inquiries. There is little law on the subject of your rights in this situation. However, it is our opinion that as you have rented the unit, including the yard, the landlord has no right to trespass and erect a sign, and if your privacy is completely ruined by repeated inquiries, you may sue for invasion of privacy, just as if the landlord personally had made repeated illegal entries.

Keep in mind that in this age of computerized multiple-listing services, many real estate offices can, and commonly do, sell houses and all sorts of other real estate without ever placing a "For sale" sign on the property, except perhaps during the hours when an open house is in progress. If a real estate office puts a sign advertising sale or rental in front of the property you rent, you should at least insist that it clearly indicate a telephone number to call and warns against disturbing the occupant in words like, "Inquire at 555-1357—Do Not Disturb Occupant." If this doesn't do the trick and informal conversations with the landlord do not result in removal of the sign, your best bet is to simply remove it yourself and return it to the landlord or to write the landlord a firm letter explaining why your privacy is being invaded and asking that the sign be removed. If the violations of your privacy continue, document them and consider suing in small claims court. Of course, you will want to show the judge a copy of the letter.

2. Giving Information About You to Strangers

Your landlord may be approached by strangers, including creditors, banks and perhaps even prospective landlords, to provide credit or other information about you. As with letting a stranger into your home, this may cause you considerable anxiety. Basically, your landlord has a legal right to give out normal business information about you as long as it's factual. However, if your landlord spreads false stories about you (e.g., says you filed for bankruptcy if this isn't true) and you are damaged as a result (e.g., your credit rating is adversely affected or you don't get a job), you have grounds to sue the landlord.

In addition, if a landlord or a manager spreads other types of gossip about you (whether or not true), such as who stayed overnight in your apartment or that you drink too much, you may be in good shape to sue and obtain a substantial recovery, especially if the gossip damages you. This is because spreading this type of information usually has nothing to do with any legitimate purpose and is just plain malicious.

3. Calling or Visiting You at Work

Should a real need arise for your landlord to call you at work (say when your Uncle Harry shows up and asks to be let into your apartment), try to be understanding. However, situations justifying a landlord calling you at work are fairly rare. If a landlord calls you to complain about late rent payments or other problems, politely tell him to talk to you at home. If this doesn't work, follow up with a brief note. If the landlord persists, or tries to talk to your boss or other employees about the problem, your privacy is definitely being invaded. Consider going to small claims court, or see a lawyer.

4. Unduly Restrictive Rules on Guests

A few landlords, overly concerned about their tenants moving new occupants into the property, go overboard in keeping tabs on the tenants' legitimate guests who stay overnight or for a few days. Often their leases, rental agreements, or rules and regulations will require you to "register" an overnight guest. While your landlord has a legitimate concern about persons who begin as "guests" becoming permanent unauthorized residents of the property (see Chapter 2), it is overkill to require you to inform your landlord of a guest whose stay is only for a day or two. As with other subjects we mention in this chapter, extreme behavior in this area—whether by an owner or a management employee—can be considered an invasion of privacy for which you may have a valid cause of action.

Chapter 7:

Repairs and Maintenance

From time to time, things need fixing and maintaining on any piece of property. Most landlords are willing to take care of the building because that is their job, because the law requires it, or because they don't want the place to become run down. Some landlords, however, are slow and reluctant to fulfill their responsibilities.

Section A of this chapter sets out the landlord's *duties*. The rest of the chapter deals with *remedies*—what you can do about a landlord who won't properly repair or maintain the place.

A. The Landlord's Duties

There are basically two sources of the landlord's duties to repair and maintain the premises: the law and the lease (or rental agreement).

1. The Law

The law is contained in the State Housing Law, the Uniform Housing Code, and local ordinances. These are described in Chapter 2, which also spells out in great detail exactly what the landlord must do. See Chapter 2, Section D, "How to Check a Place Over." These duties occur at the outset of the tenancy and also continue during the tenancy.

The law is also contained in Civil Code Section 1941.1. This is shorter than the laws described above, but it imposes basically the same requirements, in a more summary fashion. The reason it is important is that all judges have the Civil Code right on their desks, whereas very few have the Uniform Housing Code, etc., available.

Civil Code Section 1941.1 is a bit long, but it is so important that we've decided to set it out here for you. It requires the landlord to provide:

"(a) Effective waterproofing and weather protection of roof and exterior walls, including unbroken windows and doors.

(b) Plumbing or gas facilities which conformed to applicable law in effect at the time of installation, maintained in good working order.

(c) A water supply approved under applicable law, which is under the control of the tenant, capable of producing hot and cold running water, or a system which is under the control of the landlord, which produces hot and cold running water, furnished to appropriate fixtures, and connected to a sewage disposal system approved under applicable law.

(d) Heating facilities which conformed with applicable law at the time of installation, maintained in good working order.

(e) Electrical lighting, with wiring and electrical equipment which conformed with applicable law at the time of installation, maintained in good working order.

(f) Building, grounds and appurtenances at the time of the commencement of the lease or rental agreement in every part clean, sanitary, and free from all accumulations of debris, filth, rubbish, garbage, rodents and vermin, and all areas under control of the landlord kept in every part clean, sanitary, and free from all accumulations of debris, filth, rubbish, garbage, rodents, and vermin.

(g) An adequate number of appropriate receptacles for garbage and rubbish, in clean condition and good repair at the time of the commencement of the lease or rental agreement, with the landlord providing appropriate serviceable receptacles thereafter, and being responsible for the clean condition and good repair of such receptacles under his control.

(h) Floors, stairways, and railings maintained in good repair."

It's important to understand that these are minimum requiremnets. Other conditions in the property may make it not "habitable," which means that you have several legal remedies available (see Section B).

2. The Lease or Rental Agreement

As you can see, the laws discussed above deal with basic living conditions only—heat, water, weatherproofing, etc. They do not deal with "amenities"—other facilities which are not essential, but which make living a little easier. Examples are drapes, washing machines, swimming pools, saunas, parking places, intercoms, dishwashers, and the like. The law does not require the landlord to furnish these things, but if she does so, she might be required to maintain or repair them—not by the above laws, but by her own promise to do so.

This promise might be express or implied.

It is express when the lease or rental agreement contains language which says that the landlord will repair certain things or maintain them a certain way.

Such a promise may be implied when the landlord (or his rental agent, manager, etc.) said or did something which indicated that the landlord would repair or maintain something.

Example: Tina sees Larry's ad for an apartment. The ad says "heated swimming pool." After Tina moves in, Larry stops heating the pool regularly, because his utility costs have risen. Larry has violated his implied promise to keep the pool heated.

Example: When Larry's rental agent shows Tom around the building, she goes out of her way to show off the laundry room, saying, "Here's the laundry room—it's for the use of all the tenants." Tom rents the apartment. Later the washing machine in the laundry room breaks down, but Larry won't fix it. Larry has violated his implied promise to maintain the laundry room appliances in working order.

Example: Tina's apartment has a built-in dishwasher. When she rented the apartment, neither the lease nor the landlord said anything about who was to repair the dishwasher if it broke. The dishwasher has broken down a few times and whenever Tina asked Larry to fix it, he did (or tried to). By doing so, he has shown that there is a "usage" or "practice" that he—not the tenant—is responsible for repairing the dishwasher during the tenancy.

If the landlord does violate some promise relating to the condition of the premises, you may sue her for money damages. In most instances you would do this in small claims court. There is no law allowing you to use the repair-and-deduct remedy (discussed in Section B4 below) to deal with such problems. Whether you can legally use rent withholding here is not yet clear (though there are some good arguments that you should be able to, if the breach of promise really cuts into what you had a right to expect and negatively affects the habitability of the unit). If the property is subject to rent control, a decrease in promised services may be considered an illegal rent increase. See Chapter 4, Section G.

B. Remedies

1. Complain to the Landlord

If the landlord fails to meet one of his duties to repair or maintain something, talk to him. If you can, talk directly to the owner of the building, not just his manager or caretaker. Sometimes the owner wants to do the right thing, but he has a lazy or incompetent employee who doesn't. If so, the owner might appreciate your telling him, and he might get the needed work done promptly.

Your complaint should be in writing. The letter should be polite, but firm—you are not begging for charity, but insisting on your rights as a tenant.

Here is what your letter might look like:

1500 Acorn Street, #4
Cloverdale, CA
March 24, 19___

Mr. Simon Landlord
10 Jones Street
Cloverdale, CA

Dear Mr. Landlord:

I reside in apartment #4 in your building at 1500 Acorn Street and regularly pay my rent to you.

On March 19, 19___ the water heater in my unit failed to function. On that date I notified your manager, Mr. Robert Jackson, of the problem. He called PG&E on that date and they sent a man out who put a tag on the machine saying that it was no longer serviceable or safe and that it should be replaced. I gave Mr. Jackson a copy of the PG&E slip on March 20, 19___ and he said that he would see about having the heater replaced immediately.

So far the heater has not been replaced and no one has told me when it will be. I am sure you know that it is a real hardship to be without hot water.

I've read the *California Tenants Handbook*, so I know my rights and remedies.

I would appreciate hearing from you as soon as possible. My phone number at work is 657-4111.

Very truly yours,

_____

Tina Tenant

This letter might get results all by itself. Most landlords don't want further trouble from a tenant who stands up for her rights. "The squeaky wheel gets the grease!"

It is illegal for the landlord to try to evict you for complaining about the condition of the premises. *Kemp v. Schultz* (1981) 121 Cal. App. 3d Supp. 13.

The complaint letter also serves another function: it satisfies a legal precondition to your right to use other remedies, which we will now discuss.

2. Move Out

One remedy is simply to move out, even if you are in the middle of your lease or rental agreement. The law allows you to do this if the dwelling "substantially lacks" any of the things mentioned in Civil Code Section 1941.1 (see Section A1, above), and the landlord has been notified of the problem (orally or in writing), but failed to fix them in a "reasonable time." Civil Code §1942(a). If you have notified the landlord of the problems and given him a reasonable time to correct them, you don't have to give any notice that you are moving out.

This is called the doctrine of "constructive eviction," because the landlord has made things so miserable that you pretty much have to leave. Leaving might be a good idea, because if the landlord won't fix this problem, she will probably be a lousy landlord throughout your tenancy. If you leave, you may also sue her for money damages for the trouble she has caused you.

When you move out, it is a good idea to tell the landlord why you are doing so—and the legal basis for moving. This should decrease the likelihood of her suing you for violating your lease. Here is an example of a notice you might send her:

1500 Acorn Street, #4
Cloverdale, CA
March 29, 19__

Mr. Simon Landlord
10 Jones Street
Cloverdale, CA

Dear Mr. Landlord:

I have resided in apartment #4 at 1500 Acorn Street and regularly paid my rent to you.

As you know, on March 19, 19__ the water heater in my unit broke down. Although I have repeatedly requested repairs, no action has yet been taken. Because of the weather and because of the size of my family, I cannot continue to live comfortably without such an essential service, so I am therefore compelled to exercise my rights under Civil Code Section 1942 to vacate the premises.

Sincerely yours,

_____

Tina Tenant

For many tenants, however, moving out is not really a good alternative. Because of low vacancy rates in most communities, it is just too hard to find another place at a reasonable rent. If you are in this situation, you should consider the remedies we discuss next.

3. Call the Building Inspector

The State Housing Law and local housing codes are supposed to be enforced by a city or county agency. Codes are usually enforced by an agency called the "Building Inspection" or "Housing" Department (or some similar name). Violations creating immediate health hazards (such as rats or broken toilets) are also enforced by the Health Department. Violations creating fire hazards (such as trash in the basement) are also enforced by the Fire Department. State law provides jail terms of up to one year for repeated severe violations of the state housing law and fines up to $5,000. Health & Safety Code §17995.3.

These agencies have the power to close the building and even demolish it if the landlord will not comply with their orders to correct code violations. They very seldom go to this extreme, however. Usually they inspect the building, send a letter to the landlord ordering him to make repairs, and later reinspect the building and send more letters until the landlord complies.[1]

This sort of pressure works on many landlords, so your reporting code violations to the agency and asking for an inspection can sometimes help you. If you decide to do this, it is best to go to the agency and make your complaint in writing.

a. Drawbacks of Reporting Code Violations

There are, however, some things to watch out for before deciding to report code violations.

First, if the landlord owns a lot of slum property or has been in this business for a while, he probably knows what to do to keep the agency off his back. He may be friendly with the building inspectors. He may know how to take appeals which can delay enforcement of the codes for years. He may make a few repairs and let the others go, knowing just how much it takes to temporarily satisfy the agency that he is "trying." The landlord is less likely to get away with these tricks if there is a real health or fire hazard, like rats or open gasoline on the premises. The Health or Fire Department will usually be tougher than the Building Inspection Department.

Second, there is a danger that the landlord will find out that you reported her to the agency and will try to evict you because of this. This is called a "retaliatory eviction." The landlord will usually do this simply by giving you a 30-day notice terminating your month-to-month tenancy, giving no reason for doing so. Or, she might give you a 30-day notice that your rent is being increased, as an indirect way of getting you out.

Retaliatory evictions for reporting code violations are illegal for 180 days after the date the report was made (if you are paid up in your rent). Civil Code §1942.5(a)[2] Unfortunately, however,

---

[1]If the landlord has failed for six months or more to comply with agency orders to repair, the enforcement agency may notify the state's Franchise Tax Board. (Enforcement agencies have the discretion to do so in 90 days.) The Board then may deny the landlord any deduction on his state income tax form for interest, taxes, or depreciation on the building. California Revenue & Taxation Code §§17299 and 24436.5. Also, if the repairs have not been made within 60 days of the letter, the tenant may sue the landlord and recover any actual damages, plus "special damages" of between $100 and $1,000, plus attorney fees. Civil Code §1942.4. You may file such a lawsuit in Small Claims Court, so long as you do not use a lawyer and do not ask for more than $2,000. If you do file suit, be sure to ask for the full $1,000 in "special damages."

[2]Even if a retaliatory eviction occurs later than 180 days from the date of your complaint, it may be illegal under common law theories. *Glaser v. Meyers* (1982) 137 Cal. App. 3d 770.

one California case indicates that it's up to the tenant to prove that any eviction was retaliatory. *Western Land Office v. Cervantes* (1985) 175 Cal. App. 3d 724. So, if you refuse to get out and the landlord sues to evict you and you prove that he is doing it because you reported the code violation, you will win the lawsuit. The problem is that if the landlord can show that he is evicting you for some good reason (for example, you violated the rental agreement), you might lose. However, by attempting a retaliatory eviction, the landlord is taking a big chance. If you get out because of his 30-day notice but can prove it was retaliatory, you can sue for money damages later. *Aweeka v. Bonds* (1971) 20 Cal. App. 3d 278; Civil Code §1942.5(f). To prove that the landlord acted in retaliation, you will need written evidence that you complained to officials before the landlord began eviction proceedings. Keep careful records of all your contacts with government personnel, including dates and names.

If you have a lease, you are pretty well protected from retaliatory evictions, since the landlord must prove a breach in order to kick you out before your lease is up. If you have only a month-to-month rental agreement, you do face the danger of retaliatory evictions, unless you have a provision like Paragraph 16 of our Model month-to-month Rental Agreement, in Chapter 2, Section B5. That paragraph requires the landlord to state her reasons when trying to terminate your tenancy or increase the rent, and to prove that these reasons are true if you question them. Also, tenants in certain rent control cities can be evicted only for "good cause" as specified in the law (see Chapter 11).

When deciding whether to withhold rent, sue the landlord, or take other action against him, you may wish to find out if he has had trouble with the housing code inspectors before. In the past, many code inspectors have refused to show tenants their records without the landlord's permission. A state statute, however, expressly declares that all records of notices and orders directed to the landlord concerning serious code violations (those listed in Civil Code Section 1941.1) and the inspector's acts regarding those violations are public records. Government Code §6254.7(c). Every citizen has the right to inspect any public record. Government Code §6253.

b. If You Must Move Because of Code Violations

If a court rules that a building's condition "substantially endangers the health and safety of residents," the local enforcement agency will send you a copy of the court order. Then, if the owner repairs the premises and you can't live there while the renovation proceeds, the owner must pay you certain relocation benefits. If you must move, the landlord is required to:

• provide you with comparable temporary housing nearby, or if that's not possible, pay you the difference between your old and new rent for 120 days;

• pay your moving expenses, including packing and unpacking costs;

• insure your belongings in transit, or pay you the replacement value of property lost, stolen or damaged in transit;

• pay utility connection charges; and

• give you the first chance to move back into the old place when repairs are completed.

Health and Safety Code § 17980.7.

4. Repair and Deduct

When your landlord refuses to make repairs, California law gives you the right to make the repairs yourself (or hire someone to do them) and deduct the cost from your next month's rent. There are, however, some restrictions on this right, and there are certain procedures you must follow to exercise this right. The law on this subject is stated in California Civil Code Sections 1941-1942.5.

a. Restrictions on the Right to Repair and Deduct

First, this remedy can be used only for certain defects. It can be used only if your place substantially lacks any of the things listed in Civil Code Section 1941.1 (see Section A1, above).

Second, you are not allowed to use this remedy if you interfered with the landlord's attempt to repair the defect, or if the defect was caused by your violation of any of the following duties (under Civil Code Section 1941.2):

• To keep your premises clean (unless the landlord has agreed to do this);

• To properly dispose of your garbage and trash (unless the landlord has agreed to do this);

• To properly use all electrical, gas and plumbing fixtures and keep them as clean as their condition permits;

• Not to permit any person on the premises to damage the premises or the facilities wilfully, or to do so yourself;

• To use each room only for the purpose for which it was intended (for example, you can't cook on the spare heater).

Finally, your repair of a defect may not require an expenditure of more than one month's rent and you cannot use your "repair-and-deduct" remedy more than twice in any 12-month period. Civil Code §1942.

b. How to Exercise Your Right to Repair and Deduct

You can use the repair and deduct remedy if none of the above restrictions apply to you.

To do so, you must first notify the landlord of the defects she should repair. You should put this in writing, date it and keep a copy so you can later prove you did it. Below is a form notice you might use. A tear-out form appears in the appendix. (Be sure to keep a copy of this notice to use if you later go to court.)

NOTICE TO REPAIR

To _____,Landlord of the premises located at

_____.

NOTICE IS HEREBY GIVEN that unless certain defects on the premises are repaired within a reasonable time, the undersigned tenant shall exercise any and all rights accruing to him pursuant to law, including those granted by California Civil Code Sections 1941-1942.

The defects are the following:

_____

_____

_____

_____

Dated:_____   _____
                                         (signature of tenant)

Next you must wait a "reasonable time" to give the landlord a chance to make the repairs. After a reasonable time passes, you can do the repairs. What is a "reasonable time" will depend on the circumstances. If the heat doesn't work in January, a reasonable wait may mean only a few days, at most. If it breaks down in June, and it is expensive to repair quickly, you should wait a little longer. If you have complained to the landlord about the defect before, then you should not have to wait too long. The law says that 30 days is "presumed" to be a reasonable time. This means that if you do not wait 30 days, if the case goes to court, you must prove the wait was reasonable. If you wait 30 days, the landlord must prove the wait was unreasonable.

If the landlord has not made the repairs after a reasonable time, you may do the repairs or hire someone to do them. Keep a record of all the time you put in and all amounts you spend on labor and materials. When the next month's rent is due, give the landlord a written statement itemizing the expenses of the repairs, including compensation of your time. If this adds up to less than the rent, you must pay him the balance.

c. Retaliation for Using Repair and Deduct Remedy

If you have a month-to-month rental agreement instead of a lease, the landlord might try to retaliate against you by giving you a 30-day notice terminating your tenancy or raising your rent. Civil Code Section 1942.5(a) prohibits such retaliation, with the following restrictions:

• The tenant is protected for only 180 days after he gives notice of the defects. After that, the landlord can terminate the tenancy or raise the rent, even if the tenant can prove that the landlord is doing it to retaliate.

• The tenant may raise the defense of retaliatory eviction in the eviction suit only if she is paid up in her rent when she raises the defense.

• The tenant may raise the defense only if he has not raised this defense in another eviction action brought by the same landlord in the past 12 months.

5. The Implied Warranty of Habitability

Under a famous decision of the California Supreme Court—*Green v. Superior Court* (1974) 10 Cal. 3d 616—all leases and rental agreements are now deemed by law to include an "implied warranty of habitability." This means that whether it is written down or not, and whether the landlord likes it or not, he is required to keep the place in a "habitable" condition at all times.

What is "habitable"? According to the Supreme Court, this will usually mean substantial compliance with local building and health codes and with the standards set out in Civil Code Section 1941.1 (see Section A(1), above). Put differently, a "material" violation of these codes and standards will usually constitute a breach of the implied warranty of habitability.

What is a "material" violation has yet to be clearly defined by the law, but here are some guidelines the court has set out. Both the seriousness of the defect and the length of time it persists are relevant factors in deciding if it was material. Minor violations will not be considered material. Thus, failure to correct heavy rat infestation for a month would be clearly material, while a few ants which came in on one occasion when it rained would not. No heat for a week in January might be material, while a doorway an inch lower than allowed by the codes would not. Until the rules on this issue are more fully developed, you will just have to use common sense as to what is "material."

In *Green*, the Supreme Court held that the implied warranty of habitability is so important that any provision in a lease or rental agreement that forces the tenant to waive her rights under the warranty is invalid. In a later case, the Supreme Court held that the tenant does not waive his rights under the warranty simply by moving in while knowing that the place is substandard. *Knight v. Hallsthammar* (1981) 29 Cal. 3d 46.

There is no breach of the implied warranty if the defect was caused by you or someone living with you or visiting you.

The courts have not clearly decided whether the landlord must be notified of the defects before she can be found to have breached the implied warranty. Nevertheless, it is obviously a good idea to notify her. You can use the Notice to Repair form (Section 4b, above).

Suppose the landlord does breach the implied warranty of habitability. What can you do about it? The courts have established two very important remedies: rent withholding and suing the landlord for money damages.

a. Rent Withholding

The rent withholding remedy established by the courts is direct and powerful: you simply stop paying your rent until the landlord fixes the problems. The courts have reasoned that if the landlord doesn't fulfill his obligation to you, then your duty to him (to pay rent) "abates" until he shapes up. There is no requirement that you use any of your rent to make repairs. There is no requirement that you put your rent money into any bank or "escrow" account, but it is a good idea for you to set aside the rent money rather than spend it.[3] Unlike the repair-and-deduct remedy, you do not have to have all your rent paid up before you withold rent because of the condition of the premises.

This can give the landlord a much stronger incentive to repair than your use of the repair-and-deduct remedy. There, he at least gets you to make some of the repairs, and you must pay him the balance of the rent. With rent withholding, however, he gets nothing until he does his job. (Note, however, that the defects must be more "material" to justify rent withholding than to justify repair-and-deduct).

Here is how the rent withholding remedy works.

If the landlord fails to properly make the repairs, do not make your next rent payment. Although not required by law, it is an excellent idea to give the landlord a note at this time telling her what you are doing. It might look like this (A tear-out form appears in the appendix):

NOTICE OF RENT WITHHOLDING

To _____, Landlord of the premises located at
_____.

NOTICE IS HEREBY GIVEN that because of your failure to comply with your implied warranty of habitability by refusing to repair defects on the premises, as previously demanded of you, the undersigned tenant has elected to withhold this month's rent in accordance with California law. Rent payments will be resumed in the future, as they become due, only after said defects have been properly repaired.

Dated:_____   _____
                                    (signature of tenant)

Authority: *Green v. Superior Court*, 10 Cal. 3d 616 (1974), *Tenants Rights*, Chapter 7.

If the landlord then makes the repairs, you must resume your regular rent payments the next month, but you do not have to pay him the full amount of the rent you already withheld. You owe him only a "reasonable rent" out of that. What is a "reasonable rent" depends on the circumstances and has not yet been clearly defined by the law. In one New Jersey case where the landlord

---

[3]If the landlord sues to evict you for nonpayment of rent and you succeed in proving that he breached the implied warranty, the judge will determine a "reasonable" rent, which you must pay within five days to avoid eviction. See Chapter 11, Section D.

had failed to provide heat, hot water, elevator service and incinerator use, the court required the tenant to pay only 25% of the agreed rent.[4] A West Virginia case allows the "reasonable rent" to be measured by determining the tenant's damages for "discomfort and annoyance," and then subtracting this amount from the agreed rent.[5] It is not clear whether California courts will allow this, however.[6] If you and your landlord can't agree on this, you could keep the money and let him take you to court if he wants to. If he does go to court, and if you prove that he materially breached his "implied warranty of habitability," the court will decide what is a reasonable rent and make you pay only that amount.

Los Angeles Note: The City of Los Angeles has established a Rent Escrow Account Program, which lets tenants stop paying rent to landlords who don't correct health and safety violations for which they have been cited by the city. Tenants can pay rent into the city-run escrow account and will be protected from eviction for nonpayment of rent. When repairs are made, the city will return the money, minus administration fees, to the landlord.

If you follow the procedures in this section, then when you refuse to pay your rent, it is possible that the landlord will give you a "three-day notice" to pay your rent in three days or get out. Then, when you fail to do either, she'll sue to have you evicted (see Chapter 11 for a full discussion of the eviction procedure). While normally she would easily win in such a suit, in this case you have a good defense, and she will not be allowed to evict you if you can prove that she breached her implied warranty of habitability.

When you raise this defense in your case, the judge might then order you to make future rent payments into court until the lawsuit is concluded. (He may not order you to pay into court the rent you already withheld.)

On occasion, a tenant has claimed in court that she had a valid reason for withholding rent because of substandard conditions, when in fact the unit was clearly habitable. These tenants were simply trying to get out of paying rent. This has resulted in some judges being cynical about all cases where tenants have withheld rent under the theory that the landlord has breached the duty to provide a habitable dwelling. When you add this fact to another one—some judges are more likely to be sympathetic to landlords than to tenants—you can see that a tenant is sometimes at a disadvantage in a rent withholding case. We don't mean to scare you so much that you will not use the rent withholding remedy, but we do want to prepare you for what you may face. How can you counter this possible disadvantage in a rent withholding case? Make sure to tell the judge clearly that you have the money to pay the rent, have always paid rent in the past, and will immediately start paying rent as soon as the proper repairs are made. Also, be sure that you have strong documentation that the uninhabitable condition really exists. This normally involves producing photographs and witnesses (the more technically knowledgeable the better).

At the end of the trial, if you have proved your case, the court will decide what was a "reasonable rent" while the defects on the premises were not corrected. When this is decided, that portion of any rent money which you paid into court which represents "reasonable rent" will be paid to the landlord, and the balance will be returned to you.

---

[4]*Academy Spires, Inc. v. Brown,* 111 N.J. Spr. 477, 268 A.2d 556, 562 (1970). In a California case, rent was reduced by 50%. *Strickland v. Becks,* 95 Cal. App. 3d Supp. 18 (1979).

[5]*Teller v. McCoy,* 253 S.E.2d 114, 128 (W. VA Supreme Court, 1978).

[6]*Quevado v. Braga,* 72 Cal. App. 3d Supp. 1 (1977). But see *Stoiber v. Honeychuck* (1980) 101 Cal. App. 3d 903.

The judge will also order you to pay the "reasonable rent" portion of the rent which you withheld. He will give you only a few days to do this, so it's a good idea for you to keep this money put away rather than spending it. If you fail to pay this "reasonable rent" to the landlord in the time ordered by the judge, you will be deemed the loser of the lawsuit: you will be evicted, and a judgment for the landlord's costs, attorney's fees (if the lease or rental agreement so provides), and "reasonable rent" will be entered against you. If you do pay the "reasonable rent" to the landlord on time, then you are the winner and you are entitled to a judgment for your court costs and (if the lease or rental agreement so provides) attorney's fees.

If you do not have a lease, the landlord might try to retaliate against you simply by giving you a 30-day notice to vacate (rather than a 3-day notice to pay the rent or get out). If you can prove in the eviction suit he brings that he gave you the notice in order to retaliate against you for rightfully withholding your rent, then this might well be held to be an attempted illegal retaliatory eviction and you will not be evicted. See *Barela v. Superior Court*, (1981) 30 Cal. 3d 244, 178 Cal. Rptr. 618; *Robinson v. Diamond Housing Corp.*, 463 F.2d 853 (D.C. Cir. 1972). A California statute seems to protect against retaliation in such a situation, since it forbids a landlord from retaliating against a tenant's lawful exercise of his rights. Civil Code §1942.5(c).

Rent withholding is a powerful strategy. If all goes according to the law stated above, you can stay in the premises, withhold rent and win eviction actions until the premises are brought up to code. Unfortunately, you might get into a lawsuit and require an attorney's services. Quite often, however, the written threat of rent withholding is sufficient to solve the problem.

Rent withholding can be risky! **Warning:** If you withhold rent, do not pay it in response to a 3-day notice, and the landlord sues to evict, it is possible that you might then fail to convince the court that the landlord breached the implied warranty of habitability. If this happens, you will lose the action. Also, you will probably be evicted—even though your rent withholding was honest and in good faith, and even though you are now willing to pay the full rent rather than be evicted! You may ask the judge to "reinstate" your tenancy (see Chapter 11), but she is not required to do it.

So do not follow through with your threat to withhold rent unless you are pretty sure that you can prove that the defects which the landlord failed to fix were pretty serious, and you did not cause them.

A safer strategy—through not usually as immediate and powerful as rent withholding—is to keep paying the rent, but sue the landlord for money damages for his breach of the implied warranty of habitability.

b. Sue the Landlord

The courts have held that one remedy you have against the landlord who fails to obey the implied warranty is to sue him for money damages. In one leading case, the court held that the tenant might recover damages for the "discomfort and annoyance" of having to live in substandard conditions, and for punitive damages if the landlord's failure is willful! *Stoiber v. Honeychuck* (1980) 101 Cal. App. 3d 903.

If repairs have not been made within 60 days of the building inspector or housing department ordering the landlord to make necessary repairs, the tenant may sue the landlord for actual damages, and receive "special damages" of between $100 and $1,000 (in the judge's discretion) plus attorney fees (Civil Code § 1942.4).

A model complaint to use when suing a landlord for damages for breach of the implied warranty appears in the Forms section in the back of the latest supplement to the *California Eviction Defense Manual* (Continuing Education of the Bar).

You may file a suit yourself for up to $2,000 in small claims court. For how to do this, see the description of small claims courts in Chapter 10 and see Warner, *Everybody's Guide to Small Claims Court* (Nolo Press).

If the landlord's breach of warranty caused any sickness or injury to you or anyone in your family, be sure to see a lawyer. Your claim might be worth much more than $2,000, and a lawyer can help you get what you should.

You may also sue the landlord for breach of any promise (express or implied) to provide or maintain appliances, swimming pools, or anything else relating to the premises.

It is illegal for the landlord to try to evict you or raise your rent in retaliation for your exercising your right to file a lawsuit against him. Civil Code §1942.5(c).

Chapter 8:

Injuries to a Tenant Due to Substandard Housing Conditions

When we start talking about personal injuries, we get into an area that lawyers call "torts." Whole books have been written on this subject and many lawyers make a nice living filing lawsuits on behalf of people who have been injured as a result of the "negligent" or "intentional" acts of others. The last several years have seen a great increase in the ways a landlord might be held responsible for injuries caused to a tenant. Landlords are liable for physical injuries caused by faulty premises (a broken stair, for example) and for mental suffering or emotional distress caused by slum conditions, wrongful evictions, invasions of privacy and harassment. A tenant (or in some situations, a visitor) may even recover against the landlord for maintaining a nuisance, if the premises are substantially below code or abnormally messy or loud tenants are allowed to remain in other units in the building. If you are injured, either physically or mentally, as a result of some act or failure to act of your landlord, you should see a lawyer. (If your injury is worth $2,000 or less to you, you may want to go to Small Claims Court.)

A. Standard of Care Imposed on Landlords

It used to be that a landlord could put a clause in a lease or rental agreement which freed him from most responsibilities for injuries suffered by a tenant, even if the injury was a direct result of the landlord's negligence. This is no longer the law,[1] although you still find this sort of unenforceable clause in some leases and rental agreements.

---

[1]California Civil Code § 1953.

Today a landlord is held to a strict duty of care toward her tenants when defective conditions which existed at the time the tenant moved in caused an injury. Termed "strict liability," this duty of care extends to visitors. It is important to understand that this duty exists even though the land-lord did not know about the existence of the injury causing defect. Basically, when it comes to defects, the rule is that a landlord must act toward his tenants and visitors to the building like a retailer in the business of providing housing. *Becker v. IRM Corp.*, 38 Cal. 3d 454 (1985).

Because the doctrine of strict liability is so important, a few words about it are appropriate.

"Strict" liability means liability without fault. In other words, to prevail in a case based on strict liability, a plaintiff (person suing) does not have to prove that the defendant (person sued) was negligent. This doctrine is often applied in "products liability" cases, where a manufactured appliance, automobile or other device breaks for no apparent reason and causes injury or property damage. For example, if the steering mechanism on a new car fails (or an elevator falls), causing an accident, the people injured are entitled to recover damages from the manufacturer without having to prove the manufacturer was negligent. Although there are a number of reasons for applying "strict liability" in this situation, it comes down to a conclusion that steering mechanisms on new cars are supposed to work (and elevators are not supposed to fall), and if they fail, the manufacturer is legally responsible without the injured people having to mount an elaborate case proving negligence.

B. Landlord Liability for Defects in the Premises

Here are some examples of situations in which a landlord has been held liable for injuries caused by defects in the premises.

• Mental distress from slum conditions. *Stoiber v. Honeychuck*, 101 Cal. App. 3d 903 (1980).

• Fall through a handrail on stairway. *Brennan v. Cockrell*, 35 Cal. App. 3d 796 (1973).

• Fire caused by defective heater. *Golden v. Conway*, 55 Cal. App. 3d 948 (1976). This case also states that a landlord can be strictly liable (the tenant doesn't have to prove that the landlord acted in an unreasonable way) if he installs an appliance without knowing whether or not it is defective.

• Fire as a result of defective wiring. *Evans v. Thompson*, 72 Cal. App. 3d 978 (1977). Here a defective wall plug (that the tenant had asked the landlord to fix) forced the tenant to plug a refri-gerator into another socket with an extension cord, which resulted in a fire.

• Tenant trips over rock on common stairway. *Henrioulle v. Marin Ventures, Inc.*, 20 Cal. 3d 512 (1978).

• Emotional distress from intimidation by landlord in course of eviction. *Newby v. Alto Riviera Apts.*, 60 Cal. App. 3d 288 (1976).

• A man slipped on a wet bathroom floor and plunged his arm through a shower door made of untempered glass. The landlord didn't know of the defect but was nevertheless held to be liable. *Becker v. IRM Corp.*, 38 Cal. 3d 454 (1985).

C. Landlord Liability for Criminal Acts of a Third Person

What about injuries to a tenant that result from the criminal acts of other tenants or third persons who were on the premises? Is a landlord liable for these?

Until recently, the law was that if no similar episode occurred previously, the landlord was usually held to be not liable as a matter of law. This has all been changed by the California Supreme Court in the case of *Isaacs v. Huntington Memorial Hospital*, 38 Cal. 3d 112 (1985). This case held that depending on the fact situation, a landlord may be held liable for injuries resulting to tenants (or anyone else) by criminal actions committed by others, even though no prior similar acts occurred. Whether or not a landlord is legally responsible should a tenant get assaulted, raped,[2] robbed or bitten by a dog now depends on whether the landlord reasonably had a duty of care in the circumstances and whether or not she fulfilled it. Both of these questions are for a jury to decide under the facts of the case before it.

The ordinances of many cities and counties require all rental units to be equipped with deadbolt locks. If your unit is not so equipped and you are burglarized or injured by an intruder, your chances of recovering from your landlord are excellent. If the landlord won't make good your loss, see a lawyer.

A landlord may also be legally liable if there is a pattern of uncontrolled criminal activity on the premises. The owners of an East Palo Alto apartment building that was a notorious drug-dealing center were sued by the county, and in 1988 were ordered to relocate innocent tenants at a cost of about $13,000.

Note On Broken Security Systems: Security systems, such as garage doors that open on electronic signal, television monitors in lobbies and hallways, etc., are often advertised as desirable features which justify a higher-than-normal rent. While there is generally no legal requirement mandating the installation of these systems, a tenant is justified in relying on them if they exist. This raises the question of whether a landlord's legal liability increases should a tenant (or his property) be injured when a security system is broken. The answer is generally yes. It's obviously up to your landlord to fix any defective security system immediately. If she fails to do so and you or your property are injured, your chances of recovering your losses are excellent.

---

[2]*Olar v. Schroit* (1984) 155 Cal. App. 3d 861; *Frances T. v. Villiage Green Properties* (1986) 42 Cal. 3d 490 (Condominium Owners' Association held liable).

Note on Hiring an Attorney: We discuss how to deal with lawyers generally in Chapter 1. You will want to re-read that chapter, but you should also realize that personal injury cases are special in that a lawyer normally does not charge the client any money up front, but takes a portion of any recovery. This is called a "contingency fee" and means that the lawyer gets nothing if you lose. Depending on how much work is involved, the fee can typically be from 25% to 40% of the recovery. It is wise to shop around to see what various lawyers offer. If you have a strong case, you should get someone to help you for 25% of the eventual recovery.

Here is another idea that might prove helpful. Contact the landlord or his insurance company yourself and see what they will offer you without an attorney. Then, if you think you should get more, hire an attorney on a contingency fee arrangement so that he gets a cut only of the amount he can recover for you over and above what you were offered without his help.

D. Landlord Liability for Damage Sustained by Your Property

If you start a fire or let the water overflow your bathtub and your property is damaged, you, not the landlord, are responsible. For this reason, many renters buy renters' insurance, which also provides valuable personal liability protection.

But what happens if your property is damaged as a result of a cause not your fault? For example, suppose a fire starts in a common area of a multi-unit dwelling and burns down the whole building? Who is responsible? While it has not been finally ruled on by the courts, it is logical to assume the landlord is legally liable under the strict liability theory outlined in Section A above. Even if the courts do not rule that the *Becker* case applies to property damage as well as to personal injury, the landlord will be held to be liable if your loss resulted from her negligence (say flammable material was improperly stored in a common area). However, if your loss can in no way be traceable to the landlord (e.g., another tenant starts a fire in a perfectly safe fireplace and forgets to use a screen, allowing the fire to spread), the landlord is not liable. If you can demonstrate that the other tenant was negligent, you can recover a judgment against him.

Chapter 9:

Breaking a Lease, Subleasing, and Other Leasing Problems

A. What Happens When the Lease Runs Out

Often a tenant wishes to stay in a dwelling after a lease term expires. If you are in this situation, read your lease carefully, as it may have a provision covering this situation. If so, the terms of the lease control, unless they call for an illegal automatic renewal. In the absence of a lease provision, California Civil Code Section 1945 provides that if a lease runs out and the landlord thereafter accepts rent, the tenant becomes a month-to-month tenant under the same terms as are in the old lease. All the terms of the original lease, with the exception of the period-of-occupancy clause, are still binding and become what is, in effect, a written agreement (see Chapter 2, Section B). This means that either the landlord or the tenant can terminate the tenancy with a 30-day written notice; likewise, the rent can be increased after a 30-day notice.[1]

Sometimes a lease will contain a provision calling for the automatic renewal of the lease if the tenant stays beyond the end of the lease term. This would mean that if a tenant held over one day after a one-year lease expired, he would have renewed the lease for another year. This provision is legal only if the renewal or extension provision is printed in at least eight point boldface type,

---

[1]Special rules on the termination of a tenancy are in effect in some cities which have rent control ordinances containing requirements that a tenancy can be terminated only for a cause stated in the ordinance. See Chapter 4.

immediately above the place where the tenant signs the lease. If a renewal provision is not set forth in this way, it may be legally disregarded (voided) by the tenant (Civil Code § 1945.5).

B. Subleases and Assignments

A sub-tenant is a person to whom a tenant subleases all or part of the property. This can occur where the tenant moves out temporarily (e.g., for a couple of months in the summer) and rents the entire dwelling to someone else, or where he rents one or more rooms while continuing to live there. Typically, a sub-tenant does not have a separate agreement with the landlord. Their right of occupancy depends on:

• The continuing existence of the tenancy between the landlord and the tenant; and

• Whatever implied, oral or written rental agreement the sub-tenant has with the tenant, who functions as the sub-tenant's landlord.

But, what about the tenant who has no intention of returning, such as a tenant with a year lease who stays six months and sublets to someone else for the remaining six months of the lease term? According to technical lease jargon, this is not a sublet, but an "assignment," under which the tenant has legally "assigned" all her rights to the property to someone else. We distinguish the term "assignment" from "sublet" in part because lawyers often do, and to explain why many lease and rental agreement forms forbid both assignments and sublets without the owner's consent.

There is one important technical difference between an assignment and sublease. Where an assignment is involved, the new tenant (the "assignee") is responsible to the landlord for everything the original tenant was liable for—even in the absence of an agreement between that person and the landlord (Civil Code § 822). This should be distinguished from the situation in which a tenant sublets to a second tenant who is responsible to the first tenant, not the landlord.

As a tenant, you normally face the need to sublease or assign your tenancy in the following situations:

• You have a lease or a rental agreement and want to leave for some set period of time and then return and get your home back (see Section C, below);

• You have a lease and want to leave permanently before it ends (see Section D, below);

• You want to bring in a roommate (see Chapter 3).

C. Subleasing With the Idea of Returning Later

Technically speaking, you are entitled to sublease only when you have a lease yourself in the first place. In addition, most leases require the landlord's consent. There is case law that indicates that a landlord cannot unreasonably withhold consent.[2] In addition, you can't sublease what you don't have a right to. So if you have a month-to-month tenancy, you can sublet on that basis, but you can't give someone a five-year sublease. If you have a one-year lease, you can't sublease beyond that period — though in practice many landlords continue to accept monthly rent after a fixed-term lease expires. Legally, that converts the fixed-term tenancy to a month-to-month one.[3]

Whenever you let anyone move into your place for a while, it is important to have a written agreement which sets out all the terms of the arrangement. We include here an example of a possible sublease arrangement with the warning that it will have to be modified to suit your individual circumstances.

SUBLEASE AGREEMENT

This is an agreement between Patricia Parker of 1500 Acorn Street #4, Cloverdale, California and Joan Ehrman, now residing at 77 Wheat Avenue, Berkeley, California.

1. In consideration of $300 per month payable on the first day of each month, Patricia Parker agrees to sublease apartment #4 at 1500 Acorn Street, Cloverdale, California to Joan Ehrman from August 1, 19__ to December 30, 19__.

2. Patricia Parker hereby acknowledges receipt of $1,200 which represents payment of the first and last months' rent and a $600 security deposit.[4] The security deposit will be returned to Joan Ehrman on December 30, 19__ if the premises are completely clean and have suffered no damage.

3. A copy of the agreement between Smith Realty and Patricia Parker is stapled to this agreement and is incorporated as if set out in full. Joan Ehrman specifically covenants and agrees to adhere to all the rules and regulations set out in Sections 1-10 of this lease.

_____ Date	_____ Patricia Parker
_____ Date	_____ Joan Ehrman

---

[2]Civil Code § 1945.4, _Kendall v. Pestana_ (1986) 40 Cal. 3d 488. However, if your lease requires your landlord's consent for a sublease, as almost all do, and you sublease without requesting it, the sublease is probably invalid.

[3]In some communities covered by rent control ordinances which require "just cause" to evict, a determined subtenant may be able to prevent you from reclaiming your rental unit unless you can establish "just cause" under the rent control ordinance.

[4]The rules which limit the amount of money that a landlord can charge a tenant for deposits discussed in Chapter 10 also apply to sublease agreements.

D. How to Break a Lease

If you want to move out before your lease expires, you probably won't have too much of a problem. In most areas of California, the same shortage of housing that gives the landlord an advantage at the time of the original rental also makes it possible for a tenant to get out of a lease fairly easily.

1. General Rules

When you sign a lease, you promise to pay rent on certain premises for a certain time. Simply moving out does not get you off the hook as far as paying is concerned. You have made a contract and legally you are bound to fulfill it. This means that you are legally bound to pay rent for the full lease term, whether or not you continue to occupy the dwelling.[5] If you do not pay, your landlord can sue you, get a judgment and try to collect the money by doing such things as attaching your wages.

But the law requires a landlord to take all reasonable steps to keep his losses to a minimum. California Civil Code § 1951.2. This means that when a tenant leaves in the middle of the lease term, the landlord must make all reasonable efforts to rent the premises to another tenant at the best price possible.

If the landlord re-rents the property quickly, and doesn't lose any rent, the former tenant doesn't owe the landlord anything. Only if the landlord loses money because the old tenant moved out early is the landlord entitled to payment from the former tenant. Because of a general shortage of rental units in most areas of California, the landlord should be able to get a new tenant fairly quickly, for about the same rent as paid by the original tenant. The result is that the tenant who breaks the lease is obligated for little or no damages.

Example: Susan Peters rented an apartment from Steve Lee in January for a term of one year, at the monthly rent of $1,000. Everything went well until September, when Susan had to move to be closer to her invalid mother. Under the general rule, Susan is theoretically liable to Steve for $3,000—the rent for October, November, and December. However, if Steve mitigated these damages by taking out an ad and re-renting on October 15, Susan would owe much less. If the new tenant paid $500 for the last half of October and $1,000 in November and December, Steve must credit the total $2,500 he got from the new tenant against Susan's $3,000 liability. This leaves Susan liable for only $500, plus Steve's advertising costs of $20, for a total of $520.

To summarize, a fixed-term tenant who leaves before the end of the lease is responsible for:

• The remaining rent due under the lease, minus any reasonable advertising expenses incurred in finding a new tenant, and

• Any rent the landlord can collect from a new tenant between the time the original tenant leaves and the end of the lease term.

Liquidated Damages Note: If your lease contains a liquidated damages clause, requiring you to pay the landlord a certain amount of money as damages for breaking the lease, you should know that a court probably won't make you pay it. If the amount of liquidated damages far exceeds

---

[5]Civil Code § 1951.2.

the amount the landlord actually lost, the court will consider it an invalid "penalty." You will have to compensate the landlord only for his actual losses.

The landlord cannot legally take the amount of liquidated damages out of your security deposit. If the landlord keeps your deposit in payment of these damages, remind him, promptly and in writing, that state law strictly limits what the landlord can use the security deposit for (see Chapter 10, Section C).

2. Self-Protection When Breaking a Lease

Notify your landlord in writing as soon as you know that you are going to move out before the end of a lease term. The more notice you give the landlord, the better your chances are that he will find another tenant.

After sending the landlord your written notice it is wise to stop by and talk to him. He may have another tenant ready to move in and not be concerned by your moving out. In some cases the landlord may demand an amount of money to compensate him for his trouble in re-renting the place. If the amount is small, it may be easier to agree to pay rather than to become involved in a dispute. If your landlord has a deposit, you might even offer to let him keep a part of it in full settlement of all possible damage claims arising from your leaving in the middle of the lease term. As noted above, since the landlord has a duty to try and re-rent the place ("mitigate damages") and since this is reasonably easy to do, you should not agree to pay much in the way of damages. Get any agreement you make in writing. A sample agreement is shown below.

AGREEMENT

This agreement is between Patricia Parker of 1500 Acorn Street #4, Cloverdale, California, and Smith Realty Co., of 10 Jones Street, Cloverdale, California, and by its owner, B. R. Smith.

In consideration of the amount of $75, Smith Realty Co. hereby agrees to cancel the lease of Patricia Parker on Apt. #4 at 1500 Acorn Street, Cloverdale, California as of October 31, 19__. The $75 payment is hereby acknowledged to be made this date by subtracting it from Patricia Parker's $500 security deposit.

_____   _____
Date   B. R. Smith

_____   _____
Date   Patricia Parker

If it is not possible to deal rationally with your landlord, or if she won't make a written release, you should take steps to protect yourself. Don't let your landlord scare you into paying her a lot of money. Simply put an advertisement in your local paper to lease your dwelling at the same rental that you are paying. When people call, show them the place, but tell them that any lease arrangement must be worked out with your landlord. Also request that the potential tenants contact the landlord directly. To protect yourself, keep a list of all tenants who appear suitable and who express an interest in moving in. Include information on your list that shows that the potential tenants are "responsible," such as job and family. Write a letter to your landlord with a list of the names and keep a copy for your file. She has a right to approve or disapprove of whomever you suggest as a tenant, but she may not be unreasonable about it. Also, when you move out be sure the unit is clean and ready to rent to the next tenant, so that your landlord has no basis to claim that it was not in rentable condition and that you are responsible for rent during the time it took him to get it cleaned.

SAMPLE LETTER TO LANDLORD:

> 1500 Acorn Street #4
> Cloverdale, California
> October 1, 19__

Smith Realty Co.
10 Jones Street
Cloverdale, California

As I told you on September 15, 19__, I plan to move out of this apartment on October 31, 19__. Because I wish to keep damages to a minimum, I am giving you the names, addresses, and phone numbers of four people who have expressed an interest in renting this apartment on or about November 1, 19__ at the same rent that I pay. I assume that you will find one of these potential tenants to be suitable, unless of course you have already arranged to rent the apartment.

(include list of names, addresses and phone numbers)

> Very truly yours,
>
> _____
> Patricia Parker

---

3. Possible Legal Action

If you move out and break a lease, the landlord may sue you for the rent he lost and the expense of getting a new tenant. This is not likely if the landlord has gotten a new tenant to move in almost immediately after you've moved out, because in such a situation there would be little or no damages. However, occasionally it takes the landlord a little time or expense (such as advertising) to get a new tenant. This is especially likely in a resort area (off season) or near a university in the summer. In this case, a landlord may sue either in Small Claims Court or in Municipal Court.

If you are sued, you will receive legal documents setting out the landlord's claim. Read them carefully to see if the amount the landlord asks for is fair. As explained above, if you take the proper steps to protect yourself, she should be entitled to little or nothing. In unusual situations, however, the landlord may be entitled to some recovery. An example of when damages could be recovered would be where a tenant with a year's lease at a $600 per month rental moved out in mid-year and no new tenant could be found who would pay more than $575 per month. In this case, the old tenant would be liable for the $25 a month difference between what he paid and what the new tenant paid, multiplied by the number of months left in the lease at the time he moved out. A tenant might also be liable for damages if it took the landlord some period of time, such as a month, to find a new tenant. In this case the first tenant would be liable for the month's rent (*if* the landlord had made diligent efforts to find a new tenant).

If you are sued in Small Claims Court for an amount that seems excessive, simply tell the judge your side of the case and bring with you any witnesses and written documentation that help tell your story. If you are sued in Municipal Court, you may want to see a lawyer, especially if there is a lot of money involved (see Chapter 1).

E. Belongings You Leave Behind

If you leave belongings on the premises when you move out, you must ask the landlord for them, in writing, within 18 days. Your request must describe the property and give the landlord your mailing address. Within five days of receiving your request, the landlord may demand, in writing, that you pay reasonable costs of storage. You must pay the charges and pick up the property within 72 hours of receiving the landlord's demand.

If the landlord doesn't comply with your request, you can sue for your actual damages and, if the landlord acted in bad faith, for another $250 in damages. Civil Code § 1965.

Alternately, the landlord may notify you, in writing, that the property is still there. The notice should describe the property and tell you where the property can be claimed, how long you have to claim it, and that you may have to pay reasonable costs of storage. The landlord must give you at least 15 days (18 days, if the notice is mailed) to claim the property.

If the property is worth less than $300, the landlord is free to dispose of it. If it is worth more than that, the landlord must sell it at a public sale, subtract costs of sale and storage, and turn the rest over to the county. You have a year to claim it. Civil Code § 1983.

Chapter 10:

Security Deposits and "Last Month's Rent"

Almost all landlords require their tenants to put up some money before moving in. This payment might be called a "security deposit," "cleaning fee," "last month's rent," or something else by the landlord.

Security deposits can add up to a lot of money—often over $1,000. The landlord usually wants to get as much as she can so she won't have to go chasing after you for unpaid rent or any costs of repairing the premises after you leave. The tenant, who usually wants to fork over as little as possible, often finds that it's very difficult to talk a landlord into reducing a deposit. Unfortunately, there is little we can say that will help you to get a potential landlord to be reasonable in this regard, assuming the deposit he charges is within the statutory maximum discussed on the next page. However, both because security deposits constitute a big investment on your part and because historically deposits have been a major source of friction between landlord and tenant, it is essential that you understand the legal rules in this area.

A. Amount of Deposit

Civil Code Section 1950.5(c) provides that the total of all deposits and fees required by the landlord—for security, cleaning, last month's rent, etc.—may not exceed an amount equal to two months' rent, if the premises are unfurnished. If the premises are furnished, the limit is an amount equal to three months' rent.

Suppose the landlord supplies the stove and refrigerator, but no other "furniture." Does this make the place "furnished"? We don't think so—though the statute is not clear on this. If the landlord provides basic furniture (beds, tables, etc.), obviously it is furnished and she is legitimately entitled to a higher deposit because the potential for damage is high. But, in our opinion, she is not exposed to that much risk of loss if she provides only the stove and refrigerator, and therefore should be allowed to require a deposit of up to two months' rent only. Also, in the rental business, "furnished" is usually taken to mean the inclusion of all basic furniture.

Subsection (c) of Civil Code Section 1950.5 also says: "This subdivision does not preclude a landlord and a tenant from entering into a mutual agreement for the landlord, at the request of the tenant and for a specified fee or charge, to make structural, decorative, furnishing, or other similar alterations, if the alterations are other than cleaning or repairing for which the landlord may charge the previous tenant as provided by subdivision (e)." The intent of this provision is clearly to allow the landlord to require compensation for strange or unusual alterations requested by the tenant. This, of course, is reasonable. However, there is a danger that some landlords may improperly try to reintroduce all sorts of extra or nonrefundable fees under this exception to the basic deposit rules. Be awake to this possibility!

If the landlord is forced to use some of the security deposit during your tenancy (e.g., because you broke something and didn't fix it or pay for it), he may require you to replenish the security deposit.

Example: Millie the tenant pays Maury the Landlord a $700 security deposit. Millie goes on vacation, leaving the water running. By the time Maury is notified, the overflow has damaged the paint on the ceiling below. Maury repaints the ceiling at a cost of $350, taking the money out of the security deposit. Maury is entitled to ask Millie to replace that money.

Note on Paying Installments: The landlord may let you pay a hefty deposit in installments over three months or so. If you miss a scheduled payment, the landlord can evict you for breaching the lease or rental agreement.

B. Deposit Cannot Be Made "Non-Refundable"

No lease or rental agreement may call any deposit "non-refundable." Civil Code § 1950.5(l). Nor may a landlord escape this rule that all security deposits are refundable by demanding a "cleaning" or "security" or "pet" "fee" instead of a deposit. Under the law, the security deposit rules we discuss here apply to any "payment, fee, deposit, or charge." Civil Code § 1950.5(b).

For example, a San Francisco apartment complex charged tenants a $65 move-in fee and a $50 transfer fee if they moved from one apartment to another within the complex. A court ruled that the fees were "deposits" under the law, and because they weren't used for the purposes allowed by law, they had to be refunded to the tenants.[1]

---

[1]*People v. Parkmerced Co.* (1988), 244 Cal. Rptr. 22, 198 Cal. App. 3d 683.

C. What the Deposits May Be Used For

Civil Code Section 1950.5(e) says that the deposit may be used by the landlord "in only those amounts as may be reasonably necessary" to do the following four things *only:*

1. To remedy defaults in payment of rent;

2. To repair damage to the premises caused by the tenant (except for "ordinary wear and tear");

3. To clean the premises, if necessary, when the tenant leaves.

4. If the rental agreement allows it, to pay for the tenant's failure to restore or replace personal property.

One of the biggest sources of tenant-landlord dispute centers around the often vague language in leases and rental agreements regarding cleaning. For example, some provisions merely say "Cleaning deposit: $200," and nothing else in the agreement says anything about cleaning. How clean must the tenant leave the premises when he vacates? As clean as they were when the tenant moved in? "Perfectly" clean? "Reasonably" clean? May the tenant merely sweep the floor, or must the floor also be washed and waxed? Must the freezer be defrosted and the oven be cleaned? The words "cleaning deposit" do not answer any of these questions; nor does the vague language of Civil Code Section 1950.5(e) that allows the deposit to be used for such cleaning as is "reasonably necessary."

The unhappy result of all this vagueness is that there is often an argument about cleaning when a tenant moves out. The best way to avoid such a fight is to spell out clearly what you both mean by "cleaning" right in the lease or rental agreement. You and your landlord don't have to use any fancy legal language—just state exactly what you both expect to be done.

If you are stuck with an agreement which has unclear language and you want to be sure to get your deposit back, we advise that you do two things:

• Clean the place thoroughly. This doesn't normally mean you have to shampoo rugs, dry clean the drapes, or wash the ceiling. A good thorough cleaning, including the refrigerator, stove, bathroom fixtures, etc. should be adequate;

• Carefully document your cleaning work through pictures, witnesses, etc. (see Section H, below).

Also you should know that Civil Code Section 1654[2] states that where an agreement is unclear, it is interpreted most strongly against the party who caused the uncertainty to exist. Therefore, if the landlord wrote the language or provided the lease form, the language will be construed against her. "Cleaning deposit," therefore, should be interpreted to mean that the tenant would not have to do any extraordinary cleaning.

Another area of landlord-tenant disputes over the return of deposits has to do with damages to the premises. Some landlords try to charge tenants for everything from a worn spot on a hall rug to faded paint to missing light bulbs. The tenant is not responsible for any damage or wear and tear done to the premises by an earlier tenant. Civil Code § 1950.5(e).

---

[2]Civil Code Section 1442 might also help you. This statute says that any provision creating a forfeiture is interpreted most strongly against the person who would benefit from it.

D. Landlord's Duty to Return Deposit

Within two weeks after you move out, the landlord must do one of two things:

1. Return all of your deposit, or

2. Give you personally or by first-class mail, an "itemized statement"—in writing—saying why he is retaining part or all of the deposit, and return any remaining part to the tenant. Civil Code § 1950.5(f).

The bad faith retention of a security deposit, or any portion thereof, may subject the landlord to $200 punitive damages in addition to any actual damages. In addition, for rental agreements entered into or renewed on or after January 1, 1987, the tenant is entitled to 2% monthly interest on the unreturned balance of the deposit.

Suppose the landlord has the right to keep part of the deposit (e.g., because you broke something), but fails to furnish the itemized statement in two weeks. Does he lose the right to keep that part? Maybe he should, but you might not be able to collect it. If you were to sue the landlord for return of the money he kept, he might simply cross-complain (sue you back) for the same amount for the damage you caused—"offsetting" your claim by the same amount. Whether the court would award you the money, however, on the ground that allowing the landlord to cross-complain in this way would make the itemization requirement unenforceable, is subject to question.

E. Effect of Sale of Premises on Security Deposits

If the landlord sells the building, she is supposed to do one of two things: return the deposit to the tenant, or transfer it to the new owner. Civil Code § 1950.5(g).

It's been known to happen, however, that the landlord does neither—she simply walks off with the money! The tenant often never knows of this. In fact, usually the tenant doesn't even know the building was sold until sometime later.

Obviously, there is not much the tenant can do to prevent this, but the new owner can easily stop it. All he has to do is to require, as a condition to buying the property, that all security deposits be transferred to the new owner at the time of sale. The new owner should do this, as he is the one who needs the security deposit to protect against the damage or rent loss which might occur when the tenants later move out.

For these reasons, the law requires the new owner to make sure that he gets all security deposits from the old landlord. Whether he does so or not, he becomes responsible for returning the security deposit to the tenant at the end of the tenancy, just as if he were the old landlord. Civil Code § 1950.5(h). Also, the new owner cannot require the tenant to replace any security deposit kept by the old landlord. Civil Code § 1950.5(h).

F. May the Landlord Increase the Security Deposit?

Tenants often ask if it's legal for a landlord to raise their security deposits after they move in. The answer is that it depends on the situation.

• If you have a fixed-term lease (e.g., a lease for a year), the landlord may not raise the security deposit during that year unless the lease allows this.

• If you live in a city which has rent control, your ordinance probably restricts increases in security deposits while you remain a tenant of a particular landlord.

• If the security deposit and other fees already add up to twice the monthly rent (if the place is unfurnished) or three times the monthly rent (if the place is furnished), the security deposit may not be increased.

• If none of these three things applies, then the landlord may force you to pay more into the security deposit—if she does it right. To legally raise a deposit, she must give you at least 30 days' written notice of the increase and she must have it properly "served" on you. This means that she must try to have it handed to you at your residence or place of work; a notice served by mail alone is not legal unless you voluntarily go along with it. Civil Code § 827; Code of Civil Procedure § 1162. See Chapter 4 regarding the law on how the landlord may change terms of a tenancy.

G. Try to Cooperate With the Landlord to Avoid Deposit Problems

Problems involving security deposits often arise like this:

• The tenant moves out,

• The landlord keeps all or part of the deposit on the ground of damage or lack of cleaning,

• The tenant says that the place was left in good condition.

If the dispute isn't compromised, the tenant will probably sue the landlord for the money withheld, leaving it up to the judge to decide who is telling the truth. For both sides, this is a pretty risky, messy, and time-consuming way of handling things.

The best way to try to prevent this from happening is to arrange to meet with the landlord or manager after you've moved out your belongings and cleaned up, and just before you return the key. Tour the apartment together and check for any damage, dirt, etc. Assuming you made out a list of damage already there when you moved in (see "Self Protection When Moving In," in Chapter 2), pull it out now and check it against the present condition of the place. Try to work out any disputes on the spot, and ask the landlord to give you the security deposit before you leave. Be reasonable, and be willing to compromise. It is better to give up a few dollars for some questionable damage than to have to sue for the whole deposit later.

If you cannot get the landlord to meet with you when you leave, then make your own tour. Bring at least one witness (a person who helped clean often makes a very convincing one) take some photos, and keep all your receipts for cleaning and repair materials, so you will be ready to prove your case if you later have to sue in Small Claims Court to get your deposit back. (Remember, after you're out, it is usually too late to come back to take pictures.)

H. If the Landlord Won't Return Your Deposit

Let's assume now that two weeks have passed since the day you moved out and you have received neither the return of your deposit nor an itemization as to what it was used for. After you get over being mad, it's time to take action. We suggest the following step-by-step approach:

Step 1. Make a Formal Demand

If you feel that your landlord has improperly kept your deposit, the first thing you should do is ask for it, in writing. Here is a sample demand letter:

1504 Oak Street #2
Cloverdale, CA
October 15, 19__

Smith Realty Co.
10 Jones Street
Cloverdale, CA

As you know, until September 30, 19__, I resided in Apartment #4 at 1500 Acorn Street and regularly paid my rent to your office. When I moved out, I left the unit cleaner than it was when I moved in.

As of today, I have received neither my $400 security deposit, nor have I received any accounting from you for that money. Please be aware that I know about my rights under California Civil Code Sec. 1950.5, and that if I do not receive my money within the next week, I will regard the retention of these deposits as showing bad faith on your part and shall sue you not only for the $400 in deposits, but also for the $200 punitive damages allowed by Sec. 1950.5 of the California Civil Code.

May I hear from you promptly.

Very truly yours,

_____

Patricia Parker

Step 2. Consider Compromise

If the landlord offers to meet you or offers a compromise settlement, try to meet him half way, but don't go overboard. After all, the law requiring that your deposits be returned if you leave a rental property clean and undamaged is there to protect you. You might suggest that the dispute be mediated. Many cities, counties and nonprofit organizations such as San Francisco's Community Boards offer landlord-tenant mediation services designed to help you and the landlord arrive at a mutually satisfactory settlement.

Step 3. Sue In Small Claims Court

If the formal demand doesn't work and there is no reasonable prospect of compromise, you should consider suing the landlord. If you rent under a lease or rental agreement which provides for the landlord's attorney's fees, then you, too, are entitled to attorney's fees if you win your lawsuit. Civil Code § 1717. In such situations, you might ask an attorney to handle the matter for you. Be sure you thoroughly discuss her fee arrangements ahead of time, however.

In most cases, however, deposit disputes should probably be brought in Small Claims Court, where lawyers aren't allowed. The rules governing Small Claims proceedings are contained in the California Code of Civil Procedure, Section 116, et seq. The cost for filing papers and serving the landlord will be modest. The best source of information on how to prepare and present a Small Claims Court case and collect money if you win is *Everybody's Guide to Small Claims Court*, Warner (Nolo Press), which devotes a chapter to discussion of how to prepare and present a landlord-tenant deposit case.

To sue your landlord in Small Claims Court, go to your local courthouse (there may be more than one, so call first to make sure you go to the right place) and find the Clerk of the Small Claims Court. The Clerk is required by law to help you fill out the papers necessary to sue your landlord. On the court form, you must state how much you are claiming the landlord owes you. This amount cannot exceed $2,000. You figure the amount you want to claim by asking for the total deposit, less anything that should reasonably be withheld for unpaid rent, damage, or dirty conditions. Add $200 in "punitive damages" (and interest at 2% per month on the uncollected balance starting from 14 days after you moved out) if you believe the landlord's failure to return your deposit (or reasonably itemize expenses) constitutes bad faith. If this adds up to more than $2,000, then you either have to waive the excess over $2,000 or else not use the Small Claims Court. If you have to decide whether to do this or sue in regular Municipal Court for an amount more than $2,000, consider that you may not easily win the full $200 in punitive damages.

If your rental agreement is oral, you must file your lawsuit against the landlord within two years after the two weeks (for the landlord to return your deposit) run out. Code of Civil Procedure § 337. However, in either instance, we advise you not to wait, but to file promptly. Judges are just not very sympathetic to old disputes.

After you file the form with the Small Claims Clerk, he will normally send a copy of it to the landlord by certified mail, with an order for her to appear in Court for a trial on the suit at a certain date and time. To find out that date and time, ask the Clerk. That date must be not less than 10 nor more than 40 days after the date of the order to appear, if the landlord lives within the county. If she doesn't live in the county, the date must be not less than 30 nor more than 70 days after the date of the order to appear (Code of Civil Procedure § 116.4). If the landlord does not sign for the certified mail notice, you will have to arrange for a new court date and arrange to have the papers served by personal service.

Small Claims Court trials are very informal. No lawyers are present and there are no formal rules of evidence. There is no jury. When you come to court for your hearing, bring the file or envelope with your records. All papers or pictures that you believe help your case should be included. Also bring with you all witnesses who have first-hand information about the facts in dispute. If you do not have any experience with a court, you can go down a day or two before and watch a few cases. You will see that it is a very simple procedure.

If you cannot speak English and cannot find a volunteer interpreter or afford to hire an interpreter, the court will probably be able to arrange for a volunteer for you. Call the clerk about this in advance.

On the day your case is to be heard, get to the court a little early and check for your courtroom (referred to as a "department"). Tell the clerk or bailiff that you are present and sit down and wait until your case is called. When your turn comes, stand at the large table at the front of the room and tell the judge clearly what is in dispute. Remember, the judge hears many cases every day, and she will not be particularly excited by yours. If you are long-winded, she may stop listening and start thinking about what she is going to eat for lunch.

Start your presentation with the problem (e.g., "Lester Landlord has failed to return to me $500 in security deposits in the six weeks since I moved out of his house at 222 Spring Street") and then present the directly relevant facts which explain why you should win (e.g., "The house was clean, undamaged, and my rent was paid in full"). Again, be brief and to the point—don't ramble. You may show pictures and documents to the judge. When you are done with your oral presentation, tell the judge you have witnesses who want to testify.

The landlord will also have a chance to tell his side. You can expect it to be very different from yours, but stay cool! When he is done, you may ask him questions if you feel that he has not told the truth or if he has left some things out. But often asking the landlord a lot of vague questions just gives him more opportunity to tell his side of the case. It is especially important not to argue with the landlord or any of his witnesses—just get your facts out, and back them up with convincing evidence.

Example: In a case where a landlord has not returned your cleaning deposit after you have moved out and asked for it, you might present your case something like this:

"Good morning, Your Honor. My name is John Smith and I now live at 2330 Jones Street. From January 1, 19__ until July 1, 19__, I lived at 1500 Williams Street in a building owned by the Jefferson Realty Company. When I moved out, the Realty Company refused to refund my $700 cleaning deposit even though I left the place spotless. I carefully cleaned the rugs, washed and waxed the kitchen and bathroom floors, washed the inside of the cupboards and washed the windows. Your Honor, I want to show you some pictures that were taken of my apartment the day I moved out. (If you completed a checklist of the condition of the premises, you will want to show it to the judge at this time.) These were taken by Mrs. Edna Jackson, who is here today and will testify. Your Honor, I don't have much else to say, except that in addition to the amount of my deposit, I am asking for the full $200 in punitive damages allowed by law. I am entitled to these damages because I don't believe the landlord had any reason at all to withhold my deposits." (If you have any evidence that the landlord commonly withholds deposits with no good reason, be sure to introduce it.) You would then ask your witness to testify.

In most courts, your witnesses do not take the witness stand, but remain at the table in front of the judge and simply explain what they know about the dispute. Typical testimony might go like this:

"Good morning, Your Honor. My name is Mrs. Edna Jackson and I live at 1498 Williams Street. On January 1, 19__ when the plaintiff moved out, I helped him move and clean up. The place was very clean when we finished. And just to show how clean it was, I took the pictures that you were just shown. I'm sure those are the pictures I took because I signed and dated them on the back after they were developed."

Punitive Damages Note: If the landlord acts in "bad faith" and does not return the money or properly account for any part that he keeps, he may be liable for up to $200 in punitive damages over and beyond the amount of the deposits unjustly retained. As noted, Small Claims Courts may award these punitive damages. Civil Code § 1950.5(m). However, many tenants who have been through Small Claims Court have told us that an award of all, or a part, of the punitive damage amount is extremely rare because judges tend to be biased in favor of landlords. How can you counter this bias where it exists? The best way to do it is to thoroughly prepare your case and document that the landlord's failure to return your deposits within 14 days was not only a mistake, but was without any reasonable basis in fact. In addition, "bad faith" might also be shown by proof that the landlord has a practice of failing to return security deposits. This can often be done with the assistance of your local tenants' organization.

If you win in small claims court and need help collecting the money from the landlord, see *Collect Your Court Judgment* (Nolo Press).

Step 4. Call the District Attorney

If your landlord has a habit of refusing to return security deposits to tenants, your local district attorney might bring a criminal action against him for fines and an injunction. *People v. Sangiacomo* (1982) 129 Cal. App. 3d 364.

I. Rent Withholding as a Way to Get Deposits Back In Advance

Suppose, after you move in, you learn from other tenants that your landlord has a tendency to cheat tenants out of their security deposits—perhaps by inventing or exaggerating a need for repairs or cleaning after they move out. When you decide to leave, you fear the same sort of trouble, and you'd rather not deal with the risk and hassle of suing the landlord in Small Claims Court.

There is a way to handle this problem that many tenants use: a month or two before you leave, tell the landlord that you are not making your usual rent payment, and she should keep your deposit and apply it to the rent.

Your letter might look like this:

1500 Acorn Street #4
Cloverdale, CA
October 15, 19__

Smith Realty Co.
10 Jones Street
Cloverdale, CA

Dear Sirs:

As you know, I occupy Apartment #4 at 1500 Acorn Street and regularly pay rent to your office once a month.

Please take note that this is a formal written notice of my intention to vacate Apartment 34 on May 1, 19__.

In speaking to other tenants in this area, I have learned that from time to time the return of cleaning deposits has been the subject of dispute between you and your tenants. Accordingly, I have decided on the following course of action: Instead of sending you the normal $500 rent payment today, I am sending you instead $200 and ask that you apply the $300 cleaning deposit to my last month's rent.

I will leave the apartment spotless and undamaged so that you will suffer no damage whatsoever. If you should doubt this or want to discuss the matter further, please give me a call and come over. I think that you will be satisfied that I am dealing with you honestly and in good faith and that the apartment, which is clean and in perfect repair now, will be in the same condition when I leave.

Very truly yours,

_____

Patricia Parker

Technically, this type of "rent withholding" is not legal. You have no legal right to compel the landlord to apply your deposit to unpaid rent, and if you do not pay your rent on time, he can serve you with a "3-day notice" (ordering you to pay the rent or get out, in 3 days). If you do not comply with such a notice, however, it is very unlikely that the landlord will follow it up with a suit to evict you for non-payment of rent. (He cannot simply lock you out.) It would probably take him at least a few weeks to bring his case to trial, and he knows you plan to leave soon anyway.

Nevertheless, we do not recommend that you use this "rent withholding" device against a landlord unless you are pretty sure that she is the type that cheats on security deposits. The fair landlord has a legitimate right and need to get the rent on time and to keep the security deposit until she is sure that the tenant has left the place in good shape.

J. Interest on Security Deposits

As a matter of fairness, the landlord should pay you interest on your security deposit. It is your money—not his—and he is merely holding it for you. He should put it into some type of interest-bearing account and pay the interest to you.

None of the form leases and rental agreements customarily used by landlords require them to pay interest on your security deposit. In fact, the only forms we know of which require this are the Model Lease and Model Rental Agreement in the Appendix at the back of this book.

A few local rent ordinances, including those of Berkeley, Santa Monica and San Francisco, require payment of interest on security deposits.

No state law clearly says that landlords must pay interest on security deposits. But the Legislature has enacted statutes imposing such obligations on trustees—people who hold money for someone else. And the courts have held that a landlord acts as a trustee when she holds a tenant's security deposit, and the landlord cannot put it to her own use. *Ingram v. Pantages* (1927) 86 Cal. App. 41; *City Investment Co. v. Pringle* (1925) 73 Cal. App. 782, 788-789. See also Legislative Counsel Opinion #4187 (3/3/75, to Senator Petris). A trustee must invest trust funds and pay any interest or profits over to the owner of the money. Civil Code §§ 2237, 2261, 2262. Therefore, it appears to us that the law presently requires landlords to pay interest on security deposits. Unfortunately, the only court to rule on this question disagreed, concluding that landlords do not have to pay interest on deposits unless the rental agreement (or local law) says they do. The court based its decision on the fact that the legislature has repeatedly refused to pass a law requiring landlords to pay interest on deposits. *Korens v. R.W. Zukin Corp.*, (1989) 261 Cal. Rptr. 137.

Note: As discussed in Section H, Step 3, a landlord who illegally withholds all or part of your deposit after you leave is liable for interest on the withheld portion at the rate of 2% per month. Civil Code § 1950.5(k).

K. Last Month's Rent

Many landlords require some payment for "last month's rent." The legal effect of such a requirement should depend largely upon the exact language used in the lease or rental agreement.

If the lease or rental agreement says, "security for last month's rent," or has a heading called "Security" and then lists "last month's rent" as one of the items on the list, then you have not actually paid the last month's rent, but just provided security for it. So, if the landlord legally raises the rent before you move out, you must pay the difference between the final rent and your security for last month's rent. For example, suppose when you moved in the monthly rent was $400, and the rental agreement said, "Security: . . . last month's rent: $400." After two years, the rent has been raised to $500, and the tenant leaves. The tenant owes the landlord the $100 difference for the last month's rent.

If, however, the lease or rental agreement does not say that the payment is for security, but simply says "last month's rent: $400," then in our opinion, the tenant has paid the last month's rent—well in advance of the last month. This money is not a security payment, and the landlord can do what he likes with it. He does not hold it as a trustee for the tenant. However, a rent increase later on will not affect the amount of the last month's rent, which the tenant has already paid. So, in the above example, the tenant would not owe an additional $100 to the landlord.

Despite this common sense approach, some judges are inclined to rule that the tenant must pay the extra $100. If the rental agreement is unclear as to whether this payment is intended as "security," point out to the judge that since the landlord provided the form agreement, it should be interpreted against him. Civil Code § 1654.

Chapter 11:

Evictions

Many tenants become terrified when they receive a Three-Day Notice to Pay Rent or Quit from the landlord. They believe that if they do not pay or get out in three days, they will be thrown out onto the street on the fourth. The law simply does not allow this. The landlord must first file a lawsuit in court and notify you of it so that you have an opportunity to defend yourself. Even if you lose the lawsuit, the court must still issue an order authorizing a law enforcement officer to remove you from the premises. All of this takes time, often more than a month, and sometimes much more.

This chapter will help you go to court and defend yourself if you choose to do so. It will also help you understand what your lawyer is doing, if you choose to hire one.

The material set out here is by no means a complete summary of every defense or litigation device available to a tenant. To give you that would make this volume look like a metropolitan phone book. Instead, we concentrate on the basic and most commonly-used tools suitable for use in defending against most straightforward eviction proceedings. If the unexpected crops up in the course of the case, you can supplement this information by consulting the *California Eviction Defense Manual*, and the *California Residential Landlord-Tenant Practice Book*, both of which are published by C.E.B. (Continuing Education of the Bar). You should be able to find them in your county law library. Be sure you consult the latest *Supplements* to these books, to discover recent cases and statutes.[1]

Citation Note: In this chapter, we make frequent references to statutes found in the California Code of Civil Procedure. From now on, we often use the standard abbreviation "C.C.P."

---

[1] The *California Eviction Defense Manual* is the source most often used by lawyers when defending unlawful detainer cases. Unlike many law books, it is not difficult to use.

A. 'Self-Help' Evictions Are Illegal

The most basic thing a tenant should know is that California law clearly states that if a landlord wishes to evict her tenant, she must first go to court, giving the tenant prior notice of the court proceedings. She cannot legally take the law into her own hands by locking the tenant out, taking the tenant's belongings, taking off doors and windows, cutting off the utilities, or any other kind of harassment.

1. Utility Cut-Offs

California Civil Code Section 789.3 says that any landlord who causes any utility service (including water, heat, light, electricity, gas, telephone, elevator, or refrigeration) to be cut off with intent to terminate a tenant's occupancy is liable to the tenant for certain damages. This section applies whether the utilities are paid for by the landlord or the tenant, and whether the landlord cuts off the utilities directly "or indirectly" (e.g., by not paying the utility bills). The tenant may sue the landlord and recover the following damages:

• Actual (out-of-pocket) damages. This includes such things as meat spoiling in the refrigerator after the electricity was turned off, or, if the tenant has to find a temporary place to live because the utilities were turned off, motel bills;

• "Punitive" damages of up to $100 for each day or part thereof that a utility was turned off (but not less than $250 in punitive damages for each separate violation);

• A reasonable attorney fee (if the tenant wins the suit);

• A court order compelling the landlord to turn on the utilities.

You can bring your suit in Small Claims Court (for up to $2,000), or retain a lawyer to sue for you in Municipal Court (for up to $25,000), or Superior Court (over $25,000).

If you live in a rent control city, you may win even more from a landlord who tries to force tenants out by illegal methods. In 1988, 23 tenants of a San Francisco residential hotel won $4.5 million from their landlord. The landlord had cut off water, entered tenants' rooms without notice, and threatened the tenants, most of whom were elderly or disabled. (*Balmoral Tenants Association v. Lee*, San Franciso Superior Ct. No. 864398.)

2. Lock-Outs

If the landlord locks you out, removes outside doors or windows, or removes your personal property from your home with the intention of terminating your tenancy, he is in violation of Civil Code Section 789.3. The damages are the same as set out above for utility cut-offs. You can collect damages in Small Claims Court, but if you want quick action to get back into your home, see a lawyer, as the statute allows you to collect her fees. The lawyer might also sue the landlord for "forcible entry and detainer." C.C.P. Section 1159; *Jordan v. Talbot* (1961) 55 Cal. 2d 597.

You might also call the police or district attorney, since these acts are crimes (forcible entry, malicious mischief, and unauthorized entry). Even if the police won't arrest the landlord, they might persuade him to let you in. Ask them to write a report on the incident, as this might help you in a later lawsuit against the landlord.

Tenants who live in "residential hotels" (apartment buildings which are called "hotels") are also protected against lock-outs. Code of Civil Procedure Section 1159; Civil Code Section 1940.

B. Overview of Eviction Procedure

The rest of this chapter, which deals with how you can defend against a formal unlawful detainer (eviction) procedure, is pretty technical and complicated. For this reason, we believe it will help you to carefully read this overview of the eviction process first. In addition, if you live in a rent-control city listed in Chapter 2 that provides for just cause evictions, or that at least requires the landlord to petition for unit increases that exceed the amount allowed by the ordinance, it is essential that you get and study a copy of your local ordinance and regulations from your rent control board. Although we can and will remind you of the many special rights residents in cities covered by rent control enjoy when it comes to defending against eviction, it is impossible for us to deal with each city's ordinance in detail.

When you read this chapter, we urge you to keep two broad and related points in mind. The first is that time limits in eviction cases are very short. For example, the time normally given for a person being sued to respond is 30 days. In eviction cases, it's five.

The second crucial point is that in the majority of eviction cases (except possibly those in some rent-control areas), the tenant ultimately ends up moving.[2] The big question, therefore, is

---

[2]Of course, there are many exceptions to this general statement, including situations in which a landlord's attempt to evict a tenant is in retaliation for a tenant's lawful rent withholding because her unit is uninhabitable or because a tenant made a legitimate complaint to a public agency.

often not whether you will have to move, but rather, how long you can remain. The answer to this question depends heavily on whether you contest the eviction or let the law take its course (e.g., allow the landlord to obtain a default judgment). We provide a chart at the end of this section to give you some idea of how long different types of eviction cases normally take.

Now let's turn to the overview.

1. The Landlord's Notice to Quit

A landlord who wants to get you out must properly serve you with a notice and wait until the notice period expires before filing an eviction lawsuit (unless you have a fixed-term lease which has expired, in which case no notice is required unless the lease itself provides for it). For an eviction based on an alleged breach of your lease or rental agreement, the notice must give you three days to perform (e.g., pay the rent or get rid of the dog). To terminate a month-to-month tenancy, the notice need only give you 30 days to vacate, unless you live in an area which requires a just cause for eviction, in which case the just cause must also be stated. Some local rent control ordinances also require landlords to include other things — for example, the phone number of the Rent Board — in the notice.

2. Filing and Service of Summons and Complaint

If you have not met the landlord's demand when the notice period runs out, he may file a "Complaint" against you in court.[3] He will then have a copy of the Complaint served on you, together with a Summons. The Summons will tell you to respond in writing within five days.

3. Response

If you don't respond in writing to the landlord's complaint, the landlord may enter a default judgment against you, which means you lose without a trial.[4]

Your first response may be:

• A *Motion to Quash Service of Summons*—if the Summons was not properly served on you, or the wrong court is named, or for certain other technical reasons;

• A *Demurrer*—if the Complaint is not in proper technical form or does not properly allege the landlord's right to evict you; or

• An *Answer*—to deny statements in the Complaint or allege new facts showing why you should win.

---

[3]Here, we are assuming that the complaint is filed in regular Municipal Court, as the great majority are, rather than Small Claims Court, which is discussed in Section I below.

[4]The five-day period to respond is extended to 15 days when you are served by substitute service. C.C.P. 415.20(b). We discuss substitute service in Section E(2) below.

These responses (called "responsive pleadings") are not mutually exclusive. So your response may be a Motion to Quash Service of Summons, then a Demurrer, and then an Answer, depending on the court's rulings. Or, you may simply file an Answer as your response.

4. Trial

After the Answer is filed, the case will either be decided summarily by a judge or go to trial. The trial (assuming it isn't settled first) will be heard by a judge, unless either side demands a jury.

5. Actual Eviction

If you lose the trial, the judge may, in rare circumstances, allow you to stay on if you pay everything you owe the landlord. If this relief is denied (and it will be most of the time), the landlord will get a "Writ of Restitution," which the sheriff (or marshal or constable) will serve on you. This will give you five days to leave. If you are not out on the fifth day, the sheriff will physically throw you out, unless a court grants a temporary stay of the eviction to give you a few extra days to move.

You may also appeal the trial court's rulings, on the theory that the court made some error of law. Your eviction will be stayed during the appeal if you can establish that a delay will cause hardship to yourself but won't irreparably harm the landlord. During any "stay," you will have to pay reasonable rent.

Note on Bankruptcy: If the tenant files for bankruptcy, the landlord must stop all attempts to recover premises from the tenant. The landlord, however, can almost always go to the bankruptcy court and get permission to proceed again within a week or two. Some non-lawyer eviction defense organizations (operating primarily in the Los Angeles area) routinely help tenants file for bankruptcy as a means of buying a little more time to find new premises. While the extra time may seem like a minor miracle at the time, we recommend against filing for bankruptcy solely to stave off an eviction. It can hurt your credit rating and may cause you to lose property you wanted to hang onto. However, if other reasons justify filing for bankruptcy, stopping an eviction may be a beneficial side effect.

6. Timeline For Eviction

How long does this entire process take? Of course, it varies from case to case. It's rare to talk to a lawyer experienced in defending eviction cases who can't tell you a story about how he or she brilliantly created a paper blizzard and staved off an eviction for many months. On the other hand, an eviction can occur in a blindingly short period of time if the landlord does everything right and you do nothing.

Nevertheless, the time estimates we set out here should prove broadly accurate, assuming the following facts:

• You have received a 30-day notice;

• The Summons and Complaint are personally served on you;

• You contest the action;

• You employ the devices and follow the procedures mentioned in the timeline;

• All papers (after the Summons and Complaint) are served by mail where this is permitted (the usual practice); and

• The landlord (or her attorney) stays on top of her case and files all papers as fast as possible.

Eviction may occur a few days earlier if the landlord:

• Personally serves all papers on you instead of mailing them; or

• Proceeds by "summary judgment" rather than trial.

Conversely, the timeline will be longer if the landlord (or her attorney) lets time slip by between any of the procedural steps necessary to move an eviction case to final judgment and actual eviction. In our experience, this almost always happens, so you are probably safe in adding a week or two to our estimates.

Because the primary elements of a basic eviction suit are discussed in detail later on in this chapter, we suggest you look at the timeline for a general idea now, and then review it after you have had more time to study the actual process.

Eviction Timeline

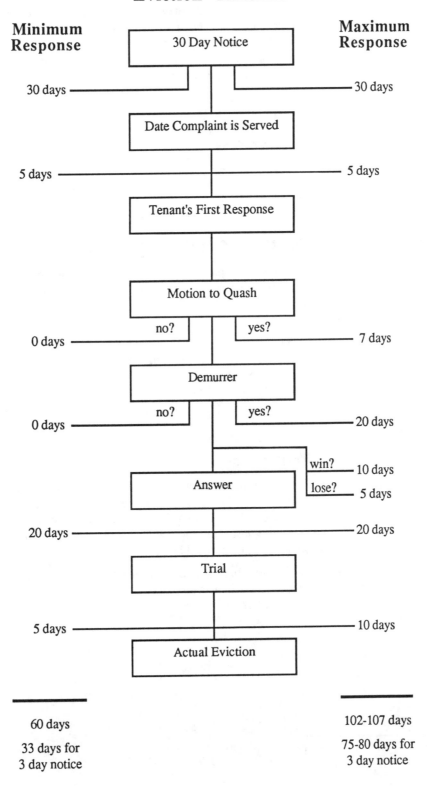

Minimum Response

30 days

5 days

0 days

0 days

20 days

5 days

60 days

33 days for
3 day notice

Maximum Response

30 Day Notice

Date Complaint is Served

Tenant's First Response

Motion to Quash

no?   yes?

Demurrer

no?   yes?

Answer

win?
lose?

Trial

Actual Eviction

30 days

5 days

7 days

20 days

10 days

5 days

20 days

10 days

102-107 days

75-80 days for
3 day notice

Again, as we've suggested, it is rare that a landlord's case marches along without one snag or another, many of them caused either by the landlord's attorney's schedule, courthouse delays, or the sheriff's backload of papers to serve. Practically speaking, if you added two (and sometimes as much as four) weeks to the timeline, you would have a better picture of how long the typical contested eviction takes. On the other hand, if you fail to take one of the steps indicated in the timeline, or you lose on your Motion to Quash or Demurrer, you should deduct the appropriate number of days.

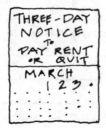

C. Notice Requirements to Legally End a Tenancy

Now that you have an overview of the eviction process, it's time to deal with the specifics. We start with the paper the landlord uses to notify you to leave. This will either be a three-day or 30-day notice and is commonly referred to as a "Notice to Quit."

One very important principle applies to all notice requirements in eviction cases: because the landlord is trying to evict you from your home, and because the law gives the landlord special privileges in eviction cases (a quicker lawsuit), the landlord must *strictly comply* with all of the law's notice requirements.[5] This means, for example, that if the landlord makes even a small mistake in a required notice, the eviction itself might be invalid and the landlord may have to start the process over.

1. Notice to End a Fixed-Term Lease

When a fixed-term lease expires, you are supposed to move out right away (unless your city has a rent-control ordinance which requires the landlord to have "just cause" to evict you). If you don't move, the landlord may file her eviction lawsuit immediately, without first serving any notice on you. In a rent-control city requiring just cause for eviction, the landlord must serve you with a notice stating one of the causes for eviction allowed by the ordinance.

If she wants to evict you during the term of your lease for your breach of the lease (such as nonpayment of rent), then she will have to serve a notice on you before suing to evict. The notice is normally a three-day notice to perform or vacate (see below).

---

[5]*Kwok v. Bergren* (1982) 130 Cal.App. 3d 596, 599.

2. The Three-Day Notice to End a Lease or Rental Agreement Because of a Tenant's Violation

You can properly be served with a three-day notice if your landlord claims you have violated the terms of your lease or rental agreement. Specifically, this means:

• If you fail to pay your rent on time, the landlord must serve a three-day notice on you before he may sue to evict you on that ground. The notice must tell you to pay the rent or move in three days. The notice must state the amount of rent you must pay to avoid eviction, and this amount may not be more than what you actually owe (the notice can ask for less than what you owe, but not more). Some judges also require landlords to include the dates for which the rent is due. Because rent is almost always due at the beginning of a month (or other rent period), the landlord is entitled to request the total rent for the period for which rent is late, less any partial payments you have made. Thus, if your $350 rent is due on the first of the month, the landlord has the right to ask you in a three-day notice for the entire $350 on the 2nd. C.C.P. Section 1161(2); *Werner v. Sargeant* (1953) 121 Cal.App. 2d 833. As stated, the notice must give you the choice of paying the rent before the end of the three days; if you pay, the notice is cancelled and you don't have to leave. C.C.P. 1161(3). After three days, the landlord may refuse your money and proceed with the eviction. If he accepts the rent after the three-day period, however, he waives his right to evict for the late payment. *EDC Associates Ltd. v. Gutierrez,* 153 Cal. App. 3d 169 (1984).

• If you are accused of violating some other provision of your lease or rental agreement, the three-day notice must tell you to stop the conduct if it's curable. For example, suppose the landlord believes that you have a dog, in violation of a lease provision which prohibits pets. The notice must say (in effect), "Either get rid of the dog in three days *or* move out in three days." In all cases, the violation of the lease or rental agreement must be substantial, not minor, in order to justify evicting you from your home.[6]

• If the landlord believes that you are committing "waste" (i.e., wrecking the place) creating a "nuisance" on the premises (e.g., dumping garbage in the backyard), or using it for an illegal purpose (e.g., to sell illegal drugs), she must serve you with a three-day notice to vacate, but in this situation, the notice need not give you the alternative of stopping your misbehavior. Code of Civil Procedure Section 1161(4).

a. Service Requirements For a Notice to Quit

To be effective, the three-day notice must be properly "served" on you. First, the landlord (or his agent) must try to find you and hand it to you. If he tries to find you at home and at work but can't, he may then hand it to someone else on your premises and also mail a copy to you. If he can't find someone on the premises to leave it with, then—and only then—he may serve it on you by the "nail and mail" method. This involves posting a copy in a conspicuous place on your premises and mailing another to you. Code of Civil Procedure Section 1162.

Landlords are often sloppy about following these procedures. It is common, for example, for a landlord to make one attempt to find the tenant at home, no attempt to find the tenant at work, and then simply nail the notice to the tenant's door and mail a copy. This is not proper service.

Sloppy landlords often fall back on a legal doctrine which states that actual receipt of an improperly served notice by the tenant "cures" any defect in service. This means that if a tenant

---

[6]*McNeece v. Wood* (1928) 204 Cal. 280, 285.

actually receives the notice, it does not matter that the landlord did not serve it in the manner required by law. Thus, if the case later goes to court, the landlord can prove you received the notice by calling you to the witness stand and asking you. For this reason, it is usually unwise for a tenant to rely on a landlord's faulty service of notice as a defense when actual notice was received.

b. Counting the Three Days After Service

As mentioned, you have three full days to comply with the demands in a three-day notice. If you do comply, then the landlord may not sue to evict you. If you don't, then he may file his lawsuit on the fourth day (or later).

To correctly count the three days, do the following:

• Ignore the date of service and start counting on the next day;

• Count three days;

• If the third day falls on a "holiday," ignore that day and move on to the next business day. A holiday is not just Christmas, Independence Day, etc., but also every Saturday and Sunday.

Example: You are served with a three-day notice on Wednesday. To count the three days, do not count Wednesday; begin with Thursday. This makes Saturday the third day. But Saturday is a holiday, and so is Sunday. So the third day is Monday. Therefore, you have until the end of Monday to comply. If the landlord files his eviction lawsuit before Tuesday, it should be thrown out of court if you raise the issue. However, if you're served on Friday, Saturday is the first day, Sunday is the second day, and Monday is the third day. In this case, neither of the weekend days extends the three-day period.

c. After the Three Days

If the three-day notice does not say that your tenancy will be "forfeited" if you don't pay the rent in three days, then you may avoid eviction by offering to pay the rent after the three days runs out—so long as you do so before the landlord files an eviction lawsuit.[7]

Example: On May 5, the landlord serves you with a three-day notice to pay $300 rent or vacate. It does not say anything about your tenancy being "forfeited," if you fail to comply with the notice. The three days run out on May 8. On May 10, you try to give the $300 to the landlord, but she returns it. On May 15, she files a lawsuit to evict you. If you can convince the judge (in your "Answer") that you tried to pay the rent on the 10th, you should win the case.

3. The 30-Day Notice To Terminate a Tenancy

To terminate a month-to-month tenancy (for reasons other than non-payment of rent or breach of a lease), the landlord must normally serve you with a notice which simply says that you are to get out in 30 days (or more). The notice need not state why the landlord wants you out, unless a rent-control ordinance requires that the notice state "good or just cause" to evict (see Section D below), or you live in "Section 8" housing and your rent is partially paid by the federal government.

---

[7]*Briggs v. Electronic Memories & Magnetics Corp.* (1975) 53 Cal.App.3d 900, 905.

A 30-day notice is not required if the landlord does not want to renew a tenant's lease, as the tenant is entitled to stay until the end of the lease term, but no longer.[8] However, many landlords use a 30-day notice near the end of a lease term as a practical way to inform the tenant that the lease will not be renewed.

The 30-day notice may also be used if your landlord's mortgage has been foreclosed upon or if the lender who has obtained title to the property wants you out in order to sell it.[9] The bank (or other buyer) may do this even in the middle of a fixed-term lease. This seems unfair, but it is your landlord's fault for not making her payments, and the bank is legally allowed to protect its interests in this fashion. If you ask it nicely for some extra time to find another place, it will probably give you some.

a. Serving a 30-Day Notice

• A 30-day notice may be served at any time of the month. It need not be served on the first day, the "rent day," or any other day;

• It may be served in the same manner as the three-day notice (see subsection 2b, just above), *or* by certified or registered mail. Civil Code Section 1946;

• When you count the 30 days, don't forget that if the 30th day falls on a Saturday, Sunday, or holiday, you have all day Monday to move (if this is what you've decided to do).

Example: Assume you have a month-to-month tenancy and pay rent on the first. If your landlord ends your month-to-month tenancy with a 30-day notice served on you on July 15, you are supposed to vacate on August 15, unless it falls on a weekend or holiday, in which case the next business day is "moving day."

b. The Implied Withdrawal of Notice Rule

Here is a rule that may help you "beat" a 30-day notice: If the landlord accepts rent covering a period beyond the 30 days, he has probably legally withdrawn the notice by implication.[10]

Example: Suppose the landlord serves you with a 30-day notice on June 10, requiring you to move on July 10. Your rent is $500 a month, due on the first. On July 1, you pay the usual $500 rent. If the landlord accepts it, he has accepted rent for the whole month of July, including the part beyond July 10. By doing so, he has probably impliedly withdrawn the notice.

c. The 30-Day Notice in Rent Control Cities With "Just Cause" Requirements

Many local rent control ordinances (including those of Los Angeles, San Francisco, Berkeley and Santa Monica) limit the landlord's right to evict. These ordinances require the landlord to have a good faith "just cause" or "good cause" reason to evict, and they specify which causes

---

[8]If the tenant lives in a city with a rent-control ordinance requiring just cause for eviction, the expiration of the lease does not by itself justify an eviction and the tenant is entitled to remain unless he or she is evicted "for cause."

[9]In a rent-control area, the 30-day notice may not be used for this purpose unless the rent-control ordinance lists it as one of the "just causes" for eviction. *Gross v. Superior Court* (1985) 171Cal. App. 3d 265.

[10]*Highland Plastics, Inc. v. Enders* (1980) 109 Cal.App.3d Supp. 1.

qualify. Note that it does not matter whether the tenant has only a month-to-month tenancy or had a fixed-term lease that has expired.

Typically, the causes that these ordinances consider "just" fall into two classes:

• Those involving some wrongdoing by the tenant—nonpayment of rent, making a nuisance of yourself, etc. As discussed in Section C(2) above, a three-day notice is typically used in this situation,[11] and

• Those involving the convenience of the landlord.

It is this latter class, where a 30-day notice is used, that has caused a lot of trouble for tenants —especially in cities whose rent control laws allow rent to be raised to the market rate when a tenant leaves (this is called "vacancy decontrol" and is explained in Chapter 4). Most "just cause" ordinances allow the landlord to evict in order to move in herself or to have certain close relatives move in if the landlord has no other comparable vacant units.[12] Some landlords have abused this provision by falsely telling the tenant that the landlord or a relative is going to move in, and later—after the tenant moves out—simply renting the place out at a higher rent.[13]

If you receive a 30-day notice of eviction for this reason, do a little checking before you decide to leave. If the landlord says he is moving in himself, find out where he lives now. If he lives in a fancy neighborhood and you live in a not-so-fancy one, maybe he really does not plan to move in. Or, if your rent is among the lowest rents in the building, the landlord may want you out pretty badly, because he can make the greatest profit by evicting you and charging a higher rent to a new tenant. In either case, see if he owns other vacant apartments he could move into instead. If there are, most ordinances require that he occupy one of these.

If a landlord claims that a relative is moving in, try to find out if the relative really exists, and if it would make sense for the relative to want to live there. For example, if the landlord's daughter is going to college in another city, it is not likely that she would want to move into your place in the middle of the semester.

If you do move out because the landlord says that she or a relative is moving in, go back and check up on whether they moved in, and if they did, how long they stayed. If it turns out that this was merely a scheme to take advantage of "vacancy decontrol," you might have a profitable lawsuit on your hands. In San Francisco, tenants' lawyers have obtained "wrongful eviction" judgments against landlords in such cases for as much as $30,000. In 1987, a San Francisco landlord settled a wrongful eviction suit for $85,000.

---

[11]Under the ordinances of some cities, including Berkeley, Santa Monica, Los Angeles, and San Francisco, the landlord must first notify the tenant of certain types of lease or rental agreement violations (e.g., moving in too many people, damaging the premises, making too much noise) and give her a chance to correct it before serving the notice.

[12]Cities define differently which relatives are eligible to evict a tenant. All include parents and children of the landlord, and some also include the landlord's brothers, sisters, and grandparents. In many cities, a landlord must own at least half of the property to qualify to move relatives in. In Los Angeles, a particular relative of a landlord may justify evicting a tenant only once, and the landlord must pay the evicted tenant's costs of finding another place to live and moving. Check your local ordinance on all of these details.

[13]In cities with ordinances providing "vacancy decontrol," such as San Francisco and Los Angeles, the landlord can raise the rent as much as she likes whenever the place becomes vacant.

Another legitimate "just cause" for eviction for which you can receive a 30-day notice is the need to make major repairs or do large-scale remodeling on the premises. However, under the terms of many ordinances, a tenant must be allowed the right of first refusal to move back in, after the remodeling is completed, at the original rent plus an extra "pass-through" increase that allows the landlord to recover part of the cost of the improvements. Here again, once the tenant has moved out, repairs aren't always made. If you suspect fraud, check with the city to see if the landlord has taken out a building permit. Also, you may want to suggest that you will let the landlord do the repairs one room at a time while you live in the others. If she declines, her supposed desire to evict "for repairs" might not be in good faith.

D. What Are Your Options After a Three-Day or 30-Day Notice is Served?

If you get a three-day or 30-day notice, sit down and think things over. Don't worry that you will be thrown out on the 4th or 31st day. As we have mentioned, the landlord must first sue to evict you, and you must be notified of the lawsuit. Only if you lose the lawsuit can you be evicted, and then only by the sheriff. As noted, at a minimum, it will take the landlord over a month to finish his lawsuit (much longer if you contest it) and (if he wins) get the sheriff to give you an eviction order.

You have several choices:

• Comply with the notice (e.g., pay the rent, get rid of the dog or simply move out). If the landlord is in the right and you are able to comply, this may be the best course.

• Negotiate a solution with the landlord, either by yourself, through a neighborhood or city-sponsored mediation program, or through your lawyer. It will cost the landlord time and money if she has to file an eviction lawsuit, so she has some incentive to work out a fair deal with you.

• Let her file her eviction lawsuit—and then fight like hell to win. The discussion in this chapter may help you decide whether you have a good chance of winning. You may also want to get some advice from a tenants' organization or an experienced tenants' lawyer.

If you decide to fight the eviction, you can represent yourself or hire a lawyer. If your lease or rental agreement requires the loser to pay the winner's attorney's fees—and your chances of winning look pretty good—you may well want to do the latter.

If you decide to represent yourself, prepare carefully. The key is to do your homework—both on the law and on the facts. Get your witnesses, receipts, photos and other evidence lined up, and learn the procedural rules set out in this chapter.

E. The Eviction Lawsuit

This section discusses evictions in Municipal Court, where most residential evictions are brought. Small Claims Court evictions are discussed in Section I below.

First, you need to know that the eviction lawsuit is technically called an "unlawful detainer" lawsuit. We use both terms interchangeably, but courts and lawyers almost always use the term "unlawful detainer."

One very important rule cuts across all other rules in an eviction case: The landlord must strictly comply with all legal requirements.[14] This is the price the landlord pays for a special, quick procedure and reflects the seriousness of the matter, which seeks to deprive you of your home.

1. The Complaint and Summons

The "Complaint" is the paper the landlord files in court to get the case going. It states the basic facts that justify eviction and asks the court to order you out and to enter a judgment against you (for unpaid rent, court costs, and sometimes attorney's fees and other damages).

Before you can be evicted, you must receive proper notice of an unlawful detainer suit by being named in the Complaint and served with a Summons. If you are living in the property but are not named as a defendant in the complaint, you may protect yourself against eviction for a while by filing a form with the court. See Section J below.

When the landlord files his Complaint with the Municipal Court clerk, the court gives him a Summons. The Summons is a notice from the court telling you that you must file a written response (Answer, Demurrer, or Motion to Quash) within five days or lose the lawsuit. The Summons also tells you whether you should give your response to the landlord's attorney or to the landlord.

---

[14]*Vasey v. California Dance Co.* (1977) 70 Cal.App.3d 742.

RESPONDING TO THE SUMMONS

When you get a Summons, you must respond by filing a document with the court. Your first response can be one of three documents, each of which is discussed below:

• Motion to Quash,

• Demurrer, or

• Answer.

You have five days to file your written response. That includes Saturdays and Sundays, but doesn't include other judicial holidays. However, if the last day you can file is a Saturday or Sunday, you can file your document the next day court is open. C.C.P. § 1167.

Example 1: Teresa is served with a Summons on Tuesday. She has five days to respond, which means her response would have to be filed on Sunday. But since court isn't open on Sunday, she can file it on Monday.

Example 2: Joe is served with a Summons on Wednesday. His five days are over on Monday, too.

Example 3: Laura is served with a Summons on Thursday. The next Monday is a court holiday. She counts Friday as day 1, Saturday as 2, Sunday as 3, Tuesday as 4, and Wednesday as 5. Wednesday is her last day to file a response.

2. The Motion to Quash

Once you are aware that the landlord has filed an unlawful detainer action against you, your first step is to decide whether the landlord has failed to comply with the strict requirements for how the Summons must be served on you. If so, you are entitled to file a paper called a "Motion to Quash Service of Summons," asking the court to rule the service of the Summons improper. If this ruling is in your favor, the landlord has to start all over again.

a. How Summons Must Be Served

The landlord must then have the Summons and a copy of the Complaint properly served on you. Unlike the case with the notice to quit (discussed in Section C(2) above), the landlord cannot get sloppy about service of the Summons and Complaint. Whether or not you receive actual notice of these documents, the landlord's failure to strictly abide by the rules governing their service means that the court has no authority (jurisdiction) to hear the case.

What are the rules governing service of a Summons and Complaint? There are two types of service—personal service and substituted service. The landlord must first attempt personal service. This, consists of having someone over the age of 18 who is not a named party to the action personally hand you the papers. Even if you don't accept the papers, service has properly been made as long as you are personally presented with them.[15]

If several unsuccessful attempts are made to personally serve you (three is the rule of thumb) the server may then effect substituted service by:

• leaving a copy of the Summons and Complaint with a competent person in your house (this can be someone less than 18 years of age), or with a person over 18 at your business; and

• explaining the nature of the papers to the person with whom they are left; and

• mailing a copy of the papers to the address where the papers were left.

If this method of service is used, your time to respond is extended from five to 15 days.

b. Should a Motion to Quash Service of Summons Be Filed?

Courts do not allow the filing of motions solely for the purpose of delay. However, if there are adequate legal grounds for a motion to be brought, the request will be granted and no inquiry into the motives behind filing the motion will be made. Simply stated, if you do file a Motion to Quash, make sure you have a valid reason. Typical grounds for a tenant's Motion to Quash based on defective service are:

• The Summons was served on one defendant but not the other;

• The wrong person was served;

• No one was served;

• The process server didn't personally serve the Summons; or

• The landlord himself served the Summons.

The main ground for a Motion to Quash based on a defect in the Summons itself is that the wrong court or judicial district is listed (this is relatively rare).

c. Overview of Motion to Quash

There are three parts to a Motion to Quash:[16]

1. *The Notice of Motion.* This notifies the other side that you are making the motion and have scheduled it to be heard by the court on a certain day.

2. *Your Declaration.* This is a written statement made under penalty of perjury stating the facts supporting your position that the service of Summons was improper.

3. *Memorandum of Points and Authorities.* This is a short statement of the legal authority for your position.

---

[15]It is a common practice, when people realize they are about to be served, to slam the door in the server's face. Forget it. The server can deposit the papers outside the door (after you slam it) and you will be considered served.

[16]The procedure discussed here is basically the same for all motions. Therefore, when we discuss other types of motions later in the book, we will often refer back to this discussion.

If you want to file this motion, be sure to do so within your five-day period to respond. Otherwise, the landlord may have a "default" entered. Once he does this, things get difficult to untangle.

The following sample Notice of Motion to Quash, Declaration, and Statement of Points and Authorities is based on the scenario that your landlord handed the Summons and Complaint to you himself (a "no-no") rather than having another person serve it. Comments keyed to the sample immediately follow it. The papers will, of course, have to be modified appropriately if you bring your motion on another ground. We also tell you how to do this, as well as how to file and serve your papers, in the comments below. If you desire more information on Motions to Quash, consult Moskovitz, *California Eviction Defense Manual* (C.E.B.), available in most law libraries.

Notice of Motion to Quash Service of Summons:

Tom Tenant
2233 Shack Lane
Anytown, CA 99000
(916) 987-6543

Defendant in pro per

In the Municipal Court of the State of California

County of _____, _____ District

Lenny Landlord,

     Plaintiff

       v.

Tom Tenant,

     Defendant

No. _____

Notice of Motion to Quash
Service of Summons

To: Lenny Landlord, plaintiff, and to Phillip Dullwrit, his attorney:

    PLEASE TAKE NOTICE THAT on [1]_____, 19_____, at [2]_____ in Department No. [3]_____ of the above-entitled court, located at [4]_____ defendant, Tom Tenant, will appear specially pursuant to Code of Civil Procedure section 418.10 and will move the court for an order quashing the service of Summons herein on the ground(s) that the Summons and Complaint in this case was personally served on him by Lenny Landlord, plaintiff in this case, in violation of Code of Civil Procedure section 418.10, which requires service of the Summons and Complaint to be served by one not a party to the action.

The motion shall be based upon this notice, the memorandum of points and authorities in support thereof, the files and records of this case, and the declaration of Tom Tenant, attached hereto.

Dated: November 29, 19__

_____
Defendant
In pro per

Declaration

Tom Tenant declares and says:

1. I am a tenant at 2233 Shack Lane, Anytown, CA 99900.

2. On November 26, 19__ I was served with the Summons and Complaint in this case by my landlord Lenny Landlord. I have not been served with those papers in any other manner or by any other person.

3. I declare under penalty of perjury under the laws of the State of California that the foregoing is true and correct.

Date: November 29, 19__

At: Anytown, California

_____
Tom Tenant

Points and Authorities

A defendant in an unlawful detainer action is entitled to file a Motion to Quash Service of Summons when service has not been validly completed. C.C.P. Section 418.10.

In this action, service of the Summons and Complaint was made personally by the plaintiff, Lenny Landlord.

Service by a party to the action violates Code of Civil Procedure Section 414.10, which requires that service of a summons and Complaint must be made by a person over 18 who is not a party to the action.

Respectfully submitted,

_____
Tom Tenant
Defendant, in pro per

d. Instructions for Preparing Papers (Motion to Quash)

Step 1: Obtain a supply of 8 1/2 by 11-inch numbered legal paper (available at most stationery stores). You will need it when you file papers with the court. If you don't have ready access to it, get at least one piece and then use a good photocopy machine to run off your own personal stock.

Step 2: Take one piece of numbered paper and put your name, address, telephone number and "Defendant in pro per" in the same location (and on approximately the same lines) as is shown in the sample.

Note: Don't go crazy about trying to line up your text exactly on the numbered lines. Just do the best you can.

Step 3: Put the county where you are being sued, the municipal court district, and the case number in the spaces as indicated on the sample. You can obtain this information from the Summons and Complaint which were served on you.

Step 4: Call the Municipal Court Clerk and ask when and in what department or division motions are heard. In large cities, this tends to be every morning. In less populous areas, motions may be heard only once or twice a week.

Step 5: Once you find out which dates and times are available, and which department hears motions, immediately do the following:

• Pick a date which is no less than eight days and no more than twelve days from the date you plan to file the motion. Put this date in the space where the [1] appears on the sample;

• Put the time the court hears motions in the space where the [2] appears on the sample;

• Put the department where motions are heard in the space where the [3] appears on the sample;

• Put the address of the court in the space where the [4] appears on the sample.

Step 6: Prepare a Declaration.

Skip a couple of lines after the last line of your Notice of Motion, type the word DECLAR-ATION in caps, and type your declaration, all as shown in the sample. Remember that the judge will be using your declaration in place of oral testimony as a basis for deciding whether to grant your motion. Therefore, use simple sentences and review your information to make sure it accurately and clearly tells the court what the landlord did wrong. Don't engage in argument. ("Just the facts, ma'am.").

Step 7: Complete your Points and Authorities.

Skip a couple of lines after the last line of your Declaration, type the words POINTS AND AUTHORITIES in caps, and then begin typing your points and authorities. To do this, use simple sentences to explain why the service didn't comply with the law, or why the Summons itself is defective (see the sample Points and Authorities). Your explanation should consist of at least three sentences providing the following information:

• That your motion is authorized by Code of Civil Procedure section 418.10;

• What the landlord did wrong; and

• The specific statute the landlord violated.

The requirement that the Summons and Complaint be served by someone over 18 and not a party to the action is found in Code of Civil Procedure Section 414.10. The requirement that substitute service may only be made after unsuccessfully attempting personal service is found in Code of Civil Procedure Section 415.20(b). The requirements for substituted service are also found in section 415.20(b).

If the landlord erred for some other reason, you will need to find a legal basis for your conclusion and put it in the Points and Authorities. Talk to a tenants' group or lawyer or research the law yourself.[17]

_____

[17]See Elias, *Legal Research: How To Find and Understand the Law* (Nolo Press).

e. Instructions For Serving the Motion to Quash

Step 1: Find the document called Proof of Service by Mail in the Appendix. Photocopy several before using it, as you may need more later. Fill it out for the day you plan to have your motion filed and served. The server must be a person over 18 and not a party to the action (i.e., not named in the Complaint as a plaintiff or defendant). As a defendant, you cannot serve your own legal papers. Leave it unsigned.

Step 2: Make two photocopies of your Notice of Motion, Motion, Declaration, Points and Authorities, and the unsigned but filled in Proof of Service by Mail. Print the name of your server on each photocopy.

Step 3: Attach a photocopy of the unsigned Proof of Service to each photocopy of your motion papers.

Step 4: Have your server mail one photocopy package (the motion papers and the Proof of Service) to the landlord's attorney (listed on the Summons) or the landlord if there is no attorney. The package must be mailed on the day indicated on the Proof of Service.

Step 5: Now have your server sign the original proof of service, stating that the mailing has occurred. Attach it to the original motion.

Step 6: Take the original package and photocopy to the Municipal Court clerk.[18] Give the original set of papers to the clerk, who will stamp (or have you stamp) your photocopy with a "filed" message. This is your proof that you filed the originals with the clerk.

Step 7: The clerk will note the date you indicated for the hearing and enter it on the court calendar after you leave.

Step 8: If the landlord desires to respond, he or she must file a response before the hearing.

Step 9: The day of the hearing, go a little early and check with the clerk's office to see that your case is on the calendar. If it isn't, find out why. If it is, go to the courtroom indicated.

Step 10: Courts in cities sometimes make a tentative decision solely on the basis of the papers filed. This tentative decision is usually posted outside the courtroom the day before your hearing. If the decision is for the landlord some courts require you to call the landlord before the hearing if you want to argue your side.

f. Instructions for the Court Hearing on a Motion to Quash

The evening before the day of the hearing, you should sit down, relax, and go over the points stated in your motion papers just to familiarize yourself with them. On the day of the hearing, you should dress conservatively, though you don't have to wear a business suit. Only lawyers are expected to wear such uniforms. Try to get to the courtroom a little early.

When your case is called, step forward. Some judges prefer to ask questions, but others prefer that the person bringing the motion (you) to talk first. In any case, don't start talking until the judge asks you to begin. Your argument should be squarely based on:

• The facts and issues set forth in your declaration and motion papers, and

---

[18] It is possible to file papers by mail, but this is not advised, especially in unlawful detainer cases being handled by a tenant without a lawyer. The time limits are so tight in these kinds of cases that a postal foul-up or a mishandling in the clerk's office can cause you no end of grief.

• The landlord's responses to your papers.

Don't refer to any facts not contained in the declarations, or state your opinion of the landlord, or argue the merits of your situation beyond what you have raised in your motion papers.

After the landlord or his lawyer has had a chance to argue his side, you will have a chance to respond. The judge will then either rule on the motion or take the matter "under submission" and decide later. If the judge denies the motion, you will then have to file your next response (or whatever other action is required at that particular phase of the case). If you win, the landlord may have another Summons ready to serve on you right there.

3. The Demurrer

Once the landlord has properly served you with a Summons and Complaint, you may file an Answer to the Complaint or you may file a Demurrer with the court clerk. You must either answer or demur within five days from the date the papers were served. If the fifth day falls on a holiday, the last day for your response is extended to the next business day (see Section 1 above).

a. What Is a Demurrer?

When you file a Demurrer, what you are really saying is, "Assuming only for the purpose of argument that everything the landlord says in her Complaint is true, it still doesn't provide legal justification for the court to order me evicted."

Note that when you file a Demurrer, you assume the facts to be true only for the purpose of the particular pleading. You are not actually conceding the truth of anything in the Complaint. Once the court rules on your Demurrer, you will still have a chance to file a written Answer in which you may deny any factual allegations in the Complaint you believe are false or don't actually know to be true.

b. When Should a Demurrer Be Filed?

Here are some of the principal legal grounds on which you may properly demur to a Complaint:

Ground 1: The three-day notice wasn't in the alternative. All three-day notices, including those based on nonpayment of rent—must be in the alternative, unless the landlord is alleging violation of a lease provision that is not curable within that time. For example, if you receive a Three-Day Notice to Quit because you have a dog (or failed to pay the rent) and the notice fails to say that you have the *alternative* of getting rid of the dog (or paying the rent) in three days, it is defective.

Ground 2: The Complaint was filed too soon. The date the Complaint was filed will be stamped on the first page of the Complaint. Look at this date. If it is before the three days or the 30 days given by the notice, you can demur.

Here is a sample Demurrer form. You will find a blank copy in the Appendix.

[PREPARE ON NUMBERED LEGAL PAPER]

Defendant's Name:_____

Address:_____

Telephone Number:_____

Defendant in Pro Per

_____

In the Municipal Court of the State of California

County of _____,_____ District

_____

Plaintiff(s)

      v.   No._____

_____   DEMURRER TO COMPLAINT

Defendant(s)

_____

Defendant(s) demur to the Complaint on the following ground(s):

1. _____

   _____

   _____.

2. _____

   _____

   _____

Date:_____   _____

                                Signature of Defendant

The Demurrer must be accompanied by the Notice of Hearing and Points and Authorities. A tear-out form for the Notice of Hearing is located in the Appendix. Immediately below, you will find instructions for filling out and filing them.

c. Filling Out the Demurrer

For instructions on how to prepare items 1 through 4, refer to Steps 1-3 for preparing the Motion to Quash set out in Section E(2)(d) above.

To fill out item 5, see the list of legal grounds for a demurrer discussed just above:

If Ground #1 applies to your situation, type in: "The three-day notice attached to the Complaint simply ordered me to vacate, without giving me the alternative of stopping any alleged breach of the rental agreement."

If Ground #2 fits your situation, type in: "The Complaint was filed prematurely, before the time set in the notice expired."

d. Filling Out the Memorandum of Points and Authorities

On a blank piece of 8 1/2 x 11-inch numbered legal paper, type "Points and Authorities in Support of Demurrer." Then skip a line and type "Code of Civil Procedure Section 430.10." Then, in numbered paragraphs, repeat each ground for your demurrer. This time, however, you should follow each ground by an appropriate legal reference. For ground #1, this is: C.C.P. 1161(3); *Feder v. Wreden Packing and Provision Co.,* 89 Cal.App. 671 (1928). For ground #2, put: C.C.P. 1161(2). When you are done, your Points and Authorities should look like this:

• The three-day notice attached to the Complaint simply ordered me to vacate, without giving me the alternative of stopping any alleged breach of the rental agreement. C.C.P. 1161(3); *Feder v. Wreden Packing and Provision Co.,* 89 Cal.App. 671 (1928); or

• The Complaint was filed prematurely, before the time set in the notice expired. C.C.P. 1161(2).

Attach your Points and Authorities to your demurrer.

e. Filling Out the Notice of Hearing On Demurrer

Turn back to Section E(2)(c) of this chapter and locate the instructions accompanying the Notice of Motion to Quash. Follow them for the Notice of Hearing on Demurrer with the following exceptions:

• Call the Municipal Court clerk and ask when Demurrers (rather than motions) are heard by the court. It may be the same or a different day.

• Select a hearing date at least 20 days after the day you plan to file your Demurrer. Put the day, the time the court hears Demurrers, the department that hears them, and the address of the court in the indicated spaces. Then, attach the Notice of Hearing to the front of the Demurrer and Points and Authorities.

f. Filing and Serving the Demurrer

Step 1: Find the document called Proof of Service by Mail in the Appendix. Photocopy several before using it, as you may need more later. Fill it out for the day you plan to have your Demurrer filed and served. The server must be a person over 18 and not a party to the action (i.e., not named in the Complaint as a plaintiff or defendant). As a defendant, you cannot serve your own legal papers. Leave it unsigned.

Step 2: Make two photocopies of your Demurrer package (Notice of Hearing, Demurrer, and Points and Authorities) and the Proof of Service. Print the name of the server on the two photocopies.

Step 3: Attach one photocopy of the Proof of Service to each photocopy of your Demurrer package.

Step 4: Have your server mail one photocopy package (your Demurrer papers and an unsigned Proof of Service) to the landlord's attorney (listed on the Summons) or the landlord if there is no attorney.

Step 5: Now have your server sign the original Proof of Service, stating that the mailing has occurred. Attach this original to your Demurrer package.

Step 6: Take the original package and photocopy to the Municipal Court clerk.[19] Give the original set of papers to the clerk, who will stamp (or have you stamp) your photocopy with a "filed" message. This is your proof that you filed the originals with the clerk.

Step 7: The clerk will note the date you indicated for the hearing and enter it on the court calendar.

If the landlord desires to respond to your Demurrer, he must file a response at least five days before the hearing. If you wish to make a written response to those papers, you must do so at least two days before the hearing.

Step 8: The day of the hearing, you should check to see that your case is on the calendar. If it isn't, ask the clerk why and get it rescheduled.

Step 9: Courts in cities sometime make a tentative decision solely on the basis of the papers filed. This tentative decision is posted outside the courtroom the day before your hearing. If you want to argue your side even if the tentative decision is against you, some courts require you to call the landlord and say you're still going to argue.

If this is your first responsive pleading, you will have to pay a filing fee. The amount depends on how many defendants there are. It will probably be between $30 and $50, payable by cash or money order only. If you win, you get this sum back from the plaintiff as "costs."

g. At the Hearing

See the discussion on this subject set out in Section E(2)(f) above.

Note: There are other motions which may be appropriate at this stage of the proceedings. For instance, a "motion to strike" might be appropriate if the landlord's complaint requests relief which is not justified by the allegations. For more on this, consult the *Eviction Defense Manual*, Moskovitz.

4. The Answer

If your Demurrer is upheld by the court, the landlord will have to amend the Complaint. Then you can demur again, if you have grounds, or file an Answer. If, on the other hand, your Demurrer is overruled, you will have to file an Answer within five days after the date of the notice of the court order overruling the demurrer. Sooner or later, unless the landlord drops the case, or you drop your contest, you will have to file an Answer.

---

[19]It is possible to file papers by mail, but this is not advised, especially in unlawful detainer cases being handled by a tenant without a lawyer. A postal service or clerk's office foul-up could cause grave problems given the short time limits in these kinds of cases.

The Answer is your chance to tell your version of what happened. It is important to realize that you must file it with the court within five days of receiving the Summons and Complaint, assuming you haven't filed a Motion to Quash or Demurrer instead.[20] If you miss the deadline, the landlord can take a default judgment against you. Defaults are discussed in subsection 5 just below.

Fortunately, a form Answer has been developed (by the California Judicial Council) specifically for unlawful detainer cases. Although you are permitted to draft your own, we think you will find the form Answer much easier to use. A tear-out copy is located in the Appendix, and you may obtain additional copies from the court for a nominal sum.

a. Filling Out the Form Answer

Top of the Form: This is self-explanatory. If you are representing yourself, put your name in both the top box and the one marked "Defendant." You will find the name of the court and the case number on the complaint.

Box 1: Fill in "2," unless you add attachments. If you do, use 8-1/2" x 11" typing paper (numbered legal paper is not required), and clearly label each attachment with the number of the paragraph on the printed form answer to which it refers (see sample attachment below). Each attachment should be on one side of a separate sheet and should be stapled to the Answer.

Box 2: Fill in your name.

Box 3: Box 3 presents a fork in the road, since the instructions say "Check only one of the next two boxes."

First, does the complaint expressly ask for more than $1,000 in damages? If it does not, check Box a. If it does, check Box b.

---

[20]Remember, however, as we stated earlier, you have 15 days if substituted service was used.

If you've checked Box b, you have a little more work to do before going to Box 4. Follow these directions and you should have no trouble:

Carefully read the complaint paragraph by paragraph. As you do, take the following actions for each paragraph.

(a) If you agree with everything in the paragraph, go on to the next one.

(b) If you disagree with any statement in a paragraph, enter the paragraph number in the space on the Answer form after 3b(1). You may very well disagree with more than one paragraph. If so, enter the numbers of all such paragraphs.

(c) If you don't have enough information to agree or disagree with a statement in a paragraph, enter the paragraph number in the space on the Answer form labeled 3b(2).

Do a careful job of reading each paragraph on the complaint. Any paragraph that isn't listed after Box 3b(1) or 3b(2) will be accepted as true by the court. This means, unless you absolutely agree with *everything* in a paragraph, the paragraph number should be entered in one of the two boxes, depending on whether you actually disagree with it or just can't say one way or the other.

Box 4: In earlier chapters, we described a number of possible defenses to evictions and referred to them as "affirmative defenses." Just to refresh your memory, an affirmative defense is any defense that involves a set of facts different than those raised in the complaint.

For example, suppose the landlord seeks to evict you because you didn't pay your rent. If your defense is that you didn't pay the rent because the rental unit was uninhabitable, as discussed in Chapter 7(B)(5), it is based on different facts than are found in the complaint and is therefore an affirmative defense.

You must raise affirmative defenses in your Answer to let the court and the other side know what your defense is about. If the grounds of your defense are adequately identified by the denials in your Answer, then you don't need to raise any affirmative defenses. For example, if the landlord says that you didn't pay your rent, and you say you did, then all you have to do is deny the allegation that you didn't pay your rent. That's what Box 3 was all about.

Rent Control Note: If you live in a rent-control area, it is possible that you have been charged more rent than the ordinance allows (See Chapter 2). If this is the case, the landlord's claim that you failed to pay rent can be defeated on the ground that the rent demanded in the three-day notice was higher than it should have been. Although this defense is technically raised by a simple denial in Box 3, it is also a good idea to describe your position in an affirmative defense.

Caution: Landlords in rent control cities that require registration of rents (Berkeley, Santa Monica, Cotati, East Palo Alto, Los Angeles, Palm Springs, Thousand Oaks, and West Hollywood) are protected against sanctions for good-faith mistakes in the amount of rent they charge. Civil Code § 1947.7. Although the statute probably doesn't apply to unlawful detainer cases, landlords may argue that it does. Your response should be that dismissal of a complaint because of a deficient three-day notice is a separate legal procedure rather than one of the "sanctions" meant by the statute. See Section C.2 above.

To raise affirmative defenses, check the box in front of every affirmative defense listed in Box 4 that describes your situation. Then, in Section 4(k), state the facts on which you base your affirmative defense. See the example below. Generally, the fewer words you use to describe your defense, the better. However, even if you try to be brief, the room provided will probably not be enough. If not, take a sheet of 8-1/2" x 11" paper, label it "4(k)" at the top, and then explain the facts regarding each affirmative defense. For example, if you need more room to explain Affirmative Defense 4(d), state your additional facts under "4(d)" on the attachment, which would look like this:

Attachment to Item 4(k)—Statement of Details of Affirmative Defenses

4(d): The reason I didn't water the lawn as required in rental agreement was that landlord never provided the hose (which she had agreed to do).

Even though we discussed many alternative defenses in earlier parts of the book, we'll give you some brief examples here as well as referring you to the specific discussions for details. If for any reason you have trouble with this Answer form, or with the idea of affirmative defenses in general, you should consult someone knowledgeable in this area.

Box 4(a): Breach of Warranty of Habitability (see Chapter 7).

If you are being evicted for nonpayment of rent and the landlord had reason to know that there are deficiencies in your apartment affecting its habitability, you should check box 4(a) and put the details in 4(k) or the attachment.

Sample Statement of Details

"On December 25, 19___, I notified my landlord (the plaintiff in this action), that the heating unit in my apartment was broken and asked that it be fixed. This was not done." Or, "On March 19, 19___, I notified my landlord that the roof was seriously leaking in three places. The roof has never been fixed."

Box 4(b): Cancellation of Notice.

Sometimes, after a three-day or 30-day notice is served, the landlord (or his agent) says something to indicate that he didn't mean it, you can have more time, or something else inconsistent with the notice. If this happens, he may have impliedly waived or cancelled the notice, so check Box 4(b).

Sample Statement of Details

"After I received the notice, Plaintiff's resident manager told me that they had served the notice on me only to scare me, and as long as I paid by the end of the month, no eviction lawsuit would be filed."

Box 4(c): Retaliatory Eviction (see Chapter 7).

In recent years, the courts have prevented evictions brought to punish tenants who:

• Complain to health authorities;

• Exercise statutory rights, such as the right to repair and deduct;

• Exercise rights under rent control ordinances;

• Organize rent strikes or other tenant protests; or

• Exercise any other statutory or constitutional right.

The general idea is that tenants should not be punished by landlords just because they are invoking rights or remedies provided to them by the law and the constitution.

Retaliatory eviction is a very common defense. If you believe that your landlord is retaliating against you for one of the activities mentioned above, check Box 4(c) and put the details in 4(k).

Sample Statement of Details

After Plaintiff twice refused to respond to our request that he fix the toilet, we complained to the city health department. Forty-five days later, we received a 30-Day Notice to Quit. We believe that we are being evicted in retaliation for our complaint to the health department.

Box 4(d): Landlord's Breach of Agreement (see Chapter 7, "Repairs and Maintenance," Section A2).

If the landlord failed to perform some promise she made regarding the premises, then your failure to pay rent may have been justified.

Sample Statement of Details

"Plaintiff had promised to provide a laundry room (with washer and dryer) for all tenants, including us, but she closed up the laundry room in July and August. Therefore, our failure to pay the agreed rent for July and August was justified."

Box 4(e): Discrimination (see Chapter 5).

The landlord may not evict you because of your race, religion, sex, sexual preference, job, because you have children, or for any other arbitrary reason.

Sample Statement of Details

"Plaintiff served me with the 30-day notice because he doesn't want black people living in his rental units."

Box 4(f): Just Cause for Eviction Ordinances (see Chapter 2 and Section D of this chapter).

If you live in a community with a rent-control ordinance that requires just cause for eviction, and you dispute the just cause alleged in the Complaint, simply deny that allegation of the complaint. If, however, the landlord committed some violation of the "just-cause" ordinance which you cannot raise by a denial, then check Box 4(f).

Sample Statements of Details

"The rent control ordinance of the City of Santa Monica says that a three-day notice must tell me of my right to call the rent board for advice. The notice served on me by Plaintiff did not say this, so it is invalid." Or,

"The rent control ordinance of the City of San Francisco requires that the three-day notice state a "just cause" to evict. The three-day notice served on me by the landlord did not do this." Or,

"Landlord has sued to evict me because she wants her mother to live in the unit. This is not a just cause to evict because under the rent control ordinance of the City of San Francisco landlord must first establish that there are no other vacant units which her mother can live in. In fact, at the time she served me with the 30-day notice, she had two equivalent vacancies."

Box 4(g): Acceptance of Rent Beyond Notice Period (see Section C3c above).

If the landlord served a 30-day notice and then accepted rent covering a period beyond the 30 days, he has impliedly withdrawn the notice, so check this box.

Box 4(h): Landlord's Refusal to Accept Rent (see Section C2d above).

If you tried to pay the rent during the time allowed you by a three-day notice but the landlord refused to accept it, check this box. If you tried to pay the rent after the three days (but before the lawsuit was filed) and the notice did not mention "forfeiture" of your tenancy, check this box.

Box 4(i): Use of Repair and Deduct Remedy (see Chapter 7, Section B4).

If you used your repair-and-deduct remedy and the landlord failed to give you credit in the three-day notice for the amount you deducted from your rent, check this box.

Box 4(j): Other Affirmative Defenses.

   Sometimes landlords orally allow tenants to get behind on their rent or to make certain repairs to their premises in exchange for free rent, or they make other agreements on which the tenant relies because of a good relationship with the landlord. Then, when a falling-out occurs, the landlord will attempt an eviction on the basis of a particular tenant default and deny that any oral agreement was made. In such a case, you have an affirmative defense based on the agreement and should check this box and place the details on 4(k).

Box 5:

   Box 5(a): If you have moved out by the time you get around to filing this answer, check this box. Remember, even though you've moved, the landlord may still be suing for money damages. It is important to file this answer to have your day in court on the money damages claim.

   Box 5(b): Add up all your deposits and list them here. Generally speaking, all your deposits must be returned if you have left the premises clean and undamaged (see Chapter 10).

   Box 5(c): Although the landlord may not accept rent after the expiration of the notice to quit, the court will award the landlord the fair market rental value of the premises for the time between the expiration of the notice and the day the judgment is entered. This is normally computed by dividing the total rent amount by 30 to arrive at a daily rental, and then multiplying this amount by the number of days in question. If you believe that the "fair rental value" stated in the complaint is too high, check this box. Then explain any habitability problems on the premises, any change in the neighborhood which might have affected rental value, or any other reason you think the landlord's estimate is excessive.

   Box 5(d): This box gives you a chance to say anything relevant and not covered by the other boxes.

   Box 6. Here you need check only Box 6(c), unless you feel you are entitled to some other remedy. You are entitled to reasonable attorney fees if you win and your rental agreement or lease provides that your landlord can recover them if she wins (see Chapter 2, Section B3).

b. Signing and Verifying Your Answer

   Here are the rules:

   Step 1: The Answer must be signed by all of the named defendants;

   Step 2: The Verification (the statement under penalty of perjury that the statements in the Answer are true) need be signed only by any one defendant;

c. Filing and Serving Your Answer

   Step 1: Find the document called Proof of Service by Mail in the Appendix. Photocopy several before using it, as you may need more later. Fill it out for the day you plan to have your answer filed and served. The server must be a person over 18 and not a party to the action (i.e., not named in the Complaint as a plaintiff or defendant). As a defendant, you cannot serve your own legal papers. Leave it unsigned.

Step 2: Make two photocopies of your Answer and the unsigned but filled in Proof of Service by Mail. Fill in the server's name on the two photocopies of the Proof of Service.

Step 3: Attach one photocopy of the Proof of Service to each photocopy of your Answer.

Step 4: Have your server mail one photocopy of the Answer and attached unsigned Proof of Service to the landlord's attorney (listed on the summons), or the landlord if there is no attorney. The package must be mailed on the day indicated on the Proof of Service.

Step 5: Now have your server sign the original Proof of Service that the mailing has occurred. Attach this original to your original Answer.

Step 6: Take the original package (Answer and Proof of Service) and a photocopy to the Municipal Court clerk.[21] Give the original set of papers to the clerk, who will stamp (or have you stamp) your photocopy package with a "filed" message. This is your proof that you filed the originals with the clerk.

Warning: Make sure your Answer is filed within five days of the day the complaint was served (or your Motion to Quash or Demurrer was overruled). If you miss this deadline, you may find yourself having to dig yourself out from under a default judgment obtained by the landlord. See Section E(1) above for how to compute the five-day period.

If this is your first responsive pleading, you will have to pay a filing fee. The amount depends on how many defendants there are. It will probably be between $30 and $50, payable by cash or money order only. If you win, you get this sum back from the plaintiff as "costs."

5. Setting Aside a Default Judgment

If the landlord obtained a default judgment against you, you may file a motion to set it aside. If the motion is granted, you may then file your Answer and have your trial.

To persuade the judge to grant your motion to set aside a default, you must show all of the following:

• That you have a pretty good excuse (such as illness) for your failure to respond to the summons in five days (e.g., "I didn't know how to respond, and it took me a few days to get hold of a copy of the *Tenants' Rights*" might work, but don't count on it).

• That you did not unnecessarily delay too long in filing your motion to set aside the default. There is no set period of time for which a delay is or is not excusable. It depends on the facts of each case.

• That you have a defense to the lawsuit.

In addition, be sure to ask for a stay of the eviction (Section G below) until the court rules on your motion to set aside the default.

---

[21]As we've indicated earlier, it is possible to file papers by mail, but this is not advised, especially if you're handling an unlawful detainer case without a lawyer.

Moving to set aside a default can be a bit tricky. We recommend that you try to get a lawyer or tenants' rights advocate to help you with it. Forms and procedures to accomplish this are contained in the *California Eviction Defense Manual* (C.E.B.) by Moskovitz, available in most county law libraries.

6. Discovery Devices You and Your Landlord Can Use to Learn More About the Other's Case

"Discovery" is the process of finding out what evidence the other side has before the trial begins, so you can prepare your own case to meet it. Discovery is conducted in two basic ways.

One is to question people face to face in a proceeding called a deposition (see Section C below).

The second is to send the other party a written document that specifies what is being sought. This document typically consists of:

- Questions (interrogatories), or
- A request that certain documents be produced for inspection, or
- A request that a physical inspection of the premises be allowed, or
- A request that certain facts be admitted as true, or
- All of the above.

The law provides a set period of time within which a party must respond to discovery requests. Usually, the response must be given within 30 days or within five days before trial, whichever is sooner.

a. Request for Inspection

A Request for Inspection is used to make the other side let you see and copy any documents or other things before trial. You may want to see copies of leases, building inspector's reports, or checks. It can also be used to get into the apartment to take photos. C.C.P. Section 2031.

The landlord must respond to your request within five days and must produce the documents for actual inspection within ten days. If the landlord refuses to respond adequately to your discovery request within that time, you may ask the court to impose sanctions on him—requiring him to pay your costs, prevent him from using certain evidence, etc. C.C.P. Section 2034.

Here is a sample Request for Inspection, plus instructions for filling it out. You will find a tear-out copy in the Appendix.

Request for Inspection:

Defendant's Name:_____

Address:_____

Telephone Number:_____

In the Municipal Court of the State of California

County of _____,_____ District

_____
Plaintiff(s)

v.   No._____

_____   Request to Inspect and for
Defendant(s)   Production of Documents
                                          Code of Civil Procedure
                                          Sec. 2031

To_____, Plaintiff, and _____, Plaintiff's attorney:

Defendant, _____, requests that you produce and permit the copying of the following documents: _____ (describe documents) _____

_____.

Defendant requests that you produce these documents at the following address:
_____ (your address or any other location) _____

_____

at the following date and time:
_____ (within 20 days, or five days before trial, which ever comes first) _____.

Defendant further requests permission to enter, inspect, and photograph the premises located at

_____ at the following date and time:

_____ (within 20 days, or five days before trial, which ever comes first) _____

Date:_____   _____
                                        Signature of Defendant

Filing and Service Instructions:

Step 1: Make one photocopy of your Request for Inspection.

Step 2: Have someone who is over 18 and not a defendant in the case prepare a Proof of Service by Mail form (you will find a tear-out in the Appendix) for the day your request is to be mailed. Don't have your server sign it yet. Make a photocopy of the Proof of Service by Mail, fill in your server's name at the bottom of the photocopy and attach it to the photocopy of your request for inspection.

Step 3: Have your server place these papers in the mail with first class postage attached.

Step 4: Have your server sign the original Proof of Service by Mail.

Step 5: Keep the originals of your Proof of Service by Mail and Request for Inspection in your records. You need not file these papers with the clerk unless a dispute arises over your request.

b. Interrogatories

The discovery device most often used in unlawful detainer cases is written interrogatories. This is a series of questions you pose which the other side must answer. The California Judicial Council has approved a set of Form Interrogatories for use in eviction cases. These are set out in the Appendix. Here is the way you use them:

• Read the interrogatories. If any is relevant to the issues in your case, check off the number of that interrogatory in the proper box of the tear-out "Form Interrogatories Request," which appears after the interrogatories.

• Do not simply check off every box in the Form Interrogatories. If you do, the landlord may take you to court and get sanctions against you (usually a fine) based on the claim that are using the interrogatories for purposes of harassment and delay. Make sure that the interrogatory pertains to some denial or affirmative defense you raised and that the landlord's answer might help you know what to expect at trial.

• Tear out the Form Interrogatories Request (and interrogatories if you wish) and follow these instructions:

Step 1: Fill out the Proof of Service by Mail for the day you plan to have your Interrogatory Request sent to the other side. Leave it unsigned. (A sample Proof of Service by Mail appears in Section E of this chapter.) Blank forms are in the Appendix.

Step 2: Make one photocopy of your Request and the Proof of Service by Mail. Fill in the server's name on the photocopy of the Proof of Service. The server must be a person over 18 and not a party to the action (i.e., not named in the complaint as a plaintiff or defendant). As a defendant, you cannot serve your own legal papers.

Step 3: Attach the photocopy of the Proof of Service to the photocopy of your Request.

Step 4: Have your server mail the photocopy package (the Request and the Proof of Service) to the landlord's attorney (listed on the summons) or the landlord, if there is no attorney. The package must be mailed on the day indicated on the Proof of Service. You may also include a full set of the interrogatories themselves if you wish.

Step 5: Now have your server sign the original Proof of Service that the mailing has occurred. Attach this original to your original Request. Place these documents in your file. You don't have to file them with the court unless a dispute arises.

c. The Deposition

Depositions are oral statements made under oath. The other party must sit down in your or your lawyer's office and answer questions. You must arrange to have a court reporter there to take down the questions and answers. The transcript can be used against the person if he tries to change his story at trial.

Explaining how to set up and conduct a deposition is beyond the scope of this book. More to the point is what happens if the landlord's attorney serves a notice of deposition on you telling you to appear somewhere at a certain time for a deposition. All you have to do is appear and answer the questions. However, you may be tricked into giving an answer that later comes back to haunt you. For this reason, if possible, it is often a good idea to have your lawyer there to help you avoid the traps set by the landlord's attorney.

d. The Request to Admit

It is possible to find out just what you and the landlord agree and disagree about by requesting her to admit certain statements that you believe to be true. If they are admitted, it saves you the trouble of having to prove them in court. If, on the other hand, the landlord denies the statement, and you later prove them to be true, the landlord can be required to reimburse you for the cost of the proof. We don't provide you the forms for this discovery device, but if you are interested in using it, consult *Modern California Discovery*, published by Continuing Education of the Bar (CEB), available in most law libraries.

7. Negotiating a Settlement

At any point in a dispute, you may negotiate a settlement with the landlord. The keys to any settlement are (1) that each side has something the other wants, and (2) that each side is willing to talk to the other in a reasonable manner.

The landlord usually wants you to get out, pay back rent, or both. She wants minimum expense and trouble. You have the power to cause her expense and trouble by your use of the defenses and procedural tools described in this chapter. Therefore, the landlord may be willing (reluctantly) to give you more time to get out, reduce the amount of her claim for back rent, or even pay your moving expenses if you are willing to give up your defenses and procedural tools and agree to get out on a specific, mutually agreeable day. If you are planning to move anyway, this sort of compromise may make excellent sense.

Of course, depending on the facts of your situation, you might instead hang tough, go to trial, and win everything. Obviously, in many situations no matter what you do you run some risk. The landlord is often in the same boat. What this amounts to is that, commonly, it may be in both of your interests to lessen your risks by negotiating a settlement both of you can live with.

Example: When Tom fails to pay his rent of $500 on May 1, Lenny serves a three-day notice on him, and when that runs out without Tom paying the rent, Lenny goes ahead and sues Tom for an eviction order and a judgment for the $500. Tom's Answer says that Lenny breached the implied warranty of habitability by not getting rid of cockroaches. Lenny (or his lawyer) tells Tom (or his lawyer) that at trial Lenny will try to prove that the cockroaches were caused by Tom's poor housekeeping. Lenny thinks he will win the trial, and Tom thinks that he will win. Each of them is sensible enough to know, however, that he has a real chance of losing—and that it is certain that a trial will take up a lot of time and energy (and maybe some costs and attorney's fees). So they (or their lawyers) get together and hammer out a settlement agreement: Tom agrees to get out by July 1, and Lenny agrees to drop his lawsuit and any claim for back rent.

Here are a few pointers about negotiation:

• As suggested, in many circumstances it is common for the tenant to receive forgiveness of past rent (or some of it) plus in some instances moving expenses and sometimes even some financial help with a new security deposit as a condition of moving out without a court fight.

• Be courteous, but don't be weak. If you have a good defense, let the landlord know that you have the resources and evidence to fight and win if she won't agree to a reasonable settlement.

• If you are in a rent-control area and your defense is that the landlord breached rent-control rules, consult the staff at your local rent board. They may be able to help.

• The settlement agreement should be in writing. If you can (and you may not be able to), try to avoid agreeing to a "stipulated judgment," which enables the landlord to get you out very quickly if he thinks you are not abiding by the settlement agreement. Also, credit reporting agencies get records of judgments, so a stipulated judgment may hurt your credit rating.

The following is a sample form settlement agreement which may be used with appropriate modification.

Settlement of Unlawful Detainer Action:

_____

1. _____ (called the "tenant" in this agreement) resides at the following premises: _____ (referred to as "premises" in this agreement).

2. _____ (referred to as "landlord" in this agreement) is the owner of the premises.

3. On _____ landlord caused a Summons and Complaint in unlawful detainer to be served on tenant. The Complaint was filed in the Municipal Court for the County of _____ , _____ District, and carries the following civil number:_____.

4. Landlord and tenant agree that tenant shall vacate the premises on or before _____ _____. In exchange for this agreement, and upon full performance by tenant, landlord agrees to file a voluntary dismissal with prejudice of the complaint specified in clause #3.

5. Also in exchange for tenant's agreement to vacate the premises on or before the date specified in clause #4, landlord agrees to:

(choose one or more of the following)

[ ] Forgive all past due rent

[ ] Forgive past due rent in the following amount: $_____

[ ] Pay the tenant $_____ to cover tenant's moving expenses, new deposit requirements, and other incidentals related to the tenant moving out.

6. Any sum specified in clause #5 to be paid by the landlord shall be paid as follows:

(choose one of the following)

[ ] Upon tenant surrendering the keys to the premises

[ ] Upon the signing of this agreement

[ ] $_____upon the signing of this agreement and $_____ upon tenant surrendering the keys.

[ ] in the following manner:_____

_____

7. The tenant's security deposit being held by landlord shall be handled as follows:

[ ] restored in full to the tenant upon surrender of the keys

[ ] treated according to law

[ ] other:_____

8. In addition to their mutual promises in this agreement, tenant and landlord agree:

a) to waive all claims and demands that each may have against the other for any transaction directly or indirectly arising from their landlord/tenant relationship;

b) that this settlement agreement not be construed as reflecting on the merits of the dispute; and

c) that landlord shall not make any negative representations to any credit reporting agency or to any other person or entity seeking information about whether tenant was a good or bad tenant.

9. Time is of the essence in this agreement. If tenant fails to timely comply with this agreement, landlord may immediately rescind this agreement in writing and proceed with his or her legal and equitable remedies.

10. This agreement was executed on _____

at _____.

Signed:_____

Signed:_____

8. Summary Judgment

Although the landlord is entitled to a trial date within three weeks after you file your Answer, she doesn't have to wait that long to obtain a judgment if she can convince the court that there is no substantial disagreement over the facts. For instance, if you both agree that you have been conducting a mail order business from your apartment, but disagree as to whether this is an illegal use of the premises, the court can decide the case without holding a full trial. This speedy procedure is termed a "summary judgment."

If the landlord files a Motion for Summary Judgment, you will be served with the Notice of Motion and an accompanying Declaration setting out the landlord's version of the facts. If you wish to contest the motion, you should file and serve a statement of your own, called a "Statement of Disputed and Undisputed Material Facts," setting forth your version of the facts. Your statement must respond specifically to the facts the landlord, in his declaration, said were undisputed. You can support your statement with declarations (from you or others) or references to other documents such as the Complaint. If your statement contradicts the landlord's facts in important particulars, and the difference in facts is important to the case, the judge should deny the motion and require the landlord to proceed to trial. Refer to the instructions for completing the Declaration accompanying the Motion to Quash (Section E(2)(d) for the required format. Your statement should be filed at least five days before the date scheduled for the summary judgment hearing (which you can find on the Notice of Motion served on you by the landlord) and should be served according to the method described for serving the Answer (Section 5b).

9. The Trial

After you file your answer, the landlord may request the court clerk to set the case for trial. This is done by filing a "Memorandum to Set for Trial" with the Municipal Court clerk. Once the clerk receives this memo from the landlord, she is supposed to set the case for trial within 20 days. Code of Civil Procedure Section 1170.5(a). You may file a motion to have this date extended, and it might be granted if you can show the judge that, for example, a key witness (such as you) must be out-of-town that day. Consult the *Calif. Eviction Defense Manual* (C.E.B.), which is available at law libraries, for how to file and serve this motion.

When you receive a copy of the landlord's memo to set, check to see whether he has requested a jury trial. If so, you needn't make a request of your own. However, the landlord usually doesn't want a jury trial, and, if you do, you will need to tell the court. Your right to demand a jury trial is secured by Code of Civil Procedure Section 1171. You probably should demand a jury if you will have a lawyer representing you at trial.[22] Requesting a trial often prompts the judge to try to get you and the landlord to settle the case before trial, which can be helpful to you. In the experience of most landlord-tenant lawyers, 12 ordinary people tend to be more sympathetic to tenants than one crusty old (or even young) judge. If, however, you will be representing yourself at trial, you might be better off having a judge decide the case. Judge trials are much more simple and informal than jury trials, which are usually too complicated for most nonlawyers to comfortably handle by themselves.

You will find the tear-out form necessary to demand a jury in the Appendix. Complete it and then follow these instructions.

Instructions to File and Serve Demand for Jury Trial

Step 1: Fill out one of the Proof of Service by Mail forms you will find in the Appendix for the day you plan to file the Demand for Jury Trial. The server must be over 18 and not a party to the action. Leave it unsigned.

Step 2: Make photocopies of Demand For Jury Trial and Proof of Service forms.

Step 3: Attach a photocopy of the unsigned Proof of Service to a photocopy of the Demand For Jury Trial.

Step 4: Have your server mail one photocopy package to the landlord or his attorney and sign the original Proof of Service.

Step 5: File the original Demand and original signed Proof of Service with the court. Have the court file stamp the second photocopy package for your files.

If you know ahead of trial which judge will hear the case, and you have reason to believe that this judge may not be fair to you, you may file a motion to disqualify the judge. Code of Civil Procedure Section 170.6. This is called a "peremptory challenge." The motion must be filed at least five days before trial, together with a statement that you believe the judge will be prejudiced against you. You need not prove that the judge is prejudiced or even state detailed reasons for your belief—the disqualification is automatic. You may do this only once in any case. If you do it, you cannot be sure which judge will replace the one you disqualified—he might even be worse! So don't use your challenge lightly.

Before the trial, carefully organize your witnesses, documents, photographs and any other evidence you think is important. Ask yourself what it would take to convince a neutral person that you are right and then organize that evidence for the judge.

At trial, be courteous and respectful to everyone. The purpose of a trial is to resolve disputes in a civilized manner; it's not a forum for yelling, sarcasm, and the like. Address yourself to the judge and the witnesses only, not the other party or his attorney. It is an advantage to be forceful and to stand up for your rights, and a serious mistake to be rude or unnecessarily hostile. The most

---

[22]If you request a jury trial, you will have to post about $125 with the court to pay for the jurors for one day of trial. If you win, you can recover these fees from the landlord. If the landlord posted the jury fee and wins, she can recover these from you.

important thing is to present your side of the case clearly and with as few complications as possible. Try not to be repetitive. If you confuse, bore, or annoy the judge, you lessen your chance of winning.

Note: We do not have the space to discuss trial tactics here. If you are worried about representing yourself, arrange to go to court and watch several contested unlawful detainer cases.

10. The Judgment

If you win, the landlord cannot evict you, and you can get a judgment for your court costs (mainly your filing fee and jury fees in case you paid them). If your lease or rental agreement provides for attorney's fees for the prevailing party—or just for the landlord—you can recover them too. Civil Code Section 1717. If the landlord wins, the judgment will award her possession of the premises. It may also award her money for unpaid rent (if the action was based on nonpayment of rent), damages, costs, and attorney's fees (if provided by the lease or rental agreement). If you asserted a habitability defense in your Answer, and the judge finds the landlord substantially breached his habitability obligations, you will be required to pay into the court within 5 days, the amount the judge determines is the reasonable rental value of the premises (in their "untenantable state") up to the time of the trial. If you don't make the payment on time, you will not be the"prevailing party" for purposes of awarding attorney fees and costs and the court must award possession of the property to the landlord, Civil Code Section 1174.2. The landlord may try to collect the money part of the judgment by garnishing your wages or by going after your bank account or other property.

F. Relief from Eviction Procedures

Even if you lose an eviction case, the judge may give you "relief from forfeiture" of your tenancy, i.e., save you from eviction. For example, suppose you didn't pay your rent because you felt the rental unit was uninhabitable, and the judge, while agreeing that there were problems, was not convinced that the rental unit was not habitable and therefore ruled against you. The judge may nonetheless grant relief from eviction whether or not the judgment declared a forfeiture of your tenancy (Code of Civil Procedure Sections 1179 and 1174(c)).

To persuade the judge to do this, you will probably have to show him two things:

• That the eviction would cause a severe hardship on you or your family (e.g., because your kids are in school, or you cannot find other housing, or you would have to move away from your job, or you are elderly or handicapped).

• That you are willing and able to pay both the money you owe the landlord (for costs, back rent, etc.) and the rent in the future. You will find a tear-out Application for Relief from Eviction form in the Appendix.

Application For Relief From Eviction:

_____

Defendant's Name:_____

Address:_____

Telephone Number:_____

In the Municipal Court of the State of California

County of _____,_____ District

_____
Plaintiff(s)

v.   No._____

_____   APPLICATION AND
Defendant(s)   DECLARATION
                                             FOR RELIEF FROM EVICTION

                                             Code of Civil Procedure
                                             Secs. 1174(c), 1179

_____

Defendant(s)_____,
hereby apply for relief from eviction, after judgment for plaintiff in this action.

If defendants are evicted, they will suffer hardship in the following way(s):_____

_____

_____

_____.

Defendants are willing and able to pay all money they presently owe to Plaintiff, as a condition to this application being granted. Defendants are also willing and able to pay the rent as it comes due in the future.

I declare under penalty of perjury that the above statements are ture and correct to the best of my knowledge.

Date:_____   _____
                                     Signature of Defendant

_____

Instructions for Serving and Filing Application for Relief From Eviction

These are the same as the instructions set out in Section E(9) above to request a jury trial.

G. Stay of Eviction Procedures

Even if the judge will not stop the eviction, she may stay it for some limited time, for a good reason—for example, to give you more time to find another place, or to let you stay in possession while you appeal. If you need time to find another place, explain how difficult it is to locate available housing in your city and ask for a stay of about 30 days. File an application for a stay as soon as possible after you receive notice of the judgment.

If you seek a stay during an appeal, you must show the court that (1) you will suffer "extreme hardship" if you are evicted, and (2) that the landlord will not be hurt by the stay. Specifically, the stay must be conditioned on your paying rent into court as it comes due thereafter. The court may also impose other conditions on the stay. If the trial court denies a stay during appeal, you may ask the appellate court to grant a stay. Code of Civil Procedure Section 1176. You will probably need a lawyer's help to accomplish this. You will find a tear-out application for Stay of Eviction form in the Appendix.

Application For Stay of Eviction:

_____

Defendant's Name:_____

Address:_____

Telephone Number:_____

In the Municipal Court of the State of California

County of _____,_____ District

_____

Plaintiff(s)

v.   No._____

_____   APPLICATION AND
          Defendant(s)   DECLARATION
                                                          FOR STAY OF EVICTION

_____

     Defendant(s)_____,
hereby apply for a stay of execution from any writ of restitution or possession in this case, for
the following period of time:_____
_____
_____.

     Such a stay is appropriate in this case for the following reason(s):_____
_____
_____.

     I declare under penalty of perjury that the above statements are true and correct to the best of
my knowledge.

Date:_____   _____
                                                          Signature of Defendant

_____

Filing and Serving Application for Relief from Eviction

Follow the instructions set out in Section E(9) above to request a jury trial.

H. Appeal From An Eviction

To appeal, you must file a paper called "Notice of Appeal" with the clerk of the Municipal Court. You must file it within 30 days of receiving notice that judgment was entered against you. The appeal is to the Appellate Department of the Superior Court. On appeal, you may argue only issues of law, not fact. This means that you may argue that the trial court erred by ruling that, for example, there can be no breach of the implied warranty of habitability if the lease says that the tenant waives his rights under this doctrine—an issue of law. But you may not argue that the judge was wrong in believing the landlord's testimony rather than yours, as this is an issue of fact. After you file your Notice of Appeal, the appellate department will notify you about when your brief (the document in which you argue points of law) must be filed in that court.

Appeals are pretty technical, and we recommend that you get a lawyer if possible. You will find a Notice of Appeal form in the Appendix.

Warning: Filing a Notice of Appeal does not automatically stop the sheriff from carrying out an eviction. To do that, you must seek a stay of the eviction from the trial court judge, as discussed in the preceding section. You should file your application stay immediately upon hearing of the judgment. If you plan to appeal, however, and feel you have a good argument that the trial court misinterpreted the law, include these facts in your application for the stay.

Notice of Appeal:

Defendant's Name:_____

Address:_____

Telephone Number:_____

In the Municipal Court of the State of California

County of _____, _____ District

_____
Plaintiff(s)

v.   No._____

_____   NOTICE OF APPEAL AND
Defendant(s)   NOTICE TO PREPARE
                                               CLERK'S TRANSCRIPT

_____

Defendant(s)_____,
hereby appeal to the Appellate Department of the Superior Court.

Defendant(s) hereby request that a Clerk's Transcript be prepared, and that this transcript include all documents filed in this action and all minute orders and other rulings and judgments issued by the court in this action..

Date:_____   _____
                                  Signature of Defendant

Instructions to File and Serve a Notice of Appeal

These are the same as the instructions set out in Section E(9) above to require a jury trial.

I. Small Claims Court Evictions

A few landlords file eviction suits in Small Claims Court, because the procedures there are simpler. Neither side may be represented by a lawyer. The landlord may file an eviction lawsuit in Small Claims Court only if:

• The tenancy is no longer than month-to-month (in other words, if you have a year's lease, the landlord can't use Small Claims Court);

• The landlord is seeking to evict you for nonpayment of rent; and

• The total amount of rent and damages she seeks does not exceed $2,000. C.C.P. Sections 86(a)(4), and 116.2.

The landlord begins a small claims lawsuit by filing an "affidavit" that sets out what she is alleging and demanding. The clerk of the court then mails a copy to you, with the date and time of the trial, which is usually 10 to 30 days later. You do not need to file a written response.

At the trial, the landlord presents her case and then you present yours. The landlord must prove that she complied with all three-day or 30-day notice requirements discussed in Section C of this chapter, and you are entitled to raise any defense discussed in this book. You and your witnesses testify under oath. Formal rules of evidence do not apply. You should be prepared to present your case persuasively, smoothly and quickly because you'll probably be given only a few minutes. Do not argue with the landlord or her witnesses. Be cool and just represent your own side as clearly as you can. After the trial, the judge will either decide immediately or mail you and the landlord the decision in a few days.

If the landlord loses, she cannot appeal. She is all through. If she still wishes to evict you, she will have to find new grounds for doing so.

If the landlord wins, she will receive a judgment exactly like the one she would get in Municipal Court, except that the money part cannot exceed $2,000. The judgment cannot be turned over to the sheriff during the 20 days after judgment is entered (30 days if you default). During this time, you may file a Notice of Appeal (or Motion To Set Aside the Default) with the Superior Court. If you file a Notice of Appeal during this period, the case is transferred to the Superior Court, where you will receive a new trial (a "trial de novo"). Until that trial, the eviction is automatically stayed. C.C.P. Section 117j. At the new trial, either side may have an attorney and may request a jury trial.

Note that, unlike the appeal from a regular Municipal Court judgment, where a stay of execution is in the "discretion" of the trial court judge, this stay is automatic, and no bond or other conditions may be placed on the stay. For this reason, the fact that the landlord uses Small Claims Court can be far more valuable to you than to him. If you win in Small Claim Court, you win, and if you lose, you get a new chance in Superior Court, and the landlord loses a lot of time. To qualify for this treatment, however, you must show up in Small Claims Court and, should you lose, file your Notice of Appeal on time. If you don't defend your Small Claims Court case in court, you can't appeal unless you get the default judgment entered against you set aside. If you lose in Superior Court, the judgment may then be turned over to the sheriff for execution.

Most Small Claims Court rules are in the California C.C.P., Section 116 et seq. They are also summarized in Warner, *Everybody's Guide to Small Claims Court* (Nolo Press), which contains much useful information on how to represent yourself in Small Claims Court.

J. After the Lawsuit—Eviction by the Sheriff

If the landlord wins the case, the judge will sign a "writ of possession." The landlord will give this writ to the civil division of the sheriff's department and pay a fee (which will be added to the judgment against you). A deputy sheriff will then serve the writ on you, along with an order that you vacate within five days. It might take the sheriff a few days to serve you with the writ. Some sheriffs serve such writs only on certain days of the week.

If you are served with the writ and are not out in five days, the sheriff will return and physically evict you and your family. He might also throw your belongings out with you, or have them stored by the landlord. (You may have to pay storage fees to get them back. See Chapter 9, Section E.)

The lesson from all this is: If you are served with a five-day notice to vacate by the sheriff, it's time to move. It is much better to manage your own moving than be thrown out by the sheriff.

If you are not named in the writ of possession, you can delay your eviction by filing a form called a "Claim of Right to Possession and Notice of Hearing" after the sheriff serves the writ of possession on you or other tenants.[23] The sheriff or marshal who serves the writ of possession is required by statute to serve a copy of the form at the same time.

The sheriff should have filled in the case number on the front of the form.

Here's how to make a claim:

1. Fill out the form.

---

[23]C.C.P. § 1174.3. This statute codifies existing case law and provides a standard form for the claim. *Arrieta v. Mahon* (1982) 31 Cal.3d 381.

2. Give the form to the sheriff or marshal. Submitting the claim form will stop the eviction. You can give the sheriff the form any time until and including when the sheriff comes back to evict you. You do not have to take it to the sheriff's office, although you may; you can just hand it to him.

3. Send the court the filing fee (or a form requesting waiver of the fee) within two court days. If you submit 15 days' rent with your filing fee, the hearing will be held within five to fifteen days. If you don't submit 15 days' rent with your filing fee, the hearing will be held in five days.

When the court holds its hearing, it will determine the validity of your claim. If the court rules in your favor, the complaint will be deemed to have been served on you at the hearing, and you will be able to respond to it in any of the ways discussed above (see Section E). If the court rules against you, it will order the sheriff to proceed with the eviction.

Sample Letter to Court:

_____

(Date)

Municipal Court of California

_____ Judicial District

_____

_____, CA _____

Re: Unlawful detainer action, Case No._____

Enclosed is a check for $_____ as payment of the fee for filing a Claim of Right to Possession. I filed a Claim of Right to Possession to the premises at_____ on _____, 19___, by giving the Claim to the sheriff/marshal of _____ County.

I have also enclosed a check for $_____, and amount equal to 15 days' rent of the premises.

Sincerely,

Tom Tenant

CLAIMANT OR CLAIMANT'S ATTORNEY (Name and Address):

TELEPHONE NO:

FOR COURT USE ONLY

ATTORNEY FOR (Name):

NAME OF COURT:
STREET ADDRESS:
MAILING ADDRESS:
CITY AND ZIP CODE:
BRANCH NAME:

PLAINTIFF:
DEFENDANT:

CLAIM OF RIGHT TO POSSESSION
AND NOTICE OF HEARING

CASE NUMBER:

(For levying officer use only)
Completed form was received on
Date: _____ Time: _____
By: _____

Complete this form only if ALL of these statements are true:
1. You are NOT named in the accompanying form called Writ of Possession.
2. You occupied the premises on or before the date the unlawful detainer (eviction) action was filed. (The date is in the accompanying Writ of Possession.)
3. You still occupy the premises.

I DECLARE THE FOLLOWING UNDER PENALTY OF PERJURY:

1. My name is (specify):
2. I reside at (street address, unit no., city and ZIP code):
3. The address of "the premises" subject to this claim is (address):
4. On (insert date): _____ , the landlord or the landlord's authorized agent filed a complaint to recover possession of the premises. (This date is in the accompanying Writ of Possession.)
5. I occupied the premises on the date the complaint was filed (the date in item 4). I have continued to occupy the premises ever since.
6. I was at least 18 years of age on the date the complaint was filed (the date in item 4).
7. I claim a right to possession of the premises because I occupied the premises on the date the complaint was filed (the date in item 4).

CLAIM OF RIGHT TO POSSESSION
AND NOTICE OF HEARING

8. I was not named in the Writ of Possession.
9. I understand that if I make this claim of possession, a court hearing will be held to decide whether my claim will be granted.
10. (Filing fee) To obtain a court hearing on my claim, I understand that after I present this form to the levying officer I must go to the court and pay a filing fee of $ _____ or file with the court "Application for Waiver of Court Fees and Costs." I understand that if I don't pay the filing fee or file the form for waiver of court fees within 2 court days, the court will immediately deny my claim.
11. (Immediate court hearing unless you deposit 15 days' rent) To obtain a court hearing on my claim, I understand I must also present a copy of this completed complaint form or a receipt from the levying officer. I also understand the date of my hearing will be set immediately if I do not deliver to the court an amount equal to 15 days' rent.

I am filing my claim in the following manner (check the box that shows how you are filing your claim. Note that you must deliver to the court a copy of the claim form or a levying officer's receipt):

a. ☐ I presented this claim form to the sheriff, marshal, or other levying officer, and within two court days I shall deliver to the court the following: (1) a copy of this completed claim form or a receipt, (2) the court filing fee or form for proceeding in forma pauperis, and (3) an amount equal to 15 days' rent; or

b. ☐ I presented this claim form to the sheriff, marshal, or other levying officer, and within two court days I shall deliver to the court (1) a copy of this completed claim form or a receipt, and (2) the court filing fee or form for proceeding in forma pauperis.

IMPORTANT: Do not take a copy of this claim form to the court unless you have first given the form to the sheriff, marshal, or other levying officer.

(To be completed by the court.)

Date of Hearing: Time: Dept. or Div.:   Room:

Address of court:

NOTICE: If you fail to appear at this hearing you will be evicted without further hearing.

CLAIM OF RIGHT TO POSSESSION
AND NOTICE OF HEARING

NOTICE TO OCCUPANTS

YOU MUST ACT AT ONCE IF ALL THE FOLLOWING ARE TRUE:

(1) You are not named in the accompanying form called Writ of Possession;

(2) You occupied the premises on or before the date the unlawful detainer (eviction) action was filed; and

(3) You still occupy the premises.

You can complete and SUBMIT THIS CLAIM FORM

(1) before the date of eviction at the sheriff's or marshal's office located at: (address)

(2) OR at the premises at the time of the eviction. (Give this form to the officer who comes to evict you.)

If you do not complete and submit this form (and pay a filing fee or file the form for proceeding in forma pauperis if you cannot pay the fee), YOU WILL BE EVICTED along with the parties named in the writ.

After this form is properly filed, A HEARING WILL BE HELD to decide your claim. If you do not appear at the hearing, you will be evicted without a further hearing.

CLAIM OF RIGHT TO POSSESSION
AND NOTICE OF HEARING

---

12. Rental agreement. I have (check all that apply to you):
   a. ☐ an oral rental agreement with the landlord.
   b. ☐ a written rental agreement with the landlord.
   c. ☐ an oral rental agreement with a person other than the landlord.
   d. ☐ a written rental agreement with a person other than the landlord.
   e. ☐ other (explain):

I declare under penalty of perjury under the laws of the State of California that the foregoing is true and correct.

WARNING: Perjury is a felony punishable by imprisonment in the state prison.

Date:

. . . . ▲ . . . .
(TYPE OR PRINT NAME)   (SIGNATURE OF CLAIMANT)

NOTICE: If your claim to possession is found to be valid, the unlawful detainer action against you will be determined at trial. At trial, you may be found liable for rent, costs, and, in some cases, treble damages.

CLAIM OF RIGHT TO POSSESSION
AND NOTICE OF HEARING

Chapter 12:

Tenants Acting Together

So far in this book all of the solutions to tenants' problems have been discussed for the tenant acting alone. Acting alone is not nearly as likely to produce results as is acting together with other people. This chapter is about methods and techniques by which tenants can gather themselves together and organize to deal with the landlord and law makers, but all the organization in the world is not worth one bit of neighborliness--and the organization is not nearly as likely to succeed without it.

In many places in California, it feels like people have forgotten what "neighbor" means, and how to be good neighbors to one another. Neighborliness is based upon caring, understanding and need. If you have caring and understanding in your heart, you don't need any of this mundane advice anyway. What about needs? If an intruder is sneaking into your place and you yell for help, it would be nice if someone came running. If Mrs. Jones next door is sick, maybe you could take her some soup or help with the kids--who knows when you will need the favor returned? And favors are not always returned by the same people who owe you, but what matter, so long as the accounts roughly balance? Help her. If your washer breaks, maybe someone in the block knows how to fix it, and maybe they'd like some of your famous pie! If all you local folks get together you can have fun. You can take turns taking all the kids to a ball game or have a picnic. You can buy food wholesale every other week and distribute it. And woe to the landlord who tries to mess with anyone in a unit full of people that get along together and who have read this book!

A. Tenant Organizing

As we have seen, the odds are often against an individual tenant getting an unreasonable landlord to be more reasonable. The landlord has most of the power. Not only is state law somewhat weighted in her favor, but she normally has far more in the way of financial resources than does the tenant. Most landlords can afford attorneys--most tenants cannot. As long as tenants are divided, she can deal with each one separately and will usually come out on top.

In many ways the landlord/tenant situation today (especially in areas without strong rent control ordinances) is similar to the labor/management situation of 1900. At the turn of the century, one worker without a union had little chance of getting better working conditions or wages from a giant corporation. Indeed, a worker who showed the bad sense to make such a request would probably be walking the bricks in a big hurry. While one tenant dealing with a small landlord might be able to work out a sensible relationship, as neither party has a great deal more power than the other, the individual tenant dealing with the large landlord has little real chance of influencing his situation very much. In fact, he is in much the same situation as was the worker before unions came on the scene. The bigger the business, the more it is run like a machine, and the more humanity is forced out. The tenant, unless she is lucky enough to live in a city with an effective rent control ordinance, either conforms to the many rules in the lease and lets her rent be raised whenever it suits the landlord, or she is out on the street trying to find another place that will probably be just as bad. This is supposed to be a "free country." Pity the poor tenant who is given life by God and freedom by the United States Constitution, only to have most of it impaired by the standard form lease. Of what value is all your freedom if the only place you can find to live will not let you have a pet, a party or hang a picture on the wall? As one tenant recently remarked, "The only thing I can do in my apartment is sleep--and if I snore, I'm in trouble."

There are two ways to restore the balance of power in landlord/tenant relationships, at least to some degree. One involves organizing to pass an effective rent control ordinance which both limits rent increases and requires just cause for eviction. We discuss rent control in some detail in Chapter 4. Suffice it to say that in many California cities rent control ordinances (which not only protect a tenant from outlandish rent increases, but also provide some security against arbitrary eviction) have been very successful. The second involves getting tenants together and bargaining with the landlord as a group. This is the subject of this chapter.

A tenant organization begins as a group of tenants who want to change their relationship with their landlord. This can involve forcing him to make repairs, stopping a rent increase in a non-rent control area, or stopping arbitrary treatment of tenants. The tenant organization may fight the landlord and force him to sign an agreement--sometimes called a collective bargaining agreement--giving the tenants all or some of what they request. If the tenant organization is together enough, it will also force the landlord to deal with it on a continuing basis.

To understand why a tenants' organization can work, consider the material in Chapter 1, Part B. As we discussed there, the landlord business--especially as it relates to large rental projects--normally operates in a way that requires the landlord to have very little of her own cash tied up in the buildings that she claims to own. Most of the time she is simply taking money from tenants in the form of rent, giving it to the bank in the form of mortgage payments and to the City in the form of taxes, and pocketing the difference. In the long run the landlord hopes that the value of the property will increase, allowing her to sell out at a substantial profit. To pay her bills in the meantime, the landlord is dependent upon the majority of her tenants paying the rent. While she can easily deal with a few tenants who hassle her, the landlord is usually not equipped to handle any sort of concerted tenant action. If all of a sudden no one pays the rent, she is in real trouble. She can, of course, bring an "unlawful detainer" suit against every tenant, but this is extremely expensive. In the meantime, she is getting no rent for a considerable period of time and her bills are piling up.

Just as to a labor union the ultimate weapon is the ability to withhold labor, so, too, the strike is the ultimate sanction of a tenants' organization. This does not mean, however, that a rent strike should be used often. Many labor unions rarely strike. They don't need to. They are well organized and able to negotiate from strength. Sensible management will often accept the fact that people have gotten together and will be willing to negotiate a contract. For this reason, tenants, like union members, should work to create a sound, well supported organization that can negotiate from strength and which seeks to arrive at understanding rather than conflict.

For example, suppose a tenants' organization identifies poor maintenance by the landlord as their major problem. This includes dirty common areas, a weed-filled yard, holes in the asphalt of the parking area, broken washing machines, etc. Chances are the amount of money necessary to deal with these problems is small as compared to the combined rent of all the tenants. A sensible landlord, then, is almost sure to clean up the problems long before the tenants ever need to carry out the threat of a strike.

Tenant organizations are usually set up in a crisis situation, when some dispute arises. This is not always the case, however. Even when no dispute is going on, a tenant organization can be a good way for neighbors to get together to organize social activities, baby-sitting cooperatives, wholesale food purchases and the like, as well as to establish a group to deal with the landlord when problems arise.

A tenant organization can also be an effective vehicle to work out problems among tenants. Face it: as any tenant in a multiunit building knows, a neighbor with a loud stereo (or kid, or dog, or spouse) can cause more day-to-day misery than the most obnoxious landlord. In this context, an effective tenants' union can set up a voluntary mediation procedure to help members settle problems before they fester. Local mediation services, such as the Community Boards program in San Francisco, can help you do this. Never overlook the importance of solving disputes between tenants before dealing with the landlord. For example, one of the authors formerly lived in a 14-unit project with an active tenants' organization. At one point there was even the hope that the tenants could buy the project and turn it into a co-op. Unfortunately, the whole organization fell apart when most meetings turned into organizational disputes between those tenants who had dogs and those who didn't, leaving not enough time or energy to deal with the landlord.

This chapter will give you some ideas on how to set up a tenant organization, tactics to use in dealing with the landlord, and how to negotiate a good agreement with him. Keep in mind, however, that a tenant organization is only as effective as the will of its members and leaders to make it effective. This takes time, energy, patience, and the willingness to take risks. Most of all, it takes a sense of community, understanding and identity between the tenants. Understanding both organizing techniques and legal rights may be helpful, but neither can replace these essential qualities. If you feel that these qualities are not there and cannot be inspired, you probably should give up the idea of forming a tenant organization. Find some way of dealing with the landlord by yourself.

B. Setting Up a Tenants' Organization

A number of organized tenants groups describe themselves as "tenants' organizations" while others use the term "tenants' union." It makes no legal difference and we use the terms interchangeably.

1. Getting the Tenants Together at a Meeting

Two or three concerned tenants can start a tenants' organization, if they are willing to do the work.

First, set a meeting time and place. Both should be convenient for most of the tenants. If everyone lives in one large building or group of buildings, this is easy. If the landlord owns several smaller scattered buildings, you will need to allow some time both to contact people and to make sure that there are enough grievances in common to make organizing possible.

Next, contact the tenants and ask them to come to the meeting. If you can possibly afford the time, do this in person, door-to-door. Recruit other tenants to help you. Use posting or distribution of notices only as a last resort or as a supplement to personal contact. If there are different races or ethnic groups in the building, you may want to get someone from each group to do the initial contacting of his own people. If more than one building is involved, make sure you have the active involvement of someone from each.

2. The First Meeting

The first meeting should be conducted informally. People should get to know each other. They should be encouraged to speak about problems they have had with the building or the landlord. This way they will see what problems they have in common.

After this, explain to people the possibilities of collective action. Through reading this Handbook, you have seen how the law and the "market-place" are stacked against the tenant if she tries to deal with the landlord individually, but effective use of tactics described in this chapter can get greater gains if the tenants act as a group. Explain some of these tactics to them. Explain that the tenants can also work out child care, wholesale food purchases, parties and the like, if they can learn to act together.

Next, try to deal with tenants' fears. People will be afraid of being evicted if they fight the landlord. Even if not expressed, these fears are there, so you had better try to bring them out and deal with them, or else you will find the tenants promising now but dropping out later when the action starts.

Explain to the tenants that while some tactics (such as the rent strike) involve a high risk of eviction, others (such as forming a tenants' organization or picketing) do not, if the group has a competent lawyer to protect it from retaliatory evictions (which are prohibited by law). Also make sure that everyone realizes that it will be up to the group to democratically decide which tactics to use. Emphasize that absolutely no action will be taken until the group is ready, having first figured out a strategy, elected leaders, made work assignments, and lined up legal representation and community support. Tell them, however, that there is always some risk of eviction or rent raise (unless you are in a city with a tight rent control ordinance), and if anyone is not willing to take it, he had better drop out now so the others don't depend on him.

From the very beginning, try to deal with the problem of internal dissension. Among the group, there are very likely to be feuds, jealousies, and maybe even racial or ethnic prejudices. Try to bring these out in the open and resolve them as soon as possible, or else they will keep the group from working together when the going gets tough.

3. Setting Up the Organization

At the first meeting, if you feel that the tenants have the qualities needed to take on the landlord, and they more or less agree as to the problems to be addressed, set up the organization of your tenant union. You might elect officers, including a president, vice president, secretary and treasurer. Or, you might elect a "steering committee" or four or five members (with a chairperson) to be responsible for running day-to-day operations, including establishing the time and place of meetings, etc.

In setting up an organization, the most important thing is to see that there is a definite person responsible for each job which is important to the group. Here are some of the jobs that will need to be done:

1. Line up a lawyer;

2. Find out the legal reality of your situation. This means learning your rights under state law. If you are in a city covered by rent control, it also means studying the ordinance and regulations;

3. Coordinate publicity;

4. Get support from other groups;

5. Handle the finances;

6. Coordinate communication among the tenants (set up further meetings, contact people, etc.);

7. Draw up a list of tenants' demands and plan negotiations with the landlord;

8. Gather information on the landlord.

Each of these jobs can be assigned to a committee chairperson, or they can be handled by certain officers. The actual work on these jobs should be done by as many people as possible, so everyone feels involved and no one feels overburdened. But make sure that there is one person responsible for seeing that each job gets done, and that the chairperson or president is responsible for seeing that they get the job done.

Before adjourning the first meeting, the group should:

1. Select a name (for example, "540 Alcatraz Ave. Tenants' Union");

2. Decide the time and place of the second meeting; and

3. Assign to specific people the jobs needed to be done before the second meeting, such as lining up a lawyer and contacting other tenants.

4. The Second Meeting

If you face serious immediate problems with the landlord, the second meeting of the tenant union should be devoted to planning a strategy. Get some agreement on what are the most serious problems the tenants want resolved. Then have your "information" chairperson report on what she found out about the landlord and to which tactics the landlord might be most vulnerable. Then the lawyer should explain the possible consequences of using certain tactics and what he can do to protect the tenants.

Make sure that both the lawyer and the tenants understand that the lawyer is there only to give advice and to help protect the tenants. She is not there to make decisions for the group--only to supply necessary information to allow the group to choose a sensible course of action. If you get a lawyer who wants to run everything, get another. Also, see that tenants do not ask the lawyer to help solve their individual problems. She is there for the group, not for individuals, and if people fall back into an "individual" rather than "group" way of trying to solve problems, the tenant organization will fail.

Then the group should formulate a strategy. Make sure that there is general agreement--a "consensus"--on whatever strategy you decide on. A simple majority vote will not do if there is strong minority feeling opposed to it.

After the strategy is formulated, make specific work assignments to specific people, with deadlines for reporting to the chairperson or the group that the job is done.

5. Contact Other Groups

Assuming your strategy involves a fairly direct confrontation with the landlord, you should try as soon as possible to get support from other groups in the community. Churches, labor unions, political clubs and social clubs can furnish money, publicity, political influence and moral support. Ask each tenant what groups he has contacts with which might help.

Be sure to contact groups which are concerned with tenants' rights. Some cities now have city-wide tenant associations. They can furnish technical advice as well as publicity and moral support. In the San Francisco Bay area, The Public Interest Clearing House publishes a directory of public interest organizations, including tenants' groups. It's available from PIC at 200 McAllister St., San Francisco, CA 94102.

6. How Many Tenants Do You Need Before Acting?

There is no set number. Sometimes only a few tenants will join initially, but many others may come in when the word spreads that the group is doing something and not just talking. If you cannot get a lot of people at first, try to get some "key" people who will influence others and bring them in later.

Obviously, the more tenants you have with you the more pressure the landlord will feel, so try to get as many tenants as you can in your tenant union.

C. Getting Information On the Landlord

In order to find out how to deal with the landlord, you will need information on her. Sometimes you need to find out who the owner is. You should try to find out what her financial situation is like to see where she is most vulnerable. You need to know something about her personality before you negotiate with her.

Here are some sources of information you might check out.

1. Tax Assessor's Office

The City or County Tax Assessor estimates the value of each piece of property and keeps a record of to whom the tax bill is sent and who pays the taxes. This information is kept according to address, so you can obtain it without first knowing the name of the owner.

This can help you identify the real owner. Usually he is the one who pays the taxes. If not, then investigating the person who does pay the taxes can lead you to the real owner.

If taxes have not been paid, this indicates either the landlord's poor financial condition or possibly her intent to abandon the building to the city or county.

The amount of the tax is a significant part of the landlord's expense in running the building. You may want to know this for negotiations.

Some assessors keep an alphabetical list of people who pay property taxes, specifying each piece of property on which they pay taxes. This can tell you how much property the landlord owns in the city or county and where it is. If he has other rental buildings, talk to the tenants there and see if they are interested in joining your effort. This can really help you increase the pressure on the landlord.

2. Local Real Estate Offices

For income tax reasons, many buildings are put up for sale rather frequently, usually six to ten years after purchase. There is a fair chance that, at any given time, your building will be on the market.

You might send some substantial-looking person into a local real estate office to ask if the building is for sale and express interest in buying it. The real estate agent might furnish him some very helpful information concerning the building, especially information relating to income and expenses. While this information may be slanted to make the building seem more profitable than it is, this bias should make the figures useful to rebut the landlord's inevitable complaints that she is suffering financially from owning the building.

3. Housing Code Inspection Departments

The city or county housing or building inspection department can be a source of information as to the condition of the building and the landlord's efforts (or lack of them) to repair.

First, since he must obtain a permit to make alterations in the building, you can find out when he last made substantial repairs and what he planned to do.

Second, find out when the agency last inspected the building and whether the violations were corrected. This documentation can be useful later for publicity or in court.

Also, find out if they have recorded any complaints by tenants. This can build your case that tenants have long been concerned about the landlord's failure to repair.

Records of the building inspector's dealings with the landlord are open to the public and may be copied. Government Code §§ 6253 and 7254.7(c).

4. Other Sources of Information

If you want to do a thorough job, here are some other sources of information you might check out.

a. County Recorder's Office

Here, if you know the name of the present owner, you can find out names of prior owners and who has mortgages, deeds of trust, or liens on the property.

b. Rent Control Board

In several California cities (including Berkeley, Santa Monica and West Hollywood), a landlord must register all rental property with the city rent control board. Comprehensive information telling you how much rent can be charged is available.

c. Title Insurance Companies

They can tell you everything about the ownership of the property, including mortgages, etc. They usually charge for their services, but some people (such as attorneys who do real estate work) can often get information from title companies for nothing.

d. Secretary of State

If the building is owned by a corporation, the Secretary of State can tell you who runs the corporation. Contact the California Secretary of State's Office, 111 Capitol Mall, Sacramento CA 95814.

e. Newspapers

A look through the local newspaper's "morgue" can sometimes produce good information on a landlord. A reporter who has covered the neighborhood for some time might also be helpful.

f. Ex-Managers and Former Tenants

These people might tell you how the landlord has treated people in the past. Since they are out, they have nothing to lose, and if they were mistreated by the landlord, they might be willing to help.

D. Tactics

1. Petition the Landlord

One good first step is to draw up a list which sets out your complaints and demands and give it to the landlord.

This document should be worded politely but firmly. Remember that it might later get into the hands of other people, such as the newspapers or the courts, so you want to sound reasonable, even if the landlord deserves something stronger.

The demands should be clearly set out, and there should be a final request for a response or a meeting by a specific time (such as a week later). Although it is probably not wise to set out at this point exactly what you intend to do if the landlord is not cooperative (since you want to leave your options open until you are ready to act), the petition should carry the clear implication that the group means business.

It is usually better if all the tenants in the group sign the petition. This lets the landlord know that the people are united and serious enough about this to sign their names and risk possible reprisals. It also tends to make the people feel more committed.

The petition is a useful starting tactic, no matter what else you later decide to do. It forces the group to stop talking about general problems and decide what issues it will focus on. Often it will impress the landlord into agreeing to solve some, or all, of the problems. Even if it doesn't, the landlord's response will give you an idea of how to deal with her in the future. Also, if you start with a reasonable petition, you are in a positive position to demonstrate later to newspapers, courts, and other groups that you made every effort to be reasonable before you had to resort to your pressure tactics.

In this context, a number of California cities and counties offer non-binding mediation programs. In some situations sitting down with your landlord to discuss the issues in this sort of forum can be a good idea. If no agreement is forthcoming in a reasonable time, you can always resort to tougher tactics later. Also, if the landlord refuses to be reasonable, it is likely to convince those tenants who are reluctant to organize and take a strong stand that doing so is the only way to accomplish your goals.

2. Call the Code Inspector

If your grievances have to do with the substandard condition of the premises, call the code inspector and ask for an inspection of the building. This can be useful for several purposes.

First, an inspection which results in a report that there are violations shows that the tenants have legitimate grievances and are not just making things up to cause trouble or withhold rent.

Second, if you end up in court, you have the inspector available as a neutral, expert witness who can testify as to conditions in the building.

Third, an inspection which results in an order from the agency that the landlord make repairs may get him to fix the place, for otherwise the agency might have it condemned. Many sophisticated landlords, however, know how to handle the agency so as to avoid making repairs until the last possible moment. They are friendly with the inspectors, know how to take appeals and get extensions, and might get the agency to hold off by doing a few things and saying he is "working on" the others. He is less likely to get away with this where there are serious health hazards, such as rats or no heat. If you have these problems, call the Health Department rather than the Building Inspection Department, as they are generally more concerned about these issues.

There are some dangers in reporting code violations. First, if the building is really in bad shape, you may get too much action. The agency may condemn the building, or the landlord might decide it is cheaper to tear it down than fix it up. In either case, the tenants might be evicted.

Second, before calling the inspector, make sure that bad conditions were not caused by tenants, even in part. If they were, the inspector will probably find out about it and her report will probably do you more harm than good.

Finally, there is a danger of eviction if the landlord finds out who reported the violations. However, because retaliatory evictions are prohibited by law, you should prevail if you bring the facts to light in court. Civil Code§1942.5. Indeed, in some instances, reporting code violations provides protection for subsequent organizing activities, since a later eviction may be inferred to be retaliatory. See Chapter 7.

Before you call out a code inspector, try to find out if there is some inspector in the agency who will be sympathetic to what you are trying to accomplish. If there is, talk to him about these problems and see what he advises. He may be able to set things up so you get the most out of the inspection with the least risk.

Rent Control Note: In a few California cities including Berkeley and Santa Monica, the existence of substandard housing conditions is a valid reason to petition the local rent control board for a rent reduction.

3. Picketing and Publicity

Landlords don't like negative publicity, particularly if it affects their business or social lives. So it can be a very useful tactic to let the world know that your landlord owns units with serious health or safety problems.

Whenever you seek publicity by any means, make sure that you make specific charges and that what you are saying is true. This will keep you out of legal trouble and keep support on your side.

There are many ways to get publicity. Here are some of them.

Picketing at the building itself involves no travel time or expense, so it is easier to get tenants out to picket. This lets tenants, prospective tenants, and the neighborhood in general know what is going on, and it can help muster support. Picketing at the landlord's office can put economic pressure on her by persuading her customers to stay away. This can be particularly effective when she is a rental agent or management company. A third possible location is the landlord's residence. This can be particularly effective if the grievances are truly serious.

Whenever you picket, be sure to have lists of your grievances available for the media. Their coverage will multiply the effect of your picketing.

Banners in the windows of tenants' apartments are another good way of letting tenants, prospective tenants, and the neighborhood know what is happening. Leaflets can also serve this purpose, and they are good to use when picketing, so people passing by (including reporters) can get the details of the dispute.

A press conference can be a good way of getting to all of the media at once. To get reporters and TV people to come, however, you will have to set up a time when they can come (that is, when nothing else of importance is happening) and call them personally, well ahead of time. Also, try to make the dispute sound dramatic. If conditions in the building are bad, have the press conference at the building and show the reporters the worst conditions.

If picketing or other publicity is hurting the landlord, he might file a lawsuit to try to stop it. He may ask the court to limit the number of pickets, stop distribution of material he claims is untrue, or stop the campaign entirely. The law on these issues is not clear, and what happens depends a lot on how the judge feels about it. Therefore, it is very helpful to have a lawyer to advise you and ready to represent you when you start a publicity campaign.

4. Rent Strikes

The rent strike can be the most powerful tactic the tenants can use. It brings direct and immediate economic pressure to bear on the landlord. Few landlords are able to pay mortgage payments, property taxes, and other expenses from sources other than rents for long. If the landlord cannot break the strike quickly, she must come to the bargaining table.

A rent strike is now legal in California, if the landlord has materially breached his "implied warranty of habitability" by failing to correct serious housing code violations. How this doctrine works and what happens if the landlord sues to evict rent strikers is more fully discussed in the section on rent withholding in Chapter 7.

If no material problems of habitability are involved in your dispute, a rent strike is not legal, but might work anyway, because the landlord might prefer to negotiate rather than try to evict.

If you decide that your landlord is being so unreasonable that no other course of action is open to you but a rent strike, there are some things you might do to minimize the danger of eviction.

First, line up a good lawyer. If she fights the eviction action very hard and takes advantage of the rights you have,[1] it might take the landlord a long time to evict anyone, if he ever can. He might not be able to wait that long, so he might be willing to negotiate.

Second, inform the landlord that you are not simply pocketing the rent money, but are putting it in an "escrow account" which will be disposed of after the dispute is settled (by using it to make repairs, turning it over to the landlord or something else). This escrow account is *not* required by law. But it is sure to impress the judge that you are not just trying to get something for nothing, so she may rule in your favor, or she may at least give you a chance to pay the rent to avoid eviction if she finds that the landlord did not materially breach his implied warranty of habitability. Also, if you dangle a large escrow account in front of a landlord, he will be more willing to deal with you than if the money is simply lost.

An escrow account can be set up as a bank savings account. Everyone deposits his rent into the account. For withdrawals, the signatures of both a tenant organization officer and the tenant should be required. This assures each tenant that her money will not be spent without her consent. An easier way to set up an escrow is to rent a safe deposit box in a bank and have each tenant put a money order (or certified check) for the amount of the rent in the box as it comes due. You might also put the money in your lawyer's account.

Whichever method you choose, make sure that every tenant follows it. If some tenants get a "free ride," morale will suffer badly and the group might easily fall apart.

Third, be sure to put together good evidence on the housing code violations. Take pictures (in color), get a housing code inspector or other expert to look at the place, and have tenants ready to testify as to the conditions.

---

[1] See *California Eviction Defense Manual* (Cont. Ed. Bar).

Finally, keep up your campaign for publicity and community support. This can help impress the judge that this is a very important issue.

5. Repair and Deduct Remedy

Another more modest form of rent strike is permitted in California. The "repair and deduct" remedy, described in detail in Chapter 7, might be used by a group of tenants to make repairs costing no more than the total of the monthly rents of the tenants participating. For example, if the plumbing doesn't work and it will cost $1,400 to fix, four tenants might notify the landlord that they will pool their next month's rent of $350 each and have it fixed, if he does not do so within a reasonable time. If he fails to do so, the tenants can have the work done, pay the bill, and deduct the amount from the next month's rent. There is presently no reported case in California where tenants have pooled their rents like this, but there seems to be nothing in Civil Code Sections 1941-1942.1 to prevent this.

Many times, of course, the threat of using this sort of remedy will produce action.

6. Lawsuits Against the Landlord

A lawsuit against the landlord can be another means of putting pressure on her so that she wants to negotiate with you. This might be done where she has locked someone out,[2] committed a retaliatory eviction or rent raise,[3] or refused to repair substantial housing code violations.[4]

A lawsuit puts the landlord on the defensive psychologically. He is in danger of having to pay substantial money damages. He will have to pay attorney's fees, which may be expensive.

If your lawsuit asks for "punitive damages," your attorney is entitled to find out the landlord's entire financial position, which he may not be anxious to reveal. Your attorney may also take the landlord's "deposition," requiring him to appear and answer questions which might make him uncomfortable.

You should be very careful about the effect on the tenant union of filing a suit, however. Often when such a suit is filed, the tenants begin to rely too much on the lawsuit and the lawyer to solve their problems for them. They tend to stop their other efforts, and the group gradually fades away. If this happens, even a victory in the lawsuit usually won't help the tenants much, since most of the tenants will probably move out before then. Be sure to tell the people (and the attorney) that the lawsuit is only one part of the campaign against the landlord to force her to negotiate with the tenant union. If they cannot accept this, then you probably should not file the suit.

---

[2]*Jordan v. Talbot*, 55 Cal. 2d 597; 12 Cal. Rptr. 488 (1961); Civil Code § 789.3.

[3]*Aweeka v. Bonds*, 20 Cal. App. 3d 278 (1971); Civil Code §1942.5(f).

[4]*Stoiber v. Honeychuck*, 101 Cal. App. 3d 903.

7. Landlord's Countertactics

There are several things the landlord is likely to try in his efforts to defeat your movement. He might file lawsuits against the tenants or try to get the police to stop the picketing. He might try to evict the leaders of the tenant union, or, thinking that if just one person is evicted the tenant union will collapse, he might try to evict one person he has good legal grounds to evict. He might try to pit certain tenants against others, making promises to some and blaming problems on others. A common tactic is to surprise the tenants by giving in to most of their demands right away with promises, then waiting for the group to fade away and then doing little or nothing.

The tenants should be aware of these possibilities and be ready to deal with them. They should remember (1) always to stick together and (2) not to relax until they have the final action they seek.

E. Negotiations

Skill in negotiating is very important to maximize the results of your campaign against the landlord. Never forget, however, that the outcome will depend much more on who has the power outside the negotiating room, that is, what you can do to the landlord if she won't give you what you want and what you can give her if she will. The most skilled negotiator can't do much for powerless people, but inarticulate amateurs can often succeed when their opponent understands that they can and will use some real power if she does not give in.

1. Preparations

The tenant organization should select a small negotiating team to speak for them.

These people should know as much as possible about the building, the tenants and the landlord. Psychologically, the landlord can gain control of the negotiating meeting if he overwhelms the tenants with his knowledge, so the tenants had better be prepared to keep up with him.

The negotiators should have a clear understanding of what their authority is, that is, what kind of deal the tenants will accept. The tenants should discuss their demands and tell the negotiators which demands are non-negotiable, which are "nice if they can get it," and which are expendable and can be traded off. In deciding this, the tenants must understand how strong they are and what they can realistically expect to get.

A role-playing session, with some tenants playing the landlord's role, can be very helpful to give the negotiators some experience.

The negotiators should have a proposed collective bargaining agreement ready at the meeting, so that they can get the landlord to commit herself in writing then and there. If there is nothing for her to sign, she might promise to sign something but change her mind later.

Finally, the negotiators should put together an overall strategy, knowing what they are after and how they are going to get there, so they can work together and not interfere with each other.

2. The Negotiating Meeting

The meeting should not take place at the landlord's office, where he will feel comfortable and the tenants intimidated. Have the meeting at the building or somewhere else in your neighborhood. In San Francisco, check with the Community Board program for help doing this. In other California cities and counties, mediation programs are available that will often help set up tenant-landlord negotiating sessions.

Have as many tenants as possible attend the meeting. This show of unity will impress the landlord and help the negotiators. It will also stimulate tenant interest and help strengthen the tenant union.

Make sure that the person you negotiate with is the owner or has the authority to make decisions binding on the owner. If this isn't made clear at the outset, they are wasting your time.

The negotiators should get across to the landlord--directly or subtly--what the union will do if negotiations break down and what they will give her if she comes to terms. On this latter point, you might tell the landlord that the tenant union and a collective bargaining agreement giving rights to tenants can increase tenant morale. This can cut down vandalism and vacancies and make rent payments more prompt.

One of the most important elements in negotiations is the psychological atmosphere. The landlord will try to be in control and keep the negotiators on on the defensive. The negotiators should realize this and try to keep the landlord on the defensive. If you work with a third party mediator, this person should help establish a neutral, cooperative atmosphere.

F. The Agreement

A written agreement (sometimes called a collective bargaining agreement) is a key goal of the tenant organization or union. Labor unions seek such agreements in order to firmly establish a continuing bargaining relationship with an employer, as well as to settle specific points of dispute. Tenant organization agreements can do the same, so that the landlord has to deal with the union rather than the isolated tenant, and so the tenant can have the power of the union behind him whenever he has a grievance.

Remember, however, that the agreement will only be as effective as the continued willingness of the tenant union to make it effective. Even though the agreement is legally binding on the landlord, experience has shown that it will simply fade away unless the tenant union (or some larger neighborhood organization) is continually around as a "watchdog" to see that the landlord complies with it.[5]

When you and your landlord sign an agreement, have the signatures notarized. Take a copy of the signed and notarized agreement to the County Recorder's Office to have it recorded. This may prevent someone who buys the building from trying to avoid the agreement.

---

[5]A model agreement, with explanatory notes, appears in the *Tenant Union Guide,* in Volume II of the *Handbook on Housing Law* (Prentice Hall), which is available at many large law libraries.

Chapter 13:

Renters Insurance

Attitudes towards insurance vary—some people wouldn't be without it while others consider it a giant rip-off. Our job is not to argue this question one way or the other, but to tell you how renters insurance works.

Renters insurance is a package of several types of insurance designed to cover tenants for more than one risk. Different insurance companies put slightly different things in their packages, both as to types of coverage, dollar amounts of coverage and especially deductible clauses. There is nothing we can tell you here that will substitute for your shopping around and comparing policies and prices. They do vary. It's a good idea to talk to friends and see if they are happy with their insurance, but realize that prices for renters insurance can be very different depending upon where you live. In certain high theft areas it is almost unobtainable.

The average renters policy covers you against losses to your belongings occurring as a result of fire and theft, up to the amount stated on the face of the policy, which is often $5,000, $10,000 or $25,000. As thefts have become more common, most policies have included "deductible" amounts of $50, $100, or even $500. This means that if you are burgled, you collect from the insurance company only for the amount of your loss over and above the "deductible" clause.

Many renters policies completely exclude certain property from theft coverage, including cash, credit cards, pets, etc., while others limit the amount of cash covered to $100, the value of manuscripts to $1,000 and jewelry and furs to $500. Make sure your policy covers what you think it does. If it doesn't, check out the policies of other companies. As a general rule, you can get whatever coverage you want if you are willing to pay for it.

If you do take out insurance on valuable items, you should inventory them. Not only should you note them down with their values, it is also an excellent idea to take photos. Keep the inven--

tory and photos at work or some other place other than your apartment, so that if there is a problem it won't have suffered the same fate as your belongings.

Some tenants don't see a reason to have fire insurance, especially if the unit is furnished, because they don't have much property to lose. This is sensible enough, but does overlook the fact that if the rental unit suffers fire (or water) damage as a result of tenant negligence (e.g., a grease fire in a frying pan spreads and damages the kitchen), the tenant is liable, and will need insurance coverage if he is to avoid having to make good the loss out of his own pocket.

In addition to fire and theft coverage, most renters policies give you (and your family living with you), personal liability coverage to a certain amount stated in the policy. This means that if you directly injure someone (e.g., you hit them on the head with a golf ball), he is injured on the rental property that you occupy through your negligence (e.g., slips on a broken front step), or you damage his belongings (e.g., your garden hose floods the neighbor's cactus garden), you are covered. There are a lot of exclusions to personal liability coverage, important among them being any damage you do with a motor vehicle, boat or through your business.

Important: Your landlord's "homeowners" insurance won't cover you. Even if you live in a duplex with your landlord and the landlord has a "homeowners" policy, this policy won't protect your belongings if there is a fire or theft. Of course, if you suffer a loss as a result of your landlord's negligence, you may have a valid claim against her. Most landlords have insurance specifically to protect against this sort of risk.

If you have a loss, be sure your insurance company treats you fairly. You are entitled to the present fair market value (what the property would sell for, not the replacement cost), of anything stolen or destroyed by fire or any other hazard covered by the policy after the deductible amount of the policy is subtracted, unless your policy specifies "replacement value." If the company won't pay you a fair amount, consider taking the dispute to Small Claims Court if it is for $2,000 or less. If the loss is a major one, you might consider seeing a lawyer, but agree to pay the lawyer only a percentage of what he can recover over and above what the insurance company offers you without the lawyer's help.

Recently many landlords have begun inserting a clause into their leases or rental agreements requiring that the tenant purchase renters insurance. This is legal under California law. The landlord's motive for doing so is threefold:

1. If the tenant's property is damaged in any way that is not the landlord's legal responsibility and the damage is covered by the renter's policy, the landlord won't have to rely on his own insurance policy;

2. Anyone who suffers a personal injury on the property in a situation where the tenant is at fault is less likely to sue the landlord also;

3. A number of landlords believe that tenants who are willing to buy insurance are more responsible than other tenants.

Chapter 14:

Condominium Conversion

Converting buildings from rental properties into condominiums was unusual several years ago. Now, however, the general shortage of new homes, coupled with favorable tax laws, has created a condominium boom.

Condominium ownership as an abstract principle can make great sense. People have a basic need to own their own spaces, and with the high cost of land and construction, condominiums are often the only way this need can find expression. But whether condominium ownership makes sense as an abstract principle need not concern us here--there are already more than enough people worrying about how to create more of them while getting paid plenty for their efforts. Our concern is with the tenants of existing rental properties who are unable or unwilling to pay large sums of money to purchase their units. Here is a little story about what this could mean to you.

One day the mailperson delivers an identical letter to all the tenants in a multiunit building. The owner, it seems, has decided to convert the building from rental units to owner-occupied condominiums. Everyone will either have to buy her apartment and a share of the common space (such as halls and grounds), or move out. Those with leases must leave when they run out, and those with month-to-month tenancies under a written rental agreement must leave in 30 days. The letter concludes politely that the owners hope that they have caused no inconvenience and are sure that many tenants will welcome this opportunity to buy their units at the rock bottom price of $200,000 each.

Is there anything a tenant can do in the above situation if he wants neither to move nor buy his unit? Can't the landlord do pretty much what she wants? At first impression, it would seem that the law favors the landlord and that the tenant is in a hopeless position, but don't give up too fast. Some very determined tenants in many cities have proved that tenants acting together aren't helpless.

The conversion of rental units to a condominium constitutes a "subdivision" under California law. This means that several local government agencies have the right to approve or disapprove the project. A public hearing must be held before the planning commission, with the right to appeal to the city council or county board of supervisors. Tenants acting together have stopped many conversions by exerting sufficient political pressure so that proposed conversions were denied the necessary approvals. One of the best ways to do this is to have the local government pass an ordinance allowing condominium conversions only if a number of conditions have been met. Your city or county may already have passed such an ordinance, and your first step is to get a copy if one exists. But beware: many ordinances purporting to strictly limit condominium conversions were, in fact, written by developers and have no real teeth.

A good condominium conversion ordinance should require most, if not all, of the following conditions to be met, before a conversion can take place:

•That existing tenants be given first right to buy their unit;

•That 50% of the existing tenants approve of the conversion;

•That all tenants over 65 or disabled to allowed to continue as tenants for life if they wish;

•That no conversions be allowed where the landlord has evicted large groups of tenants or greatly raised rents to get rid of tenants just prior to the conversion;

•That no conversions of any kind be allowed when the rental vacancy rate in a city is below 5% unless new rental units are being built at least fast enough to replace those converted;

•That special scrutiny be given to conversion of units rented to people with low and moderate incomes, to see that the units are priced at a level that the existing tenants can afford;

•That the landlord provide *adequate* relocation assistance.

To have a chance to stop a proposed condominium conversion, it is essential that tenants act together and that they create political alliances with sympathetic groups in the city. If you have not already done so, read Chapter 12. You will want to start by checking out your landlord carefully. Look for facts about the landlord that would tend to make local government agencies unsympathetic to the conversion. Among the best are the following:

•The landlord is from out of town and has recently bought your building (and perhaps others) as a speculation;

•The landlord has a long history of violating housing codes and generally is known as a "bad landlord";

•The landlord raised rents excessively, terminated tenancies for no reason, and did other things to clear out the building before the conversion was announced;

•The building is occupied by many older people (or others on fixed incomes) who have no place to go, and the landlord has made little or no effort to either allow them to stay on at terms they can afford or find them a decent place to live;

•The landlord is making an excellent return on his money as rental units and conversion to condominiums would result in huge profits.

Note: Legislation has recently been introduced in the state legislature to provide strict rules covering condominium conversions. To date, nothing has passed, largely as a result of pressure from the real estate lobby.

The only statewide law presently in effect affecting conversions is found in Government Code 66247.1. It provides that:

1. Each tenant is given 120 days' written notice of the intent to convert prior to termination of tenancy due to the conversion, and

2. Each tenant is given the first right to buy her apartment on at least the same terms that the apartment will be offered to the general public. The tenant has 90 days to decide.

So, if you are faced with a condominium conversion, don't give up. Re-read this chapter, get together with your neighbors, and organize. You will probably find that the other tenants in your city face similar situations. Together, you may be able to exert enough political pressure to save your home.

Appendix Table of Contents

Conditions of Premises Checklist
Model Lease
Model Rental Agreement
Notice to Repair
Notice of Rent Withholding
Proof of Service
Demurrer
Notice of Hearing on Demurrer
Form Answer to Unlawful Detainer Complaint
Request for Inspection
Form Interrogatories for Unlawful Detainer Cases
Settlement Agreement in Unlawful Detainer Action
Jury Demand Form
Application for Relief from Eviction
Application for Stay of Eviction
Notice of Appeal
Collective Bargaining Agreement

Checklist

The following is a summary of the conditions of the premises at

_____, California,

on the dates indicated below.

	Condition on Arrival	Condition on Departure
Living Room		
Floor & Floor Covering		
Drapes		
Walls & Ceilings		
Furniture (if any)		
Light Fixtures		
Windows, Screens & Doors		
Anything Else		
Kitchen		
Floor Covering		
Stove & Refrigerator		
Light Fixtures		
Windows, Screens & Doors		
Sink & Plumbing		
Cupboards		
Dining Room		
Floor & Floor Covering		
Drapes		
Walls & Ceilings		
Furniture (if any)		
Light Fixtures		
Windows, Screens & Doors		
Bathroom(s)		
Toilet(s)		
Sink(s)		
Shower(s)		
Floor, Walls & Ceiling		
Light Fixtures		
Windows, Screens & Doors		
Bedrooms		
Floors & Floor Covering		
Walls & Ceiling		
Furniture (if any)		
Light Fixtures		
Windows, Screens & Doors		
Other Areas		
Floors & Floor Covering		
Windows, Screens & Doors		
Walls & Ceilings		
Furnace		
Air Conditioning (if any)		
Lawn, Ground Covering		
Patio, Terrace, Deck, etc.		
Other		

Checklist filled out on moving in on _____, 19__, and approved by

_____ and _____.
              Landlord   Tenant

Checklist filled out on moving out on _____, 19__, and approved by

_____ and _____.
              Landlord   Tenant

Lease

National Housing and Economic Development Law Project Form Lease (California)

1. Parties

The parties to this Agreement are _____
_____,
hereinafter called "Landlord," and _____
_____,
hereinafter called "Tenant." If Landlord is the agent of the owner of said property, the owner's name and address is _____
_____.

2. Property

Landlord hereby lets the following property to Tenant for the term of this Agreement: (a) the property located at _____
and (b) the following furniture and appliances on said property:_____
_____
_____.

3. Term

The term of this Agreement shall be for _____
beginning on _____ and ending on _____.

4. Rent

The monthly rental for said property shall be $_____, due and payable on the first day of each month.

5. Utilities

Utilities shall be paid by the party indicated on the following chart:

	Landlord	Tenant
Electricity	_____	_____
Gas	_____	_____
Water	_____	_____
Garbage collection	_____	_____
Trash removal	_____	_____
Other	_____	_____

6. Use of Property

Tenant shall use the property only for residential purposes, except for incidental use in his trade or business (such as telephone solicitation of sales orders or arts and craft created for profit), so long as such incidental use does not violate local zoning laws or affect Landlord's ability to obtain fire or liability insurance.

7. Tenant's Duty to Maintain Premises

Tenant shall keep the dwelling unit in a clean and sanitary condition and shall otherwise comply with all state and local laws requiring tenants to maintain rented premises. If damage to the dwelling unit (other than normal wear and tear) is caused by acts or neglect of Tenant or others occupying the premises with his permission, Tenant may repair such damage at his own expense. Upon Tenant's failure to make such repairs, after reasonable notice by Landlord, Landlord may cause such repairs to be made and Tenant shall be liable to Landlord for any reasonable expense thereby incurred by Landlord.

8. Alterations

No substantial alteration, addition, or improvement shall be made by Tenant in or to the dwelling unit without the prior consent of Landlord in writing. Such consent shall not be unreasonably withheld, but may be conditioned upon Tenant's agreeing to restore the dwelling unit to its prior condition upon moving out.

9. Noise

Tenant agrees not to allow on his premises any excessive noise or other activity which disturbs the peace and quiet of other tenants in the building. Landlord agrees to prevent other tenants and other persons in the building or common areas from similarly disturbing Tenant's peace and quiet.

10. Inspection by Landlord

Unless Tenant has moved out, Landlord or his agent may enter the dwelling unit only for the following purposes: to deal with an emergency (such as fire); to make necessary or agreed repairs, decorations, alterations or improvements; to supply necessary or agreed services; or to show the unit to prospective or actual purchasers, mortgagees, tenants, workmen, or contractors. Unless there is an emergency, Landlord must give at least 24 hours prior written notice of his intent to enter and the date, time, and purpose of the intended entry. (In case of an emergency entry, Landlord shall, within 2 days thereafter, notify Tenant in writing of the date, time, and purpose of the entry.) Tenant shall have the right to refuse to allow any entry (except for an emergency) before 9 AM or after 5 PM. If Tenant objects to an intended entry between 9 AM and 5 PM, Landlord shall (where feasible) attempt to arrange a more convenient time for Tenant. Landlord's entries shall not be so frequent as to seriously disturb Tenant's peaceful enjoyment of the premises and shall not be used to harass Tenant.

11. Security Deposit

a) Upon signing this Agreement, Tenant shall deposit with Landlord the sum of $_____ as a security deposit. This deposit (with any interest accrued under the subparagraph (c) of this paragraph) may be applied by Landlord toward reimbursement for any costs reasonably necessary to repair any damage to the premises caused by Tenant, to clean the premises (where Tenant has not left the premises as clean as he found them), or for due and unpaid rent.

b) Landlord shall inspect the premises within one week prior to Tenant's vacating the premises and, before Tenant vacates, shall give Tenant a written statement of needed repairs and the estimate cost thereof.

c) Within two weeks after Tenant vacates the premises, Landlord shall return to Tenant the security deposit together with interest of one-half of one per cent for each month Landlord held the deposit, less any deductions Landlord is entitled to make under subparagraph (a) of this paragraph. If Landlord makes any such deductions, he shall, within two weeks after Tenant vacates the premises, give Tenant a written itemized statement of such deductions and explanations thereof.

12. Landlord's Obligation to Repair and Maintain Premises

a) Landlord shall maintain the building and grounds appurtenant to the dwelling unit in a decent, safe, and sanitary condition, and shall comply with all state and local laws, regulations, and ordinances concerning the condition of dwelling units.

b) Landlord shall take reasonable measures to maintain security on the premises and the building and grounds appurtenant thereto to protect Tenant and other occupants and guests of the premises from burglary, robbery, and other crimes. Tenant agrees to use reasonable care in utilizing such security measures.

c) If repairs are now needed to comply with this paragraph, Landlord specifically agrees to complete the following repairs by the following dates:

Repair	Date

d) If Landlord substantially fails to comply with any duty imposed by this paragraph, Tenant's duty to pay rent shall abate until such failure is remedied. This subparagraph shall apply to defects within Tenant's dwelling unit only if Tenant has notified Landlord or his agent of such defects. The remedy provided by this subparagraph shall not preclude Tenant from invoking any other remedy provided by law to Tenant for Landlord's violation of this Agreement.

13. Subleasing

Tenant shall not assign this Agreement or sublet the dwelling unit without the written consent of Landlord. Such consent shall not be withheld without good reason relating to the prospective tenant's ability to comply with the provisions of this Agreement. This paragraph shall not prevent Tenant from accommodating guests for reasonable periods.

14. Failure to Pay Rent

If Tenant is unable to pay rent when due, but on or before such due date he gives Landlord or his agent written notice that he is unable to pay said rent on time and the reasons therefor, Landlord shall attempt to work out with Tenant a procedure for paying such rent as soon as possible. If, after 10 days, Landlord and Tenant are unable to work out such a procedure, Landlord may serve a notice to pay rent or vacate within 3 days, as provided by California Code of Civil Procedure Section 1161.

15. Destruction of Premises

If the premises become partially or totally destroyed during the term of this Agreement, either party may thereupon terminate this Agreement upon reasonable notice.

16. Tenant's Termination for Good Cause

Upon 30 days' written notice, for good cause, Tenant may terminate this Agreement and vacate the premises. Said notice shall state good cause for termination. Good cause shall include, but not be limited to, entry into active duty with U.S. military services, employment in another community, and loss of the main source of income used to pay the rent.

17. Termination and Cleaning

Upon termination of this Agreement, Tenant shall vacate the premises, remove all personal property belonging to him, and leave the premises as clean as he found them (normal wear and tear excepted). If the property is located in an area covered by "just cause" for eviction regulations, Landlord must comply with these regulations in order to terminate or evict.

18. Lawsuits

If either party commences a lawsuit against the other to enforce any provision of this Agreement, the successful party shall be awarded court costs from the other. Landlord specifically waives any right to recover treble or other punitive damages pursuant to California Code of Civil Procedure Section 1174.

19. Notices

All notices and rent provided by this Agreement shall be in writing and shall be given to the other party as follows:

To the Tenant: at the premises.

To the Landlord: at _____.

20. Holdovers

If Tenant holds over upon termination of this Agreement and Landlord accepts Tenant's tender of the monthly rent provided by this Agreement, the Agreement shall continue to be binding on the parties as a month-to-month tenancy.

WHEREFORE We, the undersigned, do hereby execute and agree to this Lease.

LANDLORDS: TENANTS:

_____   _____
(signature)   (signature)

    _____   _____
    (date of signature)   (date of signature)

_____   _____
(signature)   (signature)

    _____   _____
    (date of signature)   (date of signature)

Rental Agreement

National Housing and Economic Development Law Project Form Lease (California)

1. Parties

The parties to this Agreement are _____
_____,
hereinafter called "Landlord," and _____
_____,
hereinafter called "Tenant." If Landlord is the agent of the owner of said property, the owner's
name and address is_____
_____.

2. Property

Landlord hereby lets the following property to Tenant for the term of this Agreement: (a) the
property located at _____
and (b) the following furniture and appliances on said property:_____
_____
_____.

3. Term

This Agreement shall run month-to-month, beginning on _____.

4. Rent

The monthly rental for said property shall be $_____, due and payable on the first
day of each month.

5. Utilities

Utilities shall be paid by the party indicated on the following chart:

	Landlord	*Tenant*
Electricity		
Gas		
Water		
Garbage collection		
Trash removal		
Other		

6. Use of Property

Tenant shall use the property only for residential purposes, except for incidental use in his trade
or business (such as telephone solicitation of sales orders or arts and craft created for profit), so
long as such incidental use does not violate local zoning laws or affect Landlord's ability to obtain
fire or liability insurance.

7. Tenant's Duty to Maintain Premises

Tenant shall keep the dwelling unit in a clean and sanitary condition and shall otherwise
comply with all state and local laws requiring tenants to maintain rented premises. If damage to
the dwelling unit (other than normal wear and tear) is caused by acts or neglect of Tenant or others
occupying the premises with his permission, Tenant may repair such damage at his own expense.

Upon Tenant's failure to make such repairs, after reasonable notice by Landlord, Landlord may cause such repairs to be made and Tenant shall be liable to Landlord for any reasonable expense thereby incurred by Landlord.

8. Alterations

No substantial alteration, addition, or improvement shall be made by Tenant in or to the dwelling unit without the prior consent of Landlord in writing. Such consent shall not be unreasonably withheld, but may be conditioned upon Tenant's agreeing to restore the dwelling unit to its prior condition upon moving out.

9. Noise

Tenant agrees not to allow on his premises any excessive noise or other activity which disturbs the peace and quiet of other tenants in the building. Landlord agrees to prevent other tenants and other persons in the building or common areas from similarly disturbing Tenant's peace and quiet.

10. Inspection by Landlord

Unless Tenant has moved out, Landlord or his agent may enter the dwelling unit only for the following purposes: to deal with an emergency (such as fire); to make necessary or agreed repairs, decorations, alterations or improvements; to supply necessary or agreed services; or to show the unit to prospective or actual purchasers, mortgagees, tenants, workmen, or contractors. Unless there is an emergency, Landlord must give at least 24 hours prior written notice of his intent to enter and the date, time, and purpose of the intended entry. (In case of an emergency entry, Landlord shall, within 2 days thereafter, notify Tenant in writing of the date, time, and purpose of the entry.) Tenant shall have the right to refuse to allow any entry (except for an emergency) before 9 AM or after 5 PM. If Tenant objects to an intended entry between 9 AM and 5 PM, Landlord shall (where feasible) attempt to arrange a more convenient time for Tenant. Landlord's entries shall not be so frequent as to seriously disturb Tenant's peaceful enjoyment of the premises and shall not be used to harass Tenant.

11. Security Deposit

a) Upon signing this Agreement, Tenant shall deposit with Landlord the sum of $_____ as a security deposit. This deposit (with any interest accrued under the subparagraph (c) of this paragraph) may be applied by Landlord toward reimbursement for any costs reasonably necessary to repair any damage to the premises caused by Tenant, to clean the premises (where Tenant has not left the premises as clean as he found them), or for due and unpaid rent.

b) Landlord shall inspect the premises within one week prior to Tenant's vacating the premises and, before Tenant vacates, shall give Tenant a written statement of needed repairs and the estimate cost thereof.

c) Within two weeks after Tenant vacates the premises, Landlord shall return to Tenant the security deposit together with interest of one-half of one per cent for each month Landlord held the deposit, less any deductions Landlord is entitled to make under subparagraph (a) of this paragraph. If Landlord makes any such deductions, he shall, within two weeks after Tenant vacates the premises, give Tenant a written itemized statement of such deductions and explanations thereof.

12. Landlord's Obligation to Repair and Maintain Premises

a) Landlord shall maintain the building and grounds appurtenant to the dwelling unit in a decent, safe, and sanitary condition, and shall comply with all state and local laws, regulations, and ordinances concerning the condition of dwelling units.

b) Landlord shall take reasonable measures to maintain security on the premises and the building and grounds appurtenant thereto to protect Tenant and other occupants and guests of the premises from burglary, robbery, and other crimes. Tenant agrees to use reasonable care in utilizing such security measures.

c) If repairs are now needed to comply with this paragraph, Landlord specifically agrees to complete the following repairs by the following dates:

Repair	Date

d) If Landlord substantially fails to comply with any duty imposed by this paragraph, Tenant's duty to pay rent shall abate until such failure is remedied. This subparagraph shall apply to defects within Tenant's dwelling unit only if Tenant has notified Landlord or his agent of such defects. The remedy provided by this subparagraph shall not preclude Tenant from invoking any other remedy provided by law to Tenant for Landlord's violation of this Agreement.

13. Subleasing

Tenant shall not assign this Agreement or sublet the dwelling unit without the written consent of Landlord. Such consent shall not be withheld without good reason relating to the prospective tenant's ability to comply with the provisions of this Agreement. This paragraph shall not prevent Tenant from accommodating guests for reasonable periods.

14. Failure to Pay Rent

If Tenant is unable to pay rent when due, but on or before such due date he gives Landlord or his agent written notice that he is unable to pay said rent on time and the reasons therefor, Landlord shall attempt to work out with Tenant a procedure for paying such rent as soon as possible. If, after 10 days, Landlord and Tenant are unable to work out such a procedure, Landlord may serve a notice to pay rent or vacate within 3 days, as provided by California Code of Civil Procedure Section 1161.

15. Destruction of Premises

If the premises become partially or totally destroyed during the term of this Agreement, either party may thereupon terminate this Agreement upon reasonable notice.

16. Notice of Termination

Tenant may terminate this Agreement upon 30 days' written notice thereof to Landlord. Landlord may terminate or change the terms of this Agreement upon 60 days' written notice thereof to Tenant unless the property is located in an area covered by "just cause" for eviction regulations, in which case those regulations control. No notice shall be valid, however, if the Landlord's dominant purpose in serving it is to retaliate against the Tenant because of Tenant's attempt to exercise or assert his rights under this Agreement or any law of the State of California, its governmental subdivisions, of the United States, or because of any other lawful act of Tenant. Any such notice shall contain a statement of the reasons for termination or change of terms, and if such statement be controverted, Landlord shall have the burden of proving its truth. This paragraph shall not affect Landlord's right to terminate for cause after expiration of a 3-day notice given pursuant to California Code of Civil Procedure Section 1161.

17. Termination and Cleaning

Upon termination of this Agreement, Tenant shall vacate the premises, remove all personal property belonging to him, and leave the premises as clean as he found them (normal wear and tear excepted). If the property is located in an area covered by "just cause" for eviction regulations, Landlord must comply with these regulations in order to terminate or evict.

18. Lawsuits

If either party commences a lawsuit against the other to enforce any provision of this Agreement, the successful party shall be awarded court costs from the other. Landlord specifically waives any right to recover treble or other punitive damages pursuant to California Code of Civil Procedure Section 1174.

19. Notices

All notices and rent provided by this Agreement shall be in writing and shall be given to the other party as follows:

To the Tenant: at the premises.

To the Landlord: at _____.

WHEREFORE We, the undersigned, do hereby execute and agree to this Lease.

LANDLORDS: TENANTS:

_____   _____
(signature)   (signature)

_____   _____
(date of signature)   (date of signature)

_____   _____
(signature)   (signature)

_____   _____
(date of signature)   (date of signature)

NOTICE TO REPAIR

To _____, Landlord of the premises located at

_____.

NOTICE IS HEREBY GIVEN that unless certain defects on the premises are repaired within a reasonable time, the undersigned tenant shall exercise any and all rights accruing to him pursuant to law, including those granted by California Civil Code Sections 1941-1942.

The defects are the following:

_____

_____

_____

_____

Dated:_____   _____
                              (signature of tenant)

NOTICE OF RENT WITHHOLDING

To _____, Landlord of the premises located at
_____.

NOTICE IS HEREBY GIVEN that because of your failure to comply with your implied warranty of habitability by refusing to repair defects on the premises, as previously demanded of you, the undersigned tenant has elected to withhold this month's rent in accordance with California law. Rent payments will be resumed in the future, as they become due, only after said defects have been properly repaired.

Dated:_____   _____
                          (signature of tenant)

PROOF OF SERVICE BY MAIL

I am a citizen of the United States and a resident of the county of_____.
I am over the age of 18 years and not a party to the above action; my residence address is:
_____, California. On :_____,
19___, I served the within Answer on the Plaintiffs in said action by placing a true copy thereof
enclosed in a sealed envelope with postage theron fully prepaid, in the United States Post Office
mail box at _____, California, addressed as follows:

_____.

I _____, certify under penalty of perjury that the
foregoing is true and correct. Executed on _____,
19___, at _____, California.

_____
Signature

1 Defendant's Name:_____

2 Address:_____

Telephone Number:_____

3 Defendant in Pro Per

4 _____

In the Municipal Court of the State of California

5 County of _____, _____ District

6 _____

Plaintiff(s)

7 v.   No._____

8 _____   DEMURRER OF

Defendant(s)   _____

9   (name of defendant)
                                            TO COMPLAINT OF

10   _____

                                            (name of plaintiff)

11 _____

Defendant(s) demur to the Complaint on the following ground(s):

12

1. _____

13 _____

14 _____.

2. _____

15 _____

16 _____

3. _____

17 _____

18 _____

19 _____

20 _____

21 _____

22 _____

23 _____

24 _____

25 Date:_____   _____

Signature of Defendant

26

27

28

Defendant's Name:_____

Address:_____

Telephone Number:_____

Defendant in Pro Per

_____

In the Municipal Court of the State of California

County of _____, _____ District

_____

Plaintiff(s)

v.   No._____

                                                      NOTICE OF HEARING ON
_____   DEMURRER OF
              Defendant(s)
                                                      _____
                                                      (name of defendant)
                                                      TO COMPLAINT OF

                                                      _____
                                                      (name of plaintiff)

_____

To:_____
                     (defendent)
    PLEASE TAKE NOTICE THAT on _____, 19____, at
_____ in Department No._____ of the above entitled court,
located at _____ a hearing will be held on defendant's
demurrer to the complaint, a copy of which is served with this notice.

Date:_____   _____
                               Defendant
                               In pro per

ATTORNEY OR PARTY WITHOUT ATTORNEY (NAME AND ADDRESS):	TELEPHONE:	FOR COURT USE ONLY

ATTORNEY FOR (NAME):

Insert name of court, judicial district or branch court, if any, and post office and street address:

PLAINTIFF:

DEFENDANT:

ANSWER— Unlawful Detainer	CASE NUMBER:

1. This pleading including attachments and exhibits consists of the following number of pages: _____

2. Defendants *(name):*

   answer the complaint as follows:

3. **Check ONLY ONE of the next two boxes:**

   a. ☐ Defendant generally denies each statement of the complaint. *(Do not check this box if the complaint demands more than $1,000.)*

   b. ☐ Defendant admits that all of the statements of the complaint are true EXCEPT:

      (1) Defendant claims the following statements of the complaint are false *(use paragraph numbers from the complaint or explain):*

      ☐ Continued on Attachment 3.b.(1).

      (2) Defendant has no information or belief that the following statements of the complaint are true, so defendant denies them *(use paragraph numbers from the complaint or explain):*

      ☐ Continued on Attachment 3.b.(2).

4. AFFIRMATIVE DEFENSES

   a. ☐ *(nonpayment of rent only)* Plaintiff has breached the warranty to provide habitable premises. *(Briefly state the facts below in item 4.k.)*

   b. ☐ Plaintiff waived, changed, or canceled the notice to quit. *(Briefly state the facts below in item 4.k.)*

   c. ☐ Plaintiff served defendant with the notice to quit or filed the complaint to retaliate against defendant. *(Briefly state the facts below in item 4.k.)*

   d. ☐ Plaintiff has failed to perform his obligations under the rental agreement. *(Briefly state the facts below in item 4.k.)*

   e. ☐ By serving defendant with the notice to quit or filing the complaint, plaintiff is arbitrarily discriminating against the defendant in violation of the constitution or laws of the United States or California. *(Briefly state the facts below in item 4.k.)*

   f. ☐ Plaintiff's demand for possession violates the local rent control or eviction control ordinance of *(city or county, title of ordinance, and date of passage):*

      (Briefly state the facts showing violation of the ordinance in item 4.k.)

   (Continued)

Form Approved by the
Judicial Council of California
Effective January 1, 1982
Rule 982.1(95)

ANSWER—Unlawful Detainer

CCP 425.12
Post Record Catalog # 982.1(95)

ANSWER—Unlawful Detainer

g. ☐ Plaintiff accepted rent from defendant to cover a period of time after the date stated in paragraph 8.b. of the complaint.

h. ☐ *(nonpayment of rent only)* On *(date):*   defendant offered the rent due but plaintiff would not accept it.

i. ☐ Defendant made needed repairs and properly deducted the cost from the rent, and plaintiff did not give proper credit.

j. ☐ Other affirmative defenses. *(Briefly state below in item 4.k.)*

k. FACTS SUPPORTING AFFIRMATIVE DEFENSES CHECKED ABOVE *(Identify each item separately.)*

☐ Continued on Attachment 4.k.

5. OTHER STATEMENTS
    a. ☐ Defendant vacated the premises on *(date):*
    b. ☐ Defendant claims a credit for deposits of $_____
    c. ☐ The fair rental value of the premises in item 12 of the complaint is excessive *(explain):*

    d. ☐ Other *(specify):*

6. DEFENDANT REQUESTS
    a. that plaintiff take nothing requested in the complaint.
    b. costs incurred in this proceeding.
    c. ☐ reasonable attorney fees.
    d. ☐ other *(specify):*

....
      (Type or print name)

_____
     (Signature of defendant or attorney)

....
      (Type or print name)

_____
     (Signature of defendant or attorney)

*(Each defendant for whom this answer is filed must be named in item 2 **and** must sign this answer unless represented by an attorney.)*

VERIFICATION

(Use a different verification form if the verification is by an attorney or for a corporation or partnership.)

I am the defendant in this proceeding and have read this answer. I declare under penalty of perjury under the laws of the State of California that this answer is true and correct.

Date:

....
      (Type or print name)

_____
     (Signature of defendant)

Defendant's Name:_____

Address:_____

Telephone Number:_____

Defendant in Pro Per

_____

In the Municipal Court of the State of California

County of _____, _____ District

_____
Plaintiff(s)

v.   No._____

_____   Request to Inspect and for
Defendant(s)   Production of Documents
                                                      Code of Civil Procedure
                                                      Sec. 2031

To _____, Plaintiff, and _____,

Plaintiff's attorney:

Defendant, _____,

requests that you produce and permit the copying of the following documents: _____

_____.

Defendant requests that you produce these documents at the following address:

_____

_____

at the following date and time: _____.

Defendant further requests permission to enter, inspect, and photograph the premises located at

_____ at the following date and time:

_____.

Date:_____   _____
                                                      Signature of Defendant

ORDER

IT IS HEREBY ORDERED that Plaintiff(s)_____

respond to Defendant's [Request for Inspection] [Written Interrogatories] no later than

_____, on condition that Defendant serve

such [Request for Inspection] [Written Interrogatories] on Plaintiff(s) no later than

_____.

Date:_____   _____

                                                                    Judge of the Municipal Court

_____

FORM INTERROGATORIES — UNLAWFUL DETAINER
Asking Party:

Answering Party:
Set No.:

CASE NUMBER:

Sec. 1. Instructions to All Parties

(a) These are general instructions. *For time limitations, requirements for service on other parties, and other details, see Code of Civil Procedure section 2030 and the cases construing it.*

(b) These interrogatories do not change existing law relating to interrogatories nor do they affect an answering party's right to assert any privilege or objection.

Sec. 2. Instructions to the Asking Party

(a) These interrogatories are designed for optional use in unlawful detainer proceedings.

(b) There are restrictions that generally limit the number of interrogatories that may be asked and the form and use of the interrogatories. For details, read Code of Civil Procedure section 2030(c).

(c) In determining whether to use these or any interrogatories, you should be aware that abuse can be punished by sanctions, including fines and attorney fees. See Code of Civil Procedure section 128.5.

(d) Check the box next to each interrogatory that you want the answering party to answer. Use care in choosing those interrogatories that are applicable to the case.

(e) Additional interrogatories may be attached.

Sec. 3. Instructions to the Answering Party

(a) An answer or other appropriate response must be given to each interrogatory checked by the asking party. Failure to respond to these interrogatories properly can be punished by sanctions, including contempt preceedings, fine, attorneys fees, and the loss of your case. See Code of Civil Procedure sections 128.5 and 2030.

(b) As a general rule, within 30 days after you are served with these interrogatories, you must serve your responses on the asking party and serve copies of your responses on all other parties to the action who have appeared. See Code of Civil Procedure section 2030 for details.

(c) Each answer must be as complete and straightforward as the information reasonably available to you permits. If an interrogatory cannot be answered completely, answer it to the extent possible.

(d) If you do not have enough personal knowledge to fully answer an interrogatory, say so, but make a reasonable and good faith effort to get the information by asking other persons or organizations, unless the information is equally available to the asking party.

(e) Whenever an interrogatory may be answered by referring to a document, the document may be attached as an exhibit to the response and referred to in the response. If the document has more than one page, refer to the page and section where the answer to the interrogatory can be found.

(f) Whenever an address and telephone number for the same person are requested in more than one interrogatory, you are required to furnish them in answering only the first interrogatory asking for that information.

(g) Your answers to these interrogatories must be verified, dated, and signed. You may wish to use the following form *at the end of your answers:*

''I declare under penalty of perjury under the laws of the State of California that the foregoing answers are true and correct.

_____   _____   ''
(DATE)   (SIGNATURE)

Sec. 4. Definitions

Words in **BOLDFACE CAPITALS** in these interrogatories are defined as follows:

(a) **PERSON** includes a natural person, firm, association, organization, partnership, business, trust, corporation, or public entity.

(b) **PLAINTIFF** includes any **PERSON** who seeks recovery of the **RENTAL UNIT** whether acting as an individual or on someone else's behalf and includes all such **PERSONS** if more than one.

Form Approved by the
Judicial Council of California
FI-128 [Rev. July 1, 1987]

**FORM INTERROGATORIES
UNLAWFUL DETAINER**

CCP 2030, 2033.5

(c) **LANDLORD** includes any **PERSON** who offered the **RENTAL UNIT** for rent and any **PERSON** on whose behalf the **RENTAL UNIT** was offered for rent and their successors in interest. **LANDLORD** includes all **PERSONS** who managed the **PROPERTY** while defendant was in possession.

(d) **RENTAL UNIT** is the premises **PLAINTIFF** seeks to recover.

(e) **PROPERTY** is the building or parcel (including common areas) of which the **RENTAL UNIT** is a part. (For example, if **PLAINTIFF** is seeking to recover possession of apartment number 12 of a 20-unit building, the building is the **PROPERTY** and apartment 12 is the **RENTAL UNIT**. If **PLAINTIFF** seeks possession of cottage number 3 in a five-cottage court or complex, the court or complex is the **PROPERTY** and cottage 3 is the **RENTAL UNIT**.)

(f) **DOCUMENT** means a writing, as defined in Evidence Code section 250, and includes the original or a copy of handwriting, typewriting, printing, photostating, photographing, and every other means of recording upon any tangible thing and form of communicating or representation, including letters, words, pictures, sounds, or symbols, or combinations of them.

(g) **NOTICE TO QUIT** includes the original or copy of any notice mentioned in Code of Civil Procedure section 1161 or Civil Code section 1946, including a 3-day notice to pay rent and quit the **RENTAL UNIT**, a 3-day notice to perform conditions or covenants or quit, a 3-day notice to quit, and a 30-day notice of termination.

(h) **ADDRESS** means the street address, including the city, state, and zip code.

Sec. 5. Interrogatories

The following interrogatories have been approved by the Judicial Council under section 2033.5 of the Code of Civil Procedure for use in unlawful detainer proceedings:

CONTENTS

70.0 General

[Either party may ask any applicable question in this section.]

☐ 70.1 State the name, **ADDRESS**, telephone number, and relationship to you of each **PERSON** who prepared or assisted in the preparation of the responses to these interrogatories. (Do not identify anyone who simply typed or reproduced the responses.)

☐ 70.2 Is **PLAINTIFF** an owner of the **RENTAL UNIT**? If so, state:
(a) the nature and percentage of ownership interest;
(b) the date **PLAINTIFF** first acquired this ownership interest.

☐ 70.3 Does **PLAINTIFF** share ownership or lack ownership? If so, state the name, the **ADDRESS**, and the nature and percentage of ownership interest of each owner.

☐ 70.4 Does **PLAINTIFF** claim the right to possession other than as an owner of the **RENTAL UNIT**? If so, state the basis of the claim.

☐ 70.5 Has **PLAINTIFF'S** interest in the **RENTAL UNIT** changed since acquisition? If so, state the nature and dates of each change.

☐ 70.6 Are there other rental units on the **PROPERTY**? If so, state how many.

☐ 70.7 During the 12 months before this proceeding was filed, did **PLAINTIFF** possess a permit or certificate of occupancy for the **RENTAL UNIT**? If so, for each state:

(a) the name and **ADDRESS** of each **PERSON** named on the permit or certificate;
(b) the dates of issuance and expiration;
(c) the permit or certificate number.

☐ 70.8 Has a last month's rent, security deposit, cleaning fee, rental agency fee, credit check fee, key deposit, or any other deposit been paid on the **RENTAL UNIT**? If so, for each item state:

(a) the purpose of the payment;
(b) the date paid;
(c) the amount;
(d) the form of payment;
(e) the name of the **PERSON** paying;
(f) the name of the **PERSON** to whom it was paid;
(g) any **DOCUMENT** which evidences payment and the name, **ADDRESS**, and telephone number of each **PERSON** who has the **DOCUMENT**;
(h) any adjustments or deductions including facts.

☐ 70.9 State the date defendant first took possession of the **RENTAL UNIT**.

☐ 70.10 State the date and all the terms of any rental agreement between defendant and the **PERSON** who rented to defendant.

☐ 70.11 For each agreement alleged in the pleadings:

(a) identify all **DOCUMENTS** that are part of the agreement and for each state the name, **ADDRESS**, and telephone number of each **PERSON** who has the **DOCUMENT**;
(b) state each part of the agreement not in writing, the name, **ADDRESS**, and telephone number of each **PERSON** agreeing to that provision, and the date that part of the agreement was made;
(c) identify all **DOCUMENTS** that evidence each part of the agreement not in writing and for each state the name, **ADDRESS**, and telephone number of each **PERSON** who has the **DOCUMENT**;
(d) identify all **DOCUMENTS** that are part of each modification to the agreement, and for each state

the name, **ADDRESS**, and telephone number of each **PERSON** who has the **DOCUMENT** (see also § 71.5);

(e) state each modification not in writing, the date, and the name, **ADDRESS**, and telephone number of the **PERSON** agreeing to the modification, and the date the modification was made (see also § 71.5);

(f) identify all **DOCUMENTS** that evidence each modification of the agreement not in writing and for each state the name, **ADDRESS**, and telephone number of each **PERSON** who has the **DOCUMENT** (see also § 71.5).

☐ 70.12 Has any **PERSON** acting on the **PLAINTIFF'S** behalf been responsible for any aspect of managing or maintaining the **RENTAL UNIT** or **PROPERTY**? If so, for each **PERSON** state:
(a) the name, **ADDRESS**, and telephone number;
(b) the dates the **PERSON** managed or maintained the **RENTAL UNIT** or **PROPERTY**;
(c) the **PERSON'S** responsibilities.

☐ 70.13 For each **PERSON** who occupies any part of the **RENTAL UNIT** (except occupants named in the complaint and occupants' children under 17) state:
(a) the name, **ADDRESS**, telephone number, and birthdate;
(b) the inclusive dates of occupancy;
(c) a description of the portion of the **RENTAL UNIT** occupied;
(d) the amount paid, the term for which it was paid, and the person to whom it was paid;
(e) the nature of the use of the **RENTAL UNIT**;
(f) the name, **ADDRESS**, and telephone number of the person who authorized occupancy;
(g) how occupancy was authorized, including failure of the **LANDLORD** or **PLAINTIFF** to protest after discovering the occupancy.

☐ 70.14 Have you or anyone acting on your behalf obtained any **DOCUMENT** concerning the tenancy between any occupant of the **RENTAL UNIT** and any **PERSON** with an ownership interest or managerial responsibility for the **RENTAL UNIT**? If so, for each **DOCUMENT** state:
(a) the name, **ADDRESS**, and telephone number of each individual from whom the **DOCUMENT** was obtained;
(b) the name, **ADDRESS**, and telephone number of each individual who obtained the **DOCUMENT**;
(c) the date the **DOCUMENT** was obtained;
(d) the name, **ADDRESS**, and telephone number of each **PERSON** who has the **DOCUMENT** (original or copy).

71.0 Notice

*[If a defense is based on allegations that the 3-day notice or 30-day **NOTICE TO QUIT** is **defective in form or content**, then either party may ask any applicable question in this section.]*

☐ 71.1 Was the **NOTICE TO QUIT** on which **PLAINTIFF** bases this proceeding attached to the complaint? If not, state the contents of this notice.

☐ 71.2 State all reasons that the **NOTICE TO QUIT** was served and for each reason:
(a) state all facts supporting **PLAINTIFF'S** decision to terminate defendant's tenancy;

(b) state the names, **ADDRESSES**, and telephone numbers of all **PERSONS** who have knowledge of the facts;
(c) identify all **DOCUMENTS** that support the facts and state the name, **ADDRESS**, and telephone number of each **PERSON** who has each **DOCUMENT**.

☐ 71.3 List all rent payments and rent credits made or claimed by or on behalf of defendant beginning 12 months before the **NOTICE TO QUIT** was served. For each payment or credit state:
(a) the amount;
(b) the date received;
(c) the form in which any payment was made;
(d) the services performed or other basis for which a credit is claimed;
(e) the period covered;
(f) the name of each **PERSON** making the payment or earning the credit;
(g) the identity of all **DOCUMENTS** evidencing the payment or credit and for each state the name, **ADDRESS**, and telephone number of each **PERSON** who has the **DOCUMENT**.

☐ 71.4 Did defendant ever fail to pay the rent on time? If so, for each late payment state:
(a) the date;
(b) the amount of any late charge;
(c) the identity of all **DOCUMENTS** recording the payment and for each state the name, **ADDRESS**, and telephone number of each **PERSON** who has the **DOCUMENT**.

☐ 71.5 Since the beginning of defendant's tenancy, has **PLAINTIFF** ever raised the rent? If so, for each rent increase state:
(a) the date the increase became effective;
(b) the amount;
(c) the reasons for the rent increase;
(d) how and when defendant was notified of the increase;
(e) the identity of all **DOCUMENTS** evidencing the increase and for each state the name, **ADDRESS**, and telephone number of each **PERSON** who has the **DOCUMENT**.
[See also section 70.11(d) − (f).]

☐ 71.6 During the 12 months before the **NOTICE TO QUIT** was served was there a period during which there was no permit or certificate of occupancy for the **RENTAL UNIT**? If so, for each period state:
(a) the inclusive dates;
(b) the reasons.

☐ 71.7 Has any **PERSON** ever reported any nuisance or disturbance at or destruction of the **RENTAL UNIT** or **PROPERTY** caused by defendant or other occupant of the **RENTAL UNIT** or their guests? If so, for each report state:
(a) a description of the disturbance or destruction;
(b) the date of the report;
(c) the name of the **PERSON** who reported;
(d) the name of the **PERSON** to whom the report was made;
(e) what action was taken as a result of the report;
(f) the identity of all **DOCUMENTS** evidencing the report and for each state the name, **ADDRESS**, and telephone number of each **PERSON** who has each **DOCUMENT**.

71.8 Does the complaint allege violation of a term of a rental agreement or lease (other than nonpayment of rent)? If so, for each covenant:
(a) identify the covenant breached;
(b) state the facts supporting the allegation of a breach;
(c) state the names, **ADDRESSES**, and telephone numbers of all **PERSONS** who have knowledge of the facts;
(d) identify all **DOCUMENTS** that support the facts and state the name, **ADDRESS**, and telephone number of each **PERSON** who has each **DOCUMENT**.

71.9 Does the complaint allege that the defendant has been using the **RENTAL UNIT** for an illegal purpose? If so, for each purpose:
(a) identify the illegal purpose;
(b) state the facts supporting the allegations of illegal use;
(c) state the names, **ADDRESSES**, and telephone numbers of all **PERSONS** who have knowledge of the facts;
(d) identify all **DOCUMENTS** that support the facts and state the name, **ADDRESS**, and telephone number of each **PERSON** who has each **DOCUMENT**.

[Additional interrogatories on this subject may be found in sections 75.0, 78.0, 79.0, and 80.0.]

72.0 Service

*[If a defense is based on allegations that the **NOTICE TO QUIT** was **defectively served**, then either party may ask any applicable question in this section.]*

72.1 Does defendant contend (or base a defense or make any allegations) that the **NOTICE TO QUIT** was defectively served? If the answer is "no," do not answer interrogatories 72.2 through 72.3.

72.2 Does **PLAINTIFF** contend that the **NOTICE TO QUIT** referred to in the complaint was served? If so, state:
(a) the kind of notice;
(b) the date and time of service;
(c) the manner of service;
(d) the name and **ADDRESS** of the person who served it:
(e) a description of any **DOCUMENT** or conversation between defendant and the person who served the notice.

72.3 Did any person receive the **NOTICE TO QUIT** referred to in the complaint? If so, for each copy of each notice state:
(a) the name of the person who received it;
(b) the kind of notice;
(c) how it was delivered;
(d) the date received;
(e) where it was delivered;
(f) the identity of all **DOCUMENTS** evidencing the notice and for each state the name, **ADDRESS**, and telephone number of each **PERSON** who has the **DOCUMENT**.

73.0 Malicious Holding Over

[If a defendant denies allegations that defendant's continued possession is malicious, then either party may ask any applicable question in this section. Additional questions in section 75.0 may also be applicable.]

73.1 If any rent called for by the rental agreement is unpaid, state the reasons and the facts upon which the reasons are based.

73.2 Has defendant made any attempts to secure other premises since the service of the **NOTICE TO QUIT** or since the service of the summons and complaint? If so, for each attempt:
(a) state all facts indicating the attempt to secure other premises;
(b) state the names, **ADDRESSES**, and telephone numbers of all **PERSONS** who have knowledge of the facts;
(c) identify all **DOCUMENTS** that support the facts and state the name, **ADDRESS**, and telephone number of each **PERSON** who has each **DOCUMENT**.

73.3 State the facts upon which **PLAINTIFF** bases the allegation of malice.

74.0 Rent Control and Eviction Control

74.1 Is there an ordinance or other local law in this jurisdiction which limits the right to evict tenants? If your answer is no, you need not answer sections 74.2 through 74.6.

74.2 For the ordinance or other local law limiting the right to evict tenants, state:
(a) the title or number of the law;
(b) the locality.

74.3 Do you contend that the **RENTAL UNIT** is exempt from the eviction provisions of the ordinance or other local law identified in section 74.2? If so, state the facts upon which you base your contention.

74.4 Is this proceeding based on allegations of a need to recover the **RENTAL UNIT** for use of the **LANDLORD** or the landlord's relative? If so, for each intended occupant state:
(a) the name;
(b) the residence **ADDRESSES** from three years ago to the present;
(c) the relationship to the **LANDLORD**;
(d) all the intended occupant's reasons for occupancy;
(e) all rental units on the **PROPERTY** that were vacated within 60 days before and after the date the **NOTICE TO QUIT** was served.

74.5 Is the proceeding based on an allegation that the **LANDLORD** wishes to remove the **RENTAL UNIT** from residential use temporarily or permanently (for example, to rehabilitate, demolish, renovate, or convert)? If so, state:
(a) each reason for removing the **RENTAL UNIT** from residential use;
(b) what physical changes and renovation will be made to the **RENTAL UNIT**;
(c) the date the work is to begin and end;
(d) the number, date, and type of each permit for the change or work;

(e) the identity of each **DOCUMENT** evidencing the intended activity (for example, blueprints, plans, applications for financing, construction contracts) and the name, **ADDRESS**, and telephone number of each **PERSON** who has each **DOCUMENT**.

☐ 74.6 Is the proceeding based on any ground other than those stated in sections 74.4 and 74.5? If so, for each:
(a) state each fact supporting or opposing the ground;
(b) state the names, **ADDRESSES**, and telephone numbers of all **PERSONS** who have knowledge of the facts;
(c) identify all **DOCUMENTS** evidencing the facts and state the name, **ADDRESS**, and telephone number of each **PERSON** who has each **DOCUMENT**.

75.0 Breach of Warranty to Provide Habitable Premises

[If plaintiff alleges nonpayment of rent and defendant bases his defense on allegations of implied or express breach of warranty to provide habitable residential premises, then either party may ask any applicable question in this section.]

☐ 75.1 Do you know of any conditions in violation of state or local building codes, housing codes, or health codes, conditions of dilapidation, or other conditions in need of repair in the **RENTAL UNIT** or on the **PROPERTY** that affected the **RENTAL UNIT** at any time defendant has been in possession? If so, state:
(a) the type of condition;
(b) the kind if corrections or repairs needed;
(c) how and when you learned of these conditions;
(d) how these conditions were caused;
(e) the name, **ADDRESS**, and telephone number of each **PERSON** who has caused these conditions.

☐ 75.2 Have any corrections, repairs, or improvements been made to the **RENTAL UNIT** since the **RENTAL UNIT** was rented to defendant? If so, for each correction, repair, or improvement state:
(a) a description giving the nature and location;
(b) the date;
(c) the name, **ADDRESS**, and telephone number of each **PERSON** who made the repairs or improvements;
(d) the cost;
(e) the identity of any **DOCUMENT** evidencing the repairs or improvements;
(f) if a building permit was issued, state the issuing agencies and the permit number of your copy.

☐ 75.3 Did defendant or any other **PERSON** during 36 months before the **NOTICE TO QUIT** was served or during defendant's possession of the **RENTAL UNIT** notify the **LANDLORD** or his agent or employee about the condition of the **RENTAL UNIT** or **PROPERTY**? If so, for each written or oral notice state:
(a) the substance;
(b) who made it;
(c) when and how it was made;
(d) the name and **ADDRESS** of each **PERSON** to whom it was made;
(e) the name and **ADDRESS** of each person who knows about it;
(f) the identity of each **DOCUMENT** evidencing the notice and the name, **ADDRESS**, and telephone number of each **PERSON** who has it;

(g) the response made to the notice;
(h) the efforts made to correct the conditions;
(i) whether the **PERSON** who gave notice was an occupant of the **PROPERTY** at the time of the complaint.

☐ 75.4 During the period beginning 36 months before the **NOTICE TO QUIT** was served to the present, was the **RENTAL UNIT** or **PROPERTY** (including other rental units) inspected for dilapidations or defective conditions by a representative of any governmental agency? If so, for each inspection state:
(a) the date;
(b) the reason;
(c) the name of the governmental agency;
(d) the name, **ADDRESS**, and telephone number of each inspector;
(e) the identity of each **DOCUMENT** evidencing each inspection and the name, **ADDRESS**, and telephone number of each **PERSON** who has it.

☐ 75.5 During the period beginning 36 months before the **NOTICE TO QUIT** was served to the present, did **PLAINTIFF** or **LANDLORD** receive a notice or other communication regarding the condition of the **RENTAL UNIT** or **PROPERTY** (including other rental units) from a governmental agency? If so, for each notice or communication state:
(a) the date received;
(b) the identity of all parties;
(c) the substance of the notice or communication;
(d) the identity of each **DOCUMENT** evidencing the notice or communication and the name, **ADDRESS**, and telephone number of each **PERSON** who has it.

☐ 75.6 Was there any corrective action taken in response to the inspection or notice or communication identified in sections 75.4 and 75.5? If so, for each:
(a) identify the notice or communication;
(b) identify the condition;
(c) describe the corrective action;
(d) identify of each **DOCUMENT** evidencing the corrective action and the name, **ADDRESS**, and telephone number of each **PERSON** who has it.

☐ 75.7 Has the **PROPERTY** been appraised for sale or loan during the period beginning 36 months before the **NOTICE TO QUIT** was served to the present? If so, for each appraisal state:
(a) the date;
(b) the name, **ADDRESS**, and telephone number of the appraiser;
(c) the purpose of the appraisal;
(d) the identity of each **DOCUMENT** evidencing the appraisal and the name, **ADDRESS**, and telephone number of each **PERSON** who has it.

☐ 75.8 Was any condition requiring repair or correction at the **PROPERTY** or **RENTAL UNIT** caused by defendant or other occupant of the **RENTAL UNIT** or their guests? If so, state:
(a) the type and location of condition;
(b) the kind of corrections or repairs needed;
(c) how and when you learned of these conditions;
(d) how and when these conditions were caused;
(e) the name, **ADDRESS**, and telephone number of each **PERSON** who caused these conditions;

(f) the identity of each **DOCUMENT** evidencing the repair (or correction) and the name, **ADDRESS**, and telephone number of each **PERSON** who has it.

[See also section 71.0 for additional questions.]

76.0 Waiver, Change, Withdrawal, or Cancellation of Notice to Quit

*[If a defense is based on waiver, change, withdrawal, or cancellation of the **NOTICE TO QUIT**, then either party may ask any applicable question in this section.]*

☐ 76.1 Did the **PLAINTIFF** or **LANDLORD** or anyone acting on his or her behalf do anything which is alleged to have been a waiver, change, withdrawal, or cancellation of the **NOTICE TO QUIT**? If so:
(a) state the facts supporting this allegation;
(b) state the names, **ADDRESSES**, and telephone numbers of all **PERSONS** who have knowledge of these facts;
(c) identify each **DOCUMENT** that supports the facts and state the name, **ADDRESS**, and telephone number of each **PERSON** who has it.

☐ 76.2 Did the **PLAINTIFF** or **LANDLORD** accept rent which covered a period after the date for vacating the **RENTAL UNIT** as specified in the **NOTICE TO QUIT**? If so:
(a) state the facts;
(b) state the names, **ADDRESSES**, and telephone numbers of all **PERSONS** who have knowledge of the facts;
(c) identify each **DOCUMENT** that supports the facts and state the name, **ADDRESS**, and telephone number of each **PERSON** who has it.

77.0 Retaliation and Arbitrary Discrimination

[If a defense is based on retaliation or arbitrary discrimination, then either party may ask any applicable question in this section.]

☐ 77.1 State all reasons that the **NOTICE TO QUIT** was served or that defendant's tenancy was not renewed and for each reason:
(a) state all facts supporting **PLAINTIFF'S** decision to terminate or not renew defendant's tenancy;
(b) state the names, **ADDRESSES**, and telephone numbers of all **PERSONS** who have knowledge of the facts;
(c) identify all **DOCUMENTS** that support the facts and state the name, **ADDRESS**, and telephone number of each **PERSON** who has it.

78.0 Nonperformance of the Rental Agreement by Landlord

*[If a defense is based on nonperformance of the rental agreement by the **LANDLORD** or someone acting on the **LANDLORD'S** behalf, then either party may ask any applicable question in this section.]*

☐ 78.1 Did the **LANDLORD** or anyone acting on the **LANDLORD'S** behalf agree to make repairs, alterations, or improvements at any time or provide services to the **PROPERTY** or **RENTAL UNIT**? If so, for each agreement state:
(a) the substance of the agreement;

(b) when it was made;
(c) whether it was written or oral;
(d) by whom and to whom;
(e) the name and **ADDRESS** of each person who knows about it;
(f) whether all promised repairs, alterations, or improvements were completed or services provided;
(g) the reasons for any failure to perform;
(h) the identity of each **DOCUMENT** evidencing the agreement or promise and the name, **ADDRESS**, and telephone number of each **PERSON** who has it.

☐ 78.2 Has **PLAINTIFF** or **LANDLORD** or any resident of the **PROPERTY** ever committed disturbances or interfered with the quiet enjoyment of the **RENTAL UNIT** (including, for example, noise, acts which threaten the loss of title to the property or loss of financing, etc.)? If so, for each disturbance or interference, state:
(a) a description of each act;
(b) the date of each act;
(c) the name, **ADDRESS**, and telephone number of each **PERSON** who acted;
(d) the name, **ADDRESS**, and telephone number of each **PERSON** who witnessed each act and any **DOCUMENTS** evidencing the person's knowledge;
(e) what action was taken by the **PLAINTIFF** or **LANDLORD** to end or lessen the disturbance or interference.

79.0 Offer of Rent by Defendant

[If a defense is based on an offer of rent by a defendant which was refused, then either party may ask any applicable question in this section.]

☐ 79.1 Has defendant or anyone acting on the defendant's behalf offered any payments to **PLAINTIFF** which **PLAINTIFF** refused to accept? If so, for each offer state:
(a) the amount;
(b) the date;
(c) purpose of offer;
(d) the manner of the offer;
(e) the identity of the person making the offer;
(f) the identity of the person refusing the offer;
(g) the date of the refusal;
(h) the reasons for the refusal.

80.0 Deduction from Rent for Necessary Repairs

[If a defense to payment of rent or damages is based on claim of retaliatory eviction, then either party may ask any applicable question in this section. Additional questions in section 75.0 may also be applicable.]

☐ 80.1 Does defendant claim to have deducted from rent any amount which was withheld to make repairs after communication to the **LANDLORD** of the need for the repairs? If the answer is ''no,'' do not answer interrogatories 80.2 through 80.6.

☐ 80.2 For each condition in need of repair for which a deduction was made, state:
(a) the nature of the condition;
(b) the location;
(c) the date the condition was discovered by defendant;
(d) the date the condition was first known by **LANDLORD** or **PLAINTIFF**;

(e) the dates and methods of each notice to the **LANDLORD** or **PLAINTIFF** of the condition;

(f) the response or action taken by the **LANDLORD** or **PLAINTIFF** to each notification;

(g) the cost to remedy the condition and how the cost was determined;

(h) the identity of any bids obtained for the repairs and any **DOCUMENTS** evidencing the bids.

☐ 80.3 Did **LANDLORD** or **PLAINTIFF** fail to respond within a reasonable time after receiving a communication of a need for repair? If so, for each communication state:

(a) the date it was made;

(b) how it was made;

(c) the response and date;

(d) why the delay was unreasonable.

☐ 80.4 Was there an insufficient period specified or actually allowed between the time of notification and the time repairs were begun by defendant to allow **LANDLORD** or **PLAINTIFF** to make the repairs? If so, state all facts on which the claim of insufficiency is based.

☐ 80.5 Does **PLAINTIFF** contend that any of the items for which rent deductions were taken were not allowable under law? If so, for each item state all reasons and facts on which you base your contention.

☐ 80.6 Has defendant vacated or does defendant anticipate vacating the **RENTAL UNIT** because repairs were requested and not made within a reasonable time? If so, state all facts on which defendant justifies having vacated the **RENTAL UNIT** or anticipates vacating the rental unit.

81.0 Fair Market Rental Value

*[If defendant denies **PLAINTIFF** allegation on the fair market rental value of the **RENTAL UNIT**, then either party may ask any applicale question in this section. If defendant claims that the fair market rental value is less because of a breach of warranty to provide habitable premises, then either party may also ask any applicable question in section 75.0]*

☐ 81.1 Do you have an opinion on the fair market rental value of the **RENTAL UNIT**? If so, state:

(a) the substance of your opinion;

(b) the factors upon which the fair market rental value is based;

(c) the method used to calculate the fair market rental value.

☐ 81.2 Has any other **PERSON** ever expressed to you an opinion on the fair market rental value of the **RENTAL UNIT**? If so, for each **PERSON**:

(a) state the name, **ADDRESS**, and telephone number;

(b) state the substance of the **PERSON's** opinion;

(c) describe the conversation or identify all **DOCUMENTS** in which the **PERSON** expressed an opinion and state the name, **ADDRESS**, and telephone number of each **PERSON** who has each **DOCUMENT**.

☐ 81.3 Do you know of any current violations of state or local building codes, housing codes, or health codes, conditions of dilapidation or other conditions in need of repair in the **RENTAL UNIT** or common areas that have affected the **RENTAL UNIT** at any time defendant has been in possession? If so, state:

(a) the conditions in need of repair;

(b) the kind of repairs needed;

(c) the name, **ADDRESS**, and telephone number of each **PERSON** who caused these conditions.

SETTLEMENT AGREEMENT

1. _____ (called the "tenant" in this agreement) resides at the following premises: _____ (referred to as "premises" in this agreement).

2. _____ (referred to as "landlord" in this agreement) is the owner of the premises.

3. On _____ landlord caused a Summons and Complaint in unlawful detainer to be served on tenant. The Complaint was filed in the Municipal Court for the County of _____ , _____ District, and carries the following civil number:_____.

4. Landlord and tenant agree that tenant shall vacate the premises on or before _____ _____. In exchange for this agreement, and upon full performance by tenant, landlord agrees to file a voluntary dismissal with prejudice of the complaint specified in clause #3.

5. Also in exchange for tenant's agreement to vacate the premises on or before the date specified in clause #4, landlord agrees to:

(choose one or more of the following)

[ ] Forgive all past due rent

[ ] Forgive past due rent in the following amount: $_____

[ ] Pay the tenant $_____ to cover tenant's moving expenses, new deposit requirements, and other incidentals related to the tenant moving out.

6. Any sum specified in clause #5 to be paid by the landlord shall be paid as follows:

(choose one of the following)

[ ] Upon tenant surrendering the keys to the premises

[ ] Upon the signing of this agreement

[ ] $_____upon the signing of this agreement and $_____ upon tenant surrendering the keys.

[ ] in the following manner:_____

_____

7. The tenant's security deposit being held by landlord shall be handled as follows:

[ ] restored in full to the tenant upon surrender of the keys

[ ] treated according to law

[ ] other:_____

8. In addition to their mutual promises in this agreement, tenant and landlord agree:

a) to waive all claims and demands that each may have against the other for any transaction directly or indirectly arising from their landlord/tenant relationship;

b) that this settlement agreement not be construed as reflecting on the merits of the dispute; and

c) that landlord shall not make any negative representations to any credit reporting agency or to any other person or entity seeking information about whether tenant was a good or bad tenant.

9. Time is of the essence in this agreement. If tenant fails to timely comply with this agreement, landlord may immediately rescind this agreement in writing and proceed with his or her legal and equitable remedies.

1

10. This agreement was executed on _____

at _____ .

2

3
Signed:_____

4

5
Signed:_____

6

7

8

9

10

11

12

13

14

15

16

17

18

19

20

21

22

23

24

25

26

27

28

Defendant's Name:_____

Address:_____

Telephone Number:_____

Defendant in Pro Per

_____

In the Municipal Court of the State of California

County of _____, _____ District

_____
Plaintiff(s)

v.

No._____

_____
Defendant(s)

DEMAND FOR JURY TRIAL

To the clerk of the above-entitled court:

Defendant(s) hereby demand a jury trial in this action.

Date:_____   _____

Signature of Defendant

10. This agreement was executed on _____
at _____

Signed:_____

Signed:_____

_____

1 | Defendant's Name:_____

2 | Address:_____

Telephone Number:_____

3 | Defendant in Pro Per

4 | _____

In the Municipal Court of the State of California

5 | County of _____, _____ District

6 | _____

7 | Plaintiff(s)

v. | No._____

8 | _____

APPLICATION AND

9 | Defendant(s) | DECLARATION

FOR RELIEF FROM EVICTION

10 | Code of Civil Procedure

Secs. 1174(c), 1179

11 |

12 | _____

13 | Defendant(s)_____,

hereby apply for relief from eviction, after judgment for plaintiff in this action.

14 | If defendants are evicted, they will suffer hardship in the following way(s):_____

15 | _____

_____

16 | _____.

17 | Defendants are willing and able to pay all money they presently owe to Plaintiff, as a condition

to this application being granted. Defendants are also willing and able to pay the rent as it comes

18 | due in the future.

19 | I declare under penalty of perjury that the above statements are true and correct to the best of

20 | my knowledge.

Date:_____ | _____

21 | Signature of Defendant

22 |

23 |

24 |

25 |

26 |

27 |

28 |

Defendant's Name:_____

Address:_____

Telephone Number:_____

Defendant in Pro Per

_____

In the Municipal Court of the State of California

County of _____, _____ District

_____

Plaintiff(s)

v.   No._____

_____   APPLICATION AND
Defendant(s)   DECLARATION
                                                    FOR STAY OF EVICTION

_____

Defendant(s)_____,

hereby apply for a stay of execution from any writ of restitution or possession in this case, for the

following period of time:_____

_____

_____.

Such a stay is appropriate in this case for the following reason(s):_____

_____

_____.

I declare under penalty of perjury that the above statements are true and correct to the best of

my knowledge.

Date:_____   _____

Signature of Defendant

Defendant's Name:_____

Address:_____

Telephone Number:_____

Defendant in Pro Per

_____

In the Municipal Court of the State of California

County of _____, _____ District

_____
Plaintiff(s)

v.   No._____

_____   NOTICE OF APPEAL AND
Defendant(s)   NOTICE TO PREPARE
                                            CLERK'S TRANSCRIPT

_____

Defendant(s)_____,

hereby appeal to the Appellate Department of the Superior Court.

Defendant(s) hereby request that a Clerk's Transcript be prepared, and that this transcript include all documents filed in this action and all minute orders and other rulings and judgments issued by the court in this action..

Date:_____   _____

                                       Signature of Defendant

Collective Bargaining Agreement

I. Parties

The parties to this Agreement are _____,
hereinafter called "Landlord," and _____,
hereinafter called "Organization." The property covered by this Agreement is located at _____
_____.

II. Purpose

It is the general purpose of this Agreement to provide a better means of communication between Landlord and his tenants, through Organization, their bargaining agent, to assure a continuous harmonious relationship and an orderly method of resolving differences and grievances, which will result in a stable tenancy, reduced expenses through greater tenant concern, and a better community.

III. Dismissal of Pending Lawsuits

All lawsuits currently pending between Landlord and Organization or Landlord and any member of Organization shall be dismissed, including the following: _____
_____.

IV. Recognition of Tenants' Organization

Landlord recognizes Organization as the sole collective bargaining agent for its members who are tenants at the property covered by this Agreement on all matters relating to their tenancies, the building, and their dealings with Landlord in his capacity as owner.

V. Landlord Security

Landlord shall in no way discriminate against or take reprisals against any person because of his involvement or sympathy with Organization. Nor shall Landlord promise or give any benefits to any person conditioned on such person's quitting, failing to join, or refusing to assist Organization in any way.

VI. Tenant Responsibilities

Organization agrees and recognizes that each tenant has certain obligations and responsibilities, including the following, and Organization agrees to take no action to discourage tenants from complying with these obligations and responsibilities:

1. To pay rent promptly when due (except where provided otherwise by law, this Agreement, or agreement between Landlord and a tenant);

2. To pay for and correct any damage to the premises or Landlord's furnishings caused by any intentional or negligent act of a tenant or any person occupying the premises with his permission, excepting damage due to normal wear and tear;

3. To place his garbage and refuse inside the containers provided therefor;

4. To refrain from acts which unduly disturb his neighbors;

5. To obey all state and local laws and regulations relating to the occupancy of residential property;

6. To comply with his obligations under his lease or rental agreement.

VII. Leases [or Rental Agreements]

A standard form Model Lease [or Model Rental Agreement] is attached to this Agreement and labelled "Exhibit A."

Within seven days of this Agreement, Landlord shall offer to sign such Model with each tenant who is a member of Organization. Landlord shall make the same offer to each new member of Organization within seven days of being notified of such membership by Organization.

The provisions of this Agreement shall be considered incorporated into and a part of each such Model signed.

VIII. Rents

1. *Rents.* The following monthly rentals shall apply to the following units:

Apartment (furn./unfurn.)	Rent	Apartment (furn./unfurn.)	Rent
_____	_____	_____	_____
_____	_____	_____	_____
_____	_____	_____	_____

2. *Appliances.* Landlord shall, without extra charge, furnish every apartment with a satisfactory stove and refrigerator, which he shall maintain in good working order.

3. *Utilities.* Landlord shall provide and pay for the following utilities, without adding to the monthly rent: gas, electricity, water, garbage collection, trash removal and sewer charges.

4. *Late Charges.* No late charges or fines shall be imposed.

5. *Rent Increases.* There shall be no rent increases during the term of this Agreement.

6. *Back Rents.* Back rents in the amount of _____ now held by Organization shall be disposed of as follows: _____
_____.

IX. Repairs and Maintenance

1. *Maintenance.* Landlord shall maintain the building and grounds in a decent, safe and sanitary condition, and shall comply with all state and local laws, regulations and ordinances concerning the maintenance of residential property. In addition, as specific maintenance problems have arisen in the past, Landlord specifically agrees to provide the following maintenance services:

[**Example:** (a) check the coin-operated washing machine and dryer at least once a week to see that they are in good operating condition;

(b) repair broken mailboxes upon notice by affected tenants.]

2. *Security.* Landlord shall take reasonable measures to maintain security in the building and grounds to protect the tenants and their guests from burglary, robbery and other crimes.

3. *Repairs.* Landlord shall complete the following repairs by the following dates:

Repair	Date

4. *Failure to Comply.* Organization shall have the right to inspect the building at reasonable times to ensure compliance with this Section. If any repair is not completed by the date specified, or if Landlord fails to comply with any maintenance duty for seven days or longer, the tenants of the building may thereafter, until completion of repairs or resumption of maintenance, pay their rent into a bank account held by Organization. Organization shall use the money to make the repairs or perform the maintenance, remitting the balance to Landlord after repairs are completed and maintenance resumed. This remedy shall be in addition to any remedies provided by law or contract for tenants receiving inadequate maintenance or repair.

X. Grievance Procedure

1. The term "grievance" shall mean any dispute between Landlord and a tenant or between Landlord and Organization involving the interpretation, application, or coverage of this Agreement or any lease or rental agreement, except that any claim for personal injuries exceeding $500 shall not be considered a "grievance" subject to this procedure.

2. Any tenant having a grievance may present his grievance, by himself or through Organization, to Landlord or his agent.

3. If the grievance has not been resolved to the satisfaction of the tenant within ten days after being presented, a grievance meeting shall be held between the tenant, Organization and Landlord within the next five days, or as soon thereafter as the parties may agree. At such meeting, the parties shall attempt to resolve the grievance to everyone's satisfaction.

4. If Landlord has a grievance against any tenant, or against Organization, he may present such grievance to Organization, which shall attempt to resolve the grievance as soon as possible.

5. If Landlord's grievance has not been resolved to his satisfaction within ten days after it has been presented to Organization, the grievance meeting provisions subsection 3 above shall apply.

6. If the grievance meeting produces no resolution of the grievance, the aggrieved party may then file suit in any court of competent jurisdiction for final determination fo the matter in dispute.

XI. Enforcement

The provisions of this Agreement may be enforced through appropriate legal action by Landlord, Organization, or any affected person. As the amount of damages attributable to violation of any provision of this Agreement may be difficult to ascertain, the parties agree that these provisions may be specifically enforced by an appropriate court.

XII. Severability

In the event that any provision of this Agreement is deemed invalid by any court of law, such determination shall not affect any other provisions of this Agreement and the Agreement shall remain binding on all parties hereto.

XIII. Organization's Right to Information

In order to enable organization to maintain a continuing interest in the present and future condition of the building and to adequately represent the interests of the tenants, Landlord shall furnish Organization with information and allow Organization to examine Landlord's records and books, upon reasonable notice by Organization, relating to the following matters:

1. Expenses of maintaining the building,

2. Income received from the building,

3. All other financial information relating to the building, including mortgages or deeds of trust on the building, and

4. All taxes affected by the building.

XIV. Duration

This Agreement shall remain in full force and effect from the date it is signed by both Landlord and Organization and until _____, 19____.

On _____, 19____, Landlord and Organization shall begin negotiations for a new agreement to go into effect at the expiration of this Agreement. Such negotiations shall continue in good faith until a new agreement is reached or this Agreement expires.

WHEREFORE, We, the undersigned, do hereby execute and agree to this Agreement.

For the Landlord:

1. _____
   (signature)

   _____
   (title)

   _____
   (date of signature)

2. _____
   (signature)

   _____
   (title)

   _____
   (date of signature)

For the Organization:

1. _____
   (signature)

   _____
   (title)

   _____
   (date of signature)

2. _____
   (signature)

   _____
   (title)

   _____
   (date of signature)

Subject Index

by Sayre VanYoung

About the Authors

Myron Moskovitz is a native San Franciscan who received his law degree (with honors) from the University of California in Berkeley in 1964. Since then, he has served as a law clerk for the California Supreme Court, directed the Marysville office of the California Rural Legal Assistance, and was the Chief Attorney of the National Housing Law Project in Berkeley and Chairman of the State's Commission of Housing and Community Development. He has written many articles and a book on tenants' rights for lawyers, and he has won several important cases establishing new rights for tenants. He is now a law professor at Golden Gate University in San Francisco.

Ralph Warner is one of the pioneers of the self-help law movement. He is the publisher of Nolo Press and an author of more than a dozen self-help law books and software programs.

SOFTWARE

willmaker

Nolo Press/Legisoft

Recent statistics say chances are better than 2 to 1 that you haven't written a will, even though you know you should. WillMaker makes the job easy, leading you step by step in a fill-in-the-blank format. Once you've gone through the program, you print out the will and sign it in front of witnesses. Because writing a will is only one step in the estate planning process, WillMaker comes with a 200-page manual providing an overview of probate avoidance and tax planning techniques. National 3rd Ed.

Apple, IBM PC 5 1/4 & 3 1/2, Macintosh	$59.95
Commodore	$39.95

california incorporator

Attorney Mancuso and Legisoft, Inc.

About half of the small California corporations formed today are done without the services of a lawyer. This easy-to-use software program lets you do the paperwork with minimum effort. Just answer the questions on the screen, and California Incorporator will print out the 35-40 pages of documents you need to make your California corporation legal.

California 1st Ed. (IBM PC 5 1/4 & 3 1/2) $129.00

the california nonprofit corporation handbook— computer edition with disk

Attorney Anthony Mancuso

This is the standard work on how to form a nonprofit corporation in California. Included on the disk are the forms for the Articles, Bylaws and Minutes you will need, as well as regular and special director and member minute forms. Also included are line-by-line instructions explaining how to apply for and obtain federal tax exempt status—this critical step applies to incorporating in all 50 states.

California 1st Ed.

Macintosh, IBM PC 5 1/4 & 3 1/2 $69.00

how to form your own texas corporation— computer edition with disk

Attorney Anthony Mancuso

how to form your own new york corporation— computer edition with disk

Attorney Anthony Mancuso

More and more business people are incorporating to qualify for tax benefits, limited liability status, the benefit of employee status and financial flexibility. These software packages contain all the instructions, tax information and forms you need to incorporate a small business. All organizational forms are on disk.

1st Edition

Macintosh, IBM PC 5 1/4 & 3 1/2 $69.00

for the record

By attorney Warner & Pladsen

A book/software package that helps to keep track of personal and financial records; create documents to give to family members in case of emergency; leave an accurate record for heirs, and allows easy access to all important records with the ability to print out any section. National 1st Ed.

Macintosh, IBM PC 5 1/4 & 3 1/2 $49.95

ESTATE PLANNING & PROBATE

nolo's simple will book

Attorney Denis Clifford

We feel it's important to remind people that if they don't make arrangements before they die, the state will give their property to certain close family members. If you want a particular person to receive a particular object, you need a will. It's easy to write a legally valid will using this book.

National 1st Ed. $17.95

plan your estate: wills, probate avoidance, trusts & taxes

Attorney Denis Clifford

A will is only one part of an estate plan. The first concern is avoiding probate so that your heirs won't receive a greatly diminished inheritance years later. This book shows you how to create a "living trust" and gives you the information you need to make sure whatever you have saved goes to your heirs, not to lawyers and the government.

National 1st Ed. $17.95

the power of attorney book

Attorney Denis Clifford

The Power of Attorney Book concerns something you've heard about but probably would rather ignore: Who will take care of your affairs, make your financial and medical decisions, if you can't? With this book you can appoint someone you trust to carry out your wishes.

National 2nd Ed. $17.95

how to probate an estate

Julia Nissley

When a close relative dies, amidst the grieving there are financial and legal details to be dealt with. The natural response is to rely on an attorney, but that response can be costly. With How to Probate an Estate, you can have the satisfaction of doing the work yourself and saving those fees.

California 4th Ed. $24.95

the california nonprofit corporation handbook

Attorney Anthony Mancuso

Used by arts groups, educators, social service agencies, medical programs, environmentalists and many others, this book explains all the legal formalities involved in forming and operating a nonprofit corporation. Included are all the forms for the Articles, Bylaws and Minutes you will need. Also included are complete instructions for obtaining federal 501(c)(3) exemptions and benefits. The tax information in this section applies wherever your corporation is formed.

California 5th Ed. $29.95

how to form your own corporation

Attorney Anthony Mancuso

More and more business people are incorporating to qualify for tax benefits, limited liability status, the benefit of employee status and the financial flexibility. These books contain the forms, instructions and tax information you need to incorporate a small business.

California 7th Ed. $29.95
Texas 4th Ed. $24.95
New York 2nd. Ed. $24.95
Florida 1st Ed. $19.95

1988 calcorp update package

Attorney Anthony Mancuso

This update package contains all the forms and instructions you need to modify your corporation's Articles of Incorporation so you can take advantage of new California laws. $25.00

california professional corporation handbook

Attorney Anthony Mancuso

Health care professionals, marriage, family and child counsellors, lawyers, accountants and members of certain other professions must fulfill special requirements when forming a corporation in California. This edition contains up-to-date tax information plus all the forms and instructions necessary to form a California professional corporation. An appendix explains the special rules that apply to each profession.

California 4th Ed. $34.95

marketing without advertising

Michael Phillips & Salli Rasberry

Every small business person knows that the best marketing plan encourages customer loyalty and personal recommendation. Phillips and Rasberry outline practical steps for building and expanding a small business without spending a lot of money.

National 1st Ed. $14.00

the partnership book

Attorneys Clifford & Warner

Lots of people dream of going into business with a friend. The best way to keep that dream from turning into a nightmare is to have a solid partnership agreement. This book shows how to write an agreement that covers evaluation of partner assets, disputes, buy-outs and the death of a partner.

National 3rd Ed. $18.95

nolo's small business start-up

Mike McKeever

Should you start a business? Should you raise money to expand your already running business? If the answers are yes, this book will show you how to write an effective business plan and loan package.

National 3rd Ed. $17.95

the independent paralegal's handbook: how to provide legal services without going to jail

Attorney Ralph Warner

A large percentage of routine legal work in this country is performed by typists, secretaries, researchers and various other law office helpers generally labeled paralegals. For those who would like to take these services out of the law office and offer them at a reasonable fee in an independent business, attorney Ralph Warner provides both legal and business guidelines.

National 1st Ed. $12.95

getting started as an independent paralegal (two audio tapes)

Attorney Ralph Warner

This set of tapes is a carefully edited version of Nolo Press founder Ralph Warner's Saturday Morning Law School class. It is designed for people who wish to go into business helping consumers prepare their own paperwork in uncontested actions such as bankruptcy, divorce, small business incorporations, landlord-tenant actions, probate, etc. Also covered are how to set up, run, and market your business, as well as a detailed discussion of Unauthorized Practice of Law.

National 1st Ed. $24.95

JUST FOR FUN

devil's advocates: the unnatural history of lawyers

Jonathan & Andrew Roth

This book is a painless and hilarious education on the legal profession from its rude beginning through its ruder history to its rudest present. Laugh or weep as you learn the historical underpinnings of how and why lawyers have solidly become their own worst enemies.

1st Ed. $12.95

29 reasons not to go to law school

Ralph Warner & Toni Ihara

Lawyers, law students, their spouses and consorts will love this little book with its zingy comments and Thurberesque cartoons, humorously zapping the life of the law.—Peninsula Times Tribune Filled with humor and piercing observations, this book can save you three years, $70,000 and your sanity.

3rd Ed. $9.95

poetic justice

Ed. by Jonathan & Andrew Roth

A unique compilation of humorous quotes about lawyers and the legal system, from Socrates to Woody Allen. $8.95

how to file for bankruptcy

Attorneys Stephen Elias, Robin Leonard & Albin Renauer
Here we show you how to decide whether or not filing for bankruptcy makes sense and if it does, we give you step-by-step instructions as to how to do it. *How To File For Bankruptcy* covers the procedure for completing a Chapter 7 and includes a discussion of Chapter 13 to help you decide which process is appropriate for you.
National 1st Ed. $24.95

collect your court judgment

Scott, Elias & Goldoftas
After you win a judgment in small claims, municipal or superior court, you still have to collect your money. Here are step-by-step instructions on how to collect your judgment from the debtor's bank accounts, wages, business receipts, real estate or other assets.
California 1st Ed. $24.95

make your own contract

Attorney Stephen Elias
Here are clearly written legal form contracts to: buy and sell property, borrow and lend money, store and lend personal property, make deposits on goods for later purchase, release others from personal liability, or pay a contractor to do home repairs.
National 1st Ed. $12.95

social security, medicare & pensions: a sourcebook for older americans

Attorney Joseph L. Matthews & Dorothy Matthews Berman
Social security, medicare and medicaid programs follow a host of complicated rules. Those over 55, or those caring for someone over 55, will find this comprehensive guidebook invaluable for understanding and utilizing their rightful benefits. A special chapter deals with age discrimination in employment and what to do about it.
National 4th Ed. $15.95

everybody's guide to small claims court

Attorney Ralph Warner
So, the dry cleaner ruined your good flannel suit. Your roof leaks every time it rains, and the contractor who supposedly fixed it won't call you back. The bicycle shop hasn't paid for the tire pumps you sold it six months ago. This book will help you decide if you have a case, show you how to file and serve papers, tell you what to bring to court, and how to collect a judgment.
California 8th Ed. $14.95
National 3rd Ed. $14.95

for sale by owner

George Devine
In 1986 about 600,000 homes were sold in California at a median price of $130,000. Most sellers worked with a broker and paid the 6% commission. For the median home that meant $7,800. Obviously, that's money that could be saved if you sell your own house. This book provides the background information and legal technicalities you will need to do the job yourself and with confidence.
California 1st Ed. $24.95

homestead your house

Attorneys Warner, Sherman & Ihara
Under California homestead laws, up to $60,000 of the equity in your home may be safe from creditors. But to get the maximum legal protection you should file a Declaration of Homestead before a judgment lien is recorded against you. This book includes complete instructions and tear-out forms.
California 7th Ed. $8.95

the landlord's law book: vol. 1, rights & responsibilities

Attorneys Brown & Warner
Every landlord should know the basics of landlord-tenant law. In short, the era when a landlord could substitute common sense for a detailed knowledge of the law is gone forever. This volume covers: deposits, leases and rental agreements, inspections (tenants' privacy rights), habitability (rent withholding), ending a tenancy, liability, and rent control.
California 2nd Ed. $24.95

the landlord's law book: vol. 2, evictions

Attorney David Brown
Even the most scrupulous landlord may sometimes need to evict a tenant. In the past it has been necessary to hire a lawyer and pay a high fee. Using this book you can handle most evictions yourself safely and economically.
California 2nd Ed. $24.95

tenants' rights

Attorneys Moskowitz & Warner
Your "security building" doesn't have a working lock on the front door. Is your landlord liable? How can you get him to fix it? Under what circumstances can you withhold rent? When is an apartment not "habitable?" This book explains the best way to handle your relationship with your landlord and your legal rights when you find yourself in disagreement.
California 10th Ed. $15.95

the deeds book: how to transfer title to california real estate

Attorney Mary Randolph
If you own real estate, you'll almost surely need to sign a new deed at one time or another. *The Deeds Book* shows you how to choose the right kind of deed, how to complete the tear-out forms, and how to record them in the county recorder's public records.
California 1st Ed. $15.95

dog law

Attorney Mary Randolph

There are 50 million dogs in the United States—and, it seems, at least that many rules and regulations for their owners to abide by. *Dog Law* covers topics that everyone who owns a dog, or lives near one, needs to know about disputes, injury or nuisance.

National 1st Ed. $12.95

the criminal records book

Attorney Warren Siegel

We've all done something illegal. If you were one of those who got caught, your juvenile or criminal court record can complicate your life years later. The good news is that in many cases your record can either be completely expunged or lessened in severity. *The Criminal Records Book* takes you step by step through the procedures to: seal criminal records, dismiss convictions, destroy marijuana records, reduce felony convictions.

California 2nd Ed. $14.95

draft, registration and the law

Attorney R. Charles Johnson

This clearly written guidebook explains the present draft law and how registration (required of all male citizens within thirty days of their eighteenth birthday) works. Every available option is presented along with a description of how a draft would work if there were a call tomorrow.

National 2nd Ed. $9.95

fight your ticket

Attorney David Brown

At a trade show in San Francisco recently, a traffic court judge (who must remain nameless) told our associate publisher that he keeps this book by his bench for easy reference.

If you think that ticket was unfair, here's the book showing you what to do to fight it.

California 3rd Ed. $16.95

how to become a united states citizen

Sally Abel Schreuder

This bilingual (English/Spanish) book presents the forms, applications and instructions for naturalization. This step-by-step guide will provide information and answers for legally admitted aliens who wish to become citizens.

National 3rd Ed. $12.95

how to change your name

Attorneys Loeb & Brown

Wish that you had gone back to your maiden name after the divorce? Tired of spelling over the phone V-e-n-k-a-t-a-r-a-m-a-n S-u-b-r-a-m-a-n-i-a-m?

This book explains how to change your name legally and provides all the necessary court forms with detailed instructions on how to fill them out.

California 4th Ed. $14.95

legal research: how to find and understand the law

Attorney Stephen Elias

Legal Research could also be called Volume-Two-for-all-Nolo-Press-Self-Help-Law-Books. A valuable tool for paralegals, law students and legal secretaries, this book provides access to legal information—the legal self-helper can find and research a case, read statutes, and make Freedom of Information Act requests.

National 2nd Ed. $14.95

family law dictionary

Attorneys Leonard and Elias

Written in plain English (as opposed to legalese), the Family Law Dictionary has been compiled to help the lay person doing research in the area of family law (i.e., marriage, divorce, adoption, etc.). Using cross referencs and examples as well as definitions, this book is unique as a reference tool.

National 1st Edition $13.95

patent, copyright & trademark: intellectual property law dictionary

Attorney Stephen Elias

This book uses simple language free of legal jargon to define and explain the intricacies of items associated with trade secrets, copyrights, trademarks and unfair competition, patents and patent procedures, and contracts and warranties.—IEEE Spectrum

If you're dealing with any multi-media product, a new business product or trade secret, you need this book.

National 1st Ed. $17.95

the living together kit

Attorneys Ihara & Warner

Few unmarried couples understand the laws that may affect them. Here are useful tips on living together agreements, paternity agreements, estate planning, and buying real estate.
National 5th Ed. $17.95

how to do your own divorce

Attorney Charles E. Sherman

This is the book that launched Nolo Press and advanced the self-help law movement. During the past 17 years, over 400,000 copies have been sold, saving consumers at least $50 million in legal fees (assuming 100,000 have each saved $500—certainly a conservative estimate).
California 15th Ed. $14.95
Texas 2nd Ed. (Sherman & Simons) $12.95

california marriage & divorce law

Attorneys Warner, Ihara & Elias

For a generation, this practical handbook has been the best resource for the Californian who wants to understand marriage and divorce laws. Even if you hire a lawyer to help you with a divorce, it's essential that you learn your basic legal rights and responsibilities.
California 10th Ed. $15.95

practical divorce solutions

Attorney Charles Ed Sherman

Written by the author of *How to Do Your Own Divorce* (with over 500,000 copies in print), this book provides a valuable guide both to the emotional process involved in divorce as well as the legal and financial decisions that have to be made.
California 1st Ed. $12.95

how to modify and collect child support in california

Attorneys Matthews, Siegel & Willis

California has established landmark new standards in setting and collecting child support. Payments must now be based on both objective need standards and the parents' combined income. Using this book, custodial parents can determine if they are entitled to higher child support payments and can implement the procedures to obtain that support.
California 2nd Ed. $17.95

the guardianship book

Lisa Goldoftas & Attorney David Brown

Thousands of children in California are left without a guardian because their parents have died, abandoned them or are unable to care for them. *The Guardianship Book* provides step-by-step instructions and the forms needed to obtain a legal guardianship without a lawyer.
California 1st Ed. $19.95

a legal guide for lesbian and gay couples

Attorneys Curry & Clifford

A Legal Guide contains crucial information on the special problems facing lesbians and gay men with children, civil rights legislation, and medical/legal issues.
National 5th Ed. $17.95

how to adopt your stepchild in california

Frank Zagone & Mary Randolph

For many families that include stepchildren, adoption is a satisfying way to guarantee the family a solid legal footing. This book provides sample forms and complete step-by-step instructions for completing a simple uncontested adoption by a stepparent.
California 3rd Ed. $19.95

PATENTS, COPYRIGHTS & TRADEMARKS

how to copyright software

Attorney M.J. Salone

Copyrighting is the best protection for any software. This book explains how to get a copyright and what a copyright can protect.
National 3rd Ed. $34.95

the inventor's notebook

Fred Grissom & Attorney David Pressman

The best protection for your patent is adequate records. The Inventor's Notebook provides forms, instructions, references to relevant areas of patent law, a bibliography of legal and non-legal aids, and more. It helps you document the activities that are normally part of successful independent inventing.
National 1st Ed. $19.95

legal care for your software

Attorneys Daniel Remer & Stephen Elias

If you write programs you intend to sell, or work for a software house that pays you for programming, you should buy this book. If you are a freelance programmer doing software development, you should buy this book.—Interface

This step-by-step guide for computer software writers covers copyright laws, trade secret protection, contracts, license agreements, trademarks, patents and more.
National 3rd Ed. $29.95

patent it yourself

Attorney David Pressman

You've invented something, or you're working on it, or you're planning to start...Patent It Yourself offers help in evaluating patentability, marketability and the protective documentation you should have. If you file your own patent application using this book, you can save from $1500 to $3500.
National 2nd Ed. $29.95

ORDER FORM

Quantity	Title	Unit Price	Total

Sales Tax (CA residents only):

7%	Alameda, Contra Costa, San Diego, San Mateo & Santa Clara counties
6 1/2%	Fresno, Inyo, LA, Sacramento, San Benito, San Francisco & Santa Cruz counties
6%	All others

Subtotal_____

Sales Tax_____

TOTAL_____

Method of Payment:

☐ Check enclosed

☐ VISA   ☐ Mastercard

Acct # _____ Exp._____

Signature _____

Phone (   )_____

Mail to:

NOLO PRESS
950 Parker Street
Berkeley CA 94710

Ship to:

Name _____

Address _____

_____

For faster service, use your credit card and our toll-free numbers:

Monday-Friday 9-5 Pacific Time

US		1-800-992-6656
CA	(outside 415 area)	1-800-445-6656
	(inside 415 area)	1-415-549-1976
General Information		**1-415-549-1976**

Prices subject to change

Please allow 1-2 weeks for delivery

Delivery is by UPS; no P.O. boxes, please

ORDER DIRECT AND WE PAY POSTAGE & HANDLING!

H A L T

A law reform organization worthy of your support

HALT (Help Abolish Legal Tyranny)—An Organization of Americans for Legal

Reform —is a nonprofit public interest group whose activities are primarily

funded by its 200,000 individual members. Like Nolo Press, HALT advocates a

number of changes in the legal system to make it possible for the average

American to reasonably and affordably manage his or her legal life. To name but

a few of their admirable activities, HALT lobbies to increase disciplinary

sanctions against dishonest and incompetent lawyers, reduce probate fees and

simplify procedures, increase the role of non-lawyer (independent paralegal)

legal service providers, and expand small claims court. To keep its members

abreast of major legal reform developments, HALT also publishes a quarterly

magazine, holds law reform conferences, and publishes excellent position

papers on legal reform issues.

Nolo Press supports HALT and its members and urges all interested citizens to

join for a $15 annual membership fee. For more information write to:

H A L T

1319 F Street, NW
Suite 300
Washington, D.C. 20004
(202)347-9600